Desert
The American Southwest

This new volume in The Naturalist's America series deals with one of the most fascinating of natural systems — the desert — stark, hot, dry, a land of extremes. The focus of the book is the Sonoran Desert, from Death Valley through Arizona, and south into Mexico and Baja California.

Noted as a nature writer and photographer, Ruth Kirk has been a lover of the desert since her childhood on the edge of this dry land in California. She has spent years roaming the flatlands and peaks, observing, photographing, studying the wealth of plant and animal life.

Here is an outer limit where plants and animals make precarious adaptations to maintain their hold on life. In *Desert: The American Southwest* we learn how creatures stay alive through the heat, conserve water, adjust their lives to the land's most favorable conditions. Also discussed are the physical characteristics of the land, and man's relation to the desert from the prehistoric past to the probable future. Drawing widely on both experience and biological research, Mrs. Kirk has combined this information with her photographer's eye and her enthusiasm for a strange and beautiful country. The result is an extraordinarily perceptive account of the living desert.

Outstanding photographs in color and black and white by Ruth and Louis Kirk.

The Naturalist's America

Desert

The American Southwest

BY RUTH KIRK

Illustrated with photographs by
Ruth and Louis Kirk

HOUGHTON MIFFLIN COMPANY BOSTON

1973

THE NATURALIST'S AMERICA

1. *The Appalachians* by Maurice Brooks
2. *Sierra Nevada* by Verna R. Johnston
3. *Desert* by Ruth Kirk

Endpaper map by Graf-Tech

The quotations on pages 309, 313, and 318–319 from *A Pima Remembers* by George Webb, copyright 1959, are reproduced by permission of the University of Arizona Press in Tucson.

The photograph on page 298 by George A. Grant is reproduced by courtesy of the United States Department of the Interior, National Park Service; the photographs on pages 294, 302, 316, and 325 by courtesy of Arizona State Museum, University of Arizona; the photograph on page 307 by courtesy of the Arizona State Museum, University of Arizona, James Manson Collection. The photographs on pages 44–45, 145, 172–173, 218, and 279 are reprinted from *Exploring Death Valley* by Ruth Kirk with the permission of the publishers, Stanford University Press. Copyright © 1956, 1965 by the Board of Trustees of the Leland Stanford Junior University.

First Printing v

Library of Congress Cataloging in Publication Data
Kirk, Ruth.
  Desert: The American Southwest.
  (The Naturalist's America)
  Bibliography: p.
  1. Desert ecology—Southwestern States. 2. Natural history—Southwestern States. I. Title.
QH104.5.S6K5   574.5'265   73-9902
ISBN 0-395-17209-8

Printed in the United States of America

*To my mother and father, who
loved the back roads of the desert
most of all*

Editors' Preface

THIS, the story of our southwestern deserts, is the third volume in a series, The Naturalist's America, designed to inform North Americans about the wildlife, plants, and geology of their continent.

It is a primary purpose of this series to recapture the inquiring spirit of the old naturalists, albeit with an eye to the findings of modern biologists. There is a growing effort to narrow the gap between the biologist and the layman, and the recent proliferation of nature books testifies to this trend. All but the most myopic citizen is now aware of his natural environment and his impact upon it. Few, however, realize that some of the more "desolate" parts of the world are also vulnerable to abuse: the polar regions, the equatorial rain forest, the desert, even the sea.

We hear much talk of the world's deserts as a vast "land bank" — millions of square miles of the earth's surface waiting for a technological breakthrough to bring distilled seawater to its arid soils. This will be a greener planet when that happens, but to many of us a less interesting one, completely domesticated.

The author of this book, Ruth Kirk, who is also a skilled professional photographer, has had a long intimacy with the desert. She knows its varied moods not as a visitor; she has lived there, making her home in two of the most spectacular deserts in our Southwest, Death Valley in California and Organ Pipe in Arizona, where her husband served as park naturalist.

Now, living in the rain-drenched Northwest they must, at times, yearn for the blazing sun (and indeed do return often on photography expeditions).

The deserts, which by definition have an average rainfall of less than 10 inches in a year, cover about 14 percent — nearly one-seventh — of the land area of the world. An approximately equal area, another 14 percent, is semi-arid, with a steppelike climate where rainfall does not exceed 20 inches. There are a dozen major desert areas in the world, and every continent has at least one. Even parts of Antarctica qualify as desert, since moisture is locked in ice and annual precipitation is very low.

The North American desert, with which this book is concerned, covers nearly 500,000 square miles of diverse landscape in the southwestern United States and northwestern Mexico and may be subdivided into five distinctive desert areas: the Great Basin, Mojave, Sonoran, Colorado Plateau, and Chihuahuan Deserts. To naturalists perhaps the Sonoran, which extends from southern Arizona into Mexico, is the most exciting; it has the greatest variety of birds, other animals, and plants.

The bird watcher does most of his field work at dawn and in the two or three hours of early morning before the summer sun has made an oven of the desert pavement. For many of the small mammals, reptiles, and some insects, nocturnal activity is the only possible means of survival, not so much because they can more readily avoid their predators (which are also night-adapted) but because of the problems of thermal regulation. Much of the noonday world in the desert is a subterranean world where wee beasties sleep comfortably in air-conditioned chambers until the shadows of evening again make it possible to venture forth.

A remarkable overview of the desert ecosystem can be gained from the displays of the Arizona-Sonora Desert Museum in Tucson, a unique experiment in ecological education — part museum, part zoo, part botanical garden. There, in a below-the-ground exhibit, you can see how desert animals spend the daylight hours.

Walk outside among the groves of saguaros. Nearly every plant, except the evanescent wildflowers, is armed to the teeth with spines, hooks, and needles, threatening and defying. Unseen cholla knuckles lying on the ground jump at the slightest touch of a shoe and sink their painful barbs into an ankle. Every plant keeps its distance, drawing the precious moisture from whatever radius it can command. This spacing of plants is dramatically evident from the windows of a passenger plane practically anywhere over the desert; the pattern below is that of dark specks, clusters, and polkadots on the bare desert pavement. There are years, however, when heavier than usual spring rains turn the desert briefly into huge flower gardens. The parched soil, rich in nutriment, requires only a good drenching to bring to life seeds that have lain dormant for years. It is a story of resurrection. These ephemeral plants waste little on stems, stalks, and leaves, but put most of their life force into showy blossoms. Soon they wither and die, their brief but gaudy show over. In that short span the cycle is completed and new seeds have been produced, to lie waiting in the naked sands while the sun burns down.

Tucson, like many another desert city, is surrounded by mountains that rise blue, purple, and brown against the afternoon sky like cardboard stage sets. Take a winding, climbing road into any of the ranges — the Santa Ritas, the Santa Catalinas, or the Huachucas — and note the changes as the car gains altitude. The desert soon drops behind. Increased precipitation permits the survival of a new galaxy of plants: oak scrub replaces cacti, then pines take over, and on the higher peaks, firs. Associated with these changes in the plant life are new birds, new mammals. But let Ruth Kirk tell about it. She has spent many years in the desert; we have been only visitors.

ROGER TORY PETERSON
JOHN A. LIVINGSTON

Foreword

THE DESERT is a fragile land. It needs to be respected for what it is, rich and varied and beautiful in its own stark way. It must no longer be regarded as land that God never quite got around to finishing.

Decades ago public reaction to the desert was to ignore it. More recently, because of technological ability to overpower the heat and dryness, man's attitude toward the desert has changed. Valleys and plains that grew creosote bush and jackrabbits have become alfalfa fields. Roads now checkerboard the land, more each year. Houses and industries sprout, their interiors regulated with the even-temperature comfort of a womb and their exteriors softened by lawns and even fountains, which are foolish in an arid setting. Man can overwhelm the desert, and because he *can* he does. We have scarcely seen this region as it truly is, yet we are willing to reshape it.

Some of the transformation comes because until now the desert has been unexploited. Some is spurred by population growth, which turns emptiness into a valuable resource; the desert becomes space available for filling. But note the statistics, harbingers of change within the change. The people of the Sonoran Desert alone (roughly from the Phoenix-Tucson region southward to about Guaymas, Mexico) each year consume more than 23 million acre feet of water, which is ten times what falls there as rain and snow each year. Ninety percent of the water used annually comes from subterranean reserves accumulated throughout the ages. It is being mined, and, like ore, it may give out. Agriculture prompts the prodigality. In Arizona alone 6 million of the 6½ million acre feet of water pumped from the ground yearly is sent flowing through the fields and groves, assuring bounteous crops. But the return is less than $20 in personal income per 326,000 gallons of water. This is selling out much too cheaply. Wells are going dry and water tables are sinking beyond economical reach. Land is subsiding, sometimes as much as 26 feet in two decades in parts of the desert-cum-farmland. Fields are being ruined by excessive salt. Hardpan layers form below the surface and moisture, unable to drain away, instead moves upward and brings with it salts dissolved from the soil.

While this is happening men also are discovering the natural desert. To some it represents a chance to pit driving skill against the odds of rugged terrain. Dune buggies, ATVs (all-terrain vehicles), four-wheel drive trucks, and two-wheel cycles have turned the desert into a giant sandbox where adults can play with their toys. As usual in play, attention is more on the toys than on the sandbox; the activity is what counts and the setting is being destroyed. This too seems a cheap sellout. In much of the desert you no longer dare spread your sleeping bag on the desert floor during holiday periods for fear of being run over in the night.

Fortunately, other desert enthusiasts are attuned in a different manner: they are catching the cadence of natural rhythms and giving in to desert beguilement. They value this land for its own sake, for its particular set of intricacies and peculiarities. Here I include the scientific investigators who probe such diverse matters as the circulatory system of a horned lizard's head, or the means by which leaf stomata hold themselves shut against the pull of the sun's rays. From this sort of discovery comes the understanding needed to deal wisely with the varied pieces of the desert puzzle. The studies clarify what the desert is and how man can fit intelligently into its fabric. My hope is that these pages can help draw together for all of us some understanding of the esoteric labors of the specialists. I hope too that the investigations recounted will be seen as parts of an ongoing, never-to-be-completed quest. Human grasp of truth is partial and tentative; data are subject to error; inferences may be correct within a narrow range but not transferable across the broad spectrum. In perusing the scientific literature my aim has been to draw from it a unified story, and also one that speaks of process, since knowledge does not arrive in men's minds full blown but builds bit by bit, subject to continual updating.

A word, also, concerning the geography of this book. It focuses mostly on the Sonoran Desert, the region of giant cacti — the saguaro, cardon, organpipe, and senita. This means ignoring most of the California desert, scene of my own earliest awareness of outdoor beauty. It means leaving out the Great Basin Desert, which reaches from Nevada northward as far as British Columbia, the Chihuahuan Desert of Texas and north-central Mexico, and the wondrous red sandstone canyon country at the southern base of the Colorado Rockies. One reason for this emphasis is that the Sonoran Desert best fits public expectations of what the American Desert should be, and we need these days to examine stereotypes of all sorts. Admittedly, the delimitation also reflects the geography of my heart. This is the desert I have roamed most widely — if one includes Death Valley, California, as an extension of the Sonoran Desert (and a few geographers do). Within this framework the desert discussed here begins just south of Reno. Driving from the north you fork off toward Las Vegas and are in desert; stay west along the scarp of the Sierra and you're on the fringe but not in true desert. Arriving from the east you meet the dividing line lying close to the Arizona–New Mexico border and south of the Navajo Reservation.

Certain qualities lace this sprawling region into a single whole. Vegetation varies greatly but bushes have a rounded form and grow widely separated. Bare brown earth shows between them; if it doesn't, you haven't yet come to the desert of this book.

Another diagnostic quality is that the flats won't be flat, at least not in the infinite manner of the prairies. In the desert, mountain ranges bristle on every horizon, dividing the vastness into a series of basins. Furthermore, the peaks have a raw, angular look. They demonstrate an abrupt upthrust; show their youth, their vigor. Desert terrain is strong. Very little about it is halfway.

My thanks for help in writing about the land and my earnest awareness of dependence on the work of others are without bounds. Major published sources are listed in the Bibliography at the back of this volume, but help and information have come from more quarters and persons than can be separately acknowledged. They range from experts in various phases of research to companions on the back roads and trails of Arizona and Sonora, from librarians who unearthed special reference materials to editors who have patiently seen the manuscript through its gestation. Most especially I should like to thank professors and specialists who have criticized individual chapters: Richard F. Logan, University of California, Los Angeles; Robert R. Humphrey, Stephen M. Russell, Emil W. Haury, and James R. Hastings, University of Arizona; Herbert L. Stahnke, Arizona State University; Vincent Roth, Southwestern Research Station of the American Museum of Natural History; Peter Sanchez, Park Naturalist, and Charles Hansen, Biologist, Death Valley National Monument; Charles P. Lyman and C. Richard Taylor, Harvard University; and Raymond M. Turner, United States Geological Survey. Any remaining inaccuracies or inadequate expression of fact or concept are of course wholly my responsibility (and my sorrow, since I know full well that the risk of error is high when generalizing from such varied studies by so many different researchers). Nomenclature for the most part follows usage in the Peterson Field Guide Series. Scientific names are listed in the appendix.

I should also acknowledge the good fortune of having belonged to the National Park Service in the days when a young ranger could take his wife along on his far-reaching patrols of desert valleys and canyons and peaks. And, in dedicating the book to my parents, I should like to thank them for having taught me early to see what I was looking at, using the desert out from Los Angeles for that particular childhood classroom.

RUTH KIRK

Tacoma, Washington

Contents

A section of color photographs follows page 140

Desert
The American Southwest

1. What Is Desert?

It MAY BE a characteristic of desert country that appreciation comes most fully only after an accretion of experience, built layer on layer through the years of a person's life. A dry land, hot by day and cold by night, desert strikes the initiate as scarcely more than sand and rock and wind and sun — whether the desert of Arizona, or of southeastern California, or the Sahara. No meadows of lush grass. Few lakes or even ponds. Trees little taller than what is brush in more favored lands. Flowers only briefly colorful, and then only if various factors combine in just the right way. Yet live awhile in the desert, where every road and neighbor is known for a hundred miles around, and all other terrain except perhaps the tundra seems crowded. Or visit the desert *seeing* it rather than merely looking at it, and you find yourself going back time and again.

The borderlands between Arizona and Sonora, Mexico, are such a stretch, sure to stay in mind and to draw the beholder back. A paved road parallels the international border for 200 miles, beginning just south of San Diego and striking out for the sunrise. The first portion crosses high chaparral and pine forestland. Then comes a plunge down out of the mountains and into desolate low desert. At least by God's design the land is desert, although fields of grain and cotton now checkerboard square miles, and at times the whole expanse sparkles with water brought by irrigation ditches from the Colorado River. The flooding suggests oriental paddies yet actually is not to supply moisture to roots but to leach salts from the soil. The desert can be made to bloom, but only by flushing the soil as well as wetting it. The cost in water is high.

Beyond the fields lies wild desert — sere, essentially forbidding, and bounded by mountains that rise like a wall and separate this long barren stretch from more typical desert to the east. No preparatory foothills soften the transition from flatness to slopes. Instead, the mountains thrust themselves up abruptly, barely allowing a pass to cut the range and let the highway slip through. We often have camped after dark within these mountains, feeling out a favorite set of tire tracks that angles from the road and leads to a broad basin ringed by jagged peaks. There we spread bedrolls and sleep with the falling stars and the nighttime silhouettes of saguaro cactus and ocotillo. On our first night back in the desert after a long absence we came to this spot. We had lived in Death Valley, California, and at Organ Pipe Cactus National Monument, Arizona (not far from these mountains), then had transferred north to other national park areas, where my husband continued serving as ranger and naturalist. This particular trip was a sentimental one, and so the first sign of dawn flushing against the eastern horizon lured me from sleeping bag to a high ridge that promised a view.

Light had caught the topmost crags as I finished climbing, and would soon wash down to the desert floor. I remembered the motion as a steady sliding of light from the crest of a range to the toe, but that morning I looked closely and realized that what actually happens is a sudden flaring from one rock face to another. Entire cliffs receive the sun's rays and burst from shadow into brilliance. Desert light leaps rather than slides. Surely light must rank alongside Sun and Moon in the pantheon of gods belonging to this land. Light that comes softly at dawn and blares stridently at noon. Light that penetrates the consciousness as in no other land except perhaps the high mountains and the Far North — and there for the same reasons of a broad empty land set with angular lines.

Silence should be another desert god. Below me, where shadow still held the desert, a bobcat was ambling home to sleep off its night-wandering; and close by, a rock wren started to sing. Mostly, however, it was silence that filled the dawn and not creatures or motion. When sound did come it rang within the context of the silence, syncopating the hush rather than negating it. Not until light again embraces the entire desert world does a true chorus of sound begin. In the spruce and fir forests of the North this is not the way. Robins and varied thrushes and juncos carol there while morning is an opalescent promise; but in the desert, birds wait for full light and then call and sing, fifteen or twenty species at a time. Their number is great because the desert offers a multitude of habitats. For example, below the ridge where I sat, the rocky hillside gave on to a plain of creosote bush and cholla cactus, and at one edge of the plain was the mesquite-lined wash where we were camped. Above me were the peaks, here lifting a scant 4000 or 5000 feet but with views to other peaks of nearly 10,000 feet.

The various habitats spread over many square miles, all within unobstructed sight yet involving greater distances than strong binoculars can fully bridge. On such a tapestry, even fair-sized creatures become ill-defined dots, and "watching" becomes a matter of the ears more than the eyes. Fortunately, sound carries sweet and clear in the desert, not muffled by heavy vegetation or overpowered by waterfalls or surf or roaring freeways. From the peaks that morning came the croak of a raven; from the wash below, the call of Gambel's quail and the *chit* of a cardinal. Among the creosote bushes lark sparrows were lisping, their sound reaching easily to where I sat; and from the bushes also came the two-toned throaty whistle of a curve-billed thrasher, exactly like a human "wolf" whistle. On the slope, the wren continued its tinkling song. None of these were visible. In fact, my binoculars discovered only two birds: the distant swooping flight of a woodpecker, which I assumed to be a Gila woodpecker, and a phainopepla so backlit by the low sun that its wings and tail were translucent as it flew and its crest had turned into a halo. An awareness of the lean vastness of the desert comes

Gila woodpecker

to you, sitting alone in such a sunrise. It is a land that stretches
the soul and lifts the mind far beyond the minuscule perspective
of individual life. Harsh, to be sure; but a harshness underlain
and intermixed with harmonies. The common stereotype of
desert as too severe for life simply reflects human familiarity
with gentler lands. It is an outsider's point of view. Plants and
animals and people living in the desert are attuned to its
extremes. They accept life as they find it, and have no time
or energy or reason to chafe under its terms.

Many desert natives can also flourish elsewhere. At a zoo
a Gila monster (a foot-long lizard) will lie happily in its water
dish like a miniature alligator, and a pet horned lizard that
we moved with us to the soggy coolness of the Pacific Northwest
tripled its appetite and forswore winter hibernation in favor of
year-round activity. Even within the desert, a horned lizard

may climb into a yucca or an agave after a thunderstorm and lick droplets from the spiny tips of the plants, or bathe in the rainpools held by the stiff leaves. However, such behavior does not imply suffering under the usual dry circumstances of the desert. The Papago Indians we knew in Arizona, farming the upper slopes made briefly moist by summer rains and returning to lowland villages for the winter, did not feel that they suffered. Neither did the Panamint Indians who lived near us in Death Valley, in the old days moving seasonally from the summer crucible of the valley floor to the pinyon pine forests of the surrounding mountains. For these people, as for the animals of the desert, the land and the life are natural. The desert is home.

In a similar way the Spanish conquistadors, the first outsiders to contend with the deserts of the New World, were undismayed by what they found. The windswept uplands of central Mexico suggested the high plains of home to them, and as they worked north this was the concept they brought. The Sonoran and Chihuahuan regions were *altiplanos* or *desiertos,* the words used interchangeably and carrying the same connotation. The lands were dry — hot in summer and cold in winter — and that was that. Emotion did not enter in. Then came the Yankees, cultural progeny of Britain's damp greenness, and the American Southwest became "desert" with a different meaning. Originally the English word (and its French equivalent) had not been limited to a hot and dry land, but applied to any empty, "deserted" land. Yet when the Yankee newcomers took over from the Spanish, their eyes saw the word *desierto* on the maps and their minds translated it into terms of the Sahara — the sandy barrenness of northern Africa that was the desert familiar to men of English heritage. "Wasteland" became a virtual synonym for "desert," and "appalling," "dreadful," and "lifeless" became the standard adjectives in spite of the fact that much of the North American desert is remarkable for both beauty and life. It differs radically from the Sahara, as from each of the other deserts of the world.

Perhaps the chief attribute shared by deserts is that for the most part they ring the globe along the Tropic of Cancer and the Tropic of Capricorn. This is because the spinning of the earth sets up surface speeds of 25,000 miles per hour at the equator, and practically zero at the poles, a gigantic differential that fosters a circulation pattern within the atmosphere and largely determines world climate. In the case of deserts, this circulation produces a belt of dry, hot, descending air at latitudes of roughly 15 to 30 degrees on each side of the equator. There the deserts are found, although marking their precise boundaries, or defining exactly what a desert is and what it is not, cannot be done. Various systems have been worked out, none fully satisfactory; the one most commonly used is a method developed in 1918 by Wladimir Köppen. This classification mathematically combines temperature and precipitation, and defines desert as those regions where the moisture that could evaporate if it were available is at least double the amount that actually falls as rain or snow. This requisite is exceeded many times over by much of the American Southwest, for whole regions of California, Arizona, and northern Mexico are so dry that the ratio of potential evaporation to actual precipitation works out at one hundred to one. Seven or eight *feet* of water could evaporate for each one *inch* that falls, and some parts of the desert, in some years, exceed even these figures.

Other systems of identifying deserts go beyond Köppen's considerations of temperature and moisture, and also account for factors such as vegetation, soil, landscape features, and possible use by man. Some systems consider only the amount of moisture available to plants and animals instead of total moisture, since the single factor of availability also reflects how much rain has fallen, at what temperature, onto which type of soil, under what conditions. By another set of criteria, vast regions of the earth may properly be termed "physiological deserts," such as the poles and high mountaintops, where water is locked in ice and is largely unavailable to life. Other expanses are "edaphic deserts," where porous soil causes rapid percolation and a loss of water. There are even "indoor deserts." Consider a clothes moth living in the closet of a Manhattan apartment. It must cope with more heat and less hope of moisture than any insect living in true desert as conventionally defined.

Depending on what system is followed, about one-seventh of the earth's land surface — ten million square miles — is considered desert, much of it devoid of plants and therefore of animals. This total area is slightly larger than that of perpetual frost, about two-thirds the expanse of the earth's grassland and one-half of its forest land. The largest of the deserts is the Sahara, 3.5 million square miles, approximately the size of all the United States of America, including Alaska. The Sahara spreads across the whole of northern Africa and is essentially contiguous with the Arabian, Iranian, and Indian (Thar) deserts to the east. Nor is this all. The same hot and dry climate that produces the deserts extends beyond the African coast, reaching across the Atlantic nearly to the Virgin Islands. The idea of an ocean desert may seem a contradiction of terms but is valid from the standpoint of climate. It is all too real as "desert" for shipwreck survivors bobbing on a life raft. For them, heat and thirst are as crucial in mid-ocean as for any camel caravaner crossing the Saharan sand dunes where oases lie separated by four or five days' travel. Actually, arid climates span oceans westward from each major land mass (and on this basis the American desert reaches to within about a hundred miles of Hawaii).

Along with the Sahara, two other deserts parch the African continent: the Namib, on the southwestern coast, and the Kalahari, lying inland. The Namib is practically rainless but has the distinction of staying perpetually foggy. Cold offshore ocean currents chill the air and prevent winds from blowing in with enough moisture to supply significant rain. They hold vapor for fog, but not for rain. The Kalahari is really two deserts in one. In its northwestern portion clouds drip 8 to 20 inches of rain yearly, which is more moisture than most classification systems accept as true desert. However, the rain falls onto porous sand and sinks beyond reach of both roots and man, rendering

the land desert at least until the government finishes its effort
to reverse the situation through the provision of modern wells
and pumps. In the southwest, the Kalahari is desert by virtue
of little rain and great heat.

Nearly half of Australia classifies as desert, 1.3 million square
miles, the second largest desert in the world and covering a far
greater proportion of the continent than anywhere else. (The
North American desert covers only about 5 percent of the
continent even when generously calculated.) In Australia, air
moving across the ocean arrives laden with moisture and rain
falls along the coast; but not inland. The clouds wring themselves
out without lifting over the mountains, and the vast Outback
is left to spread dry and sparsely vegetated. Here live the
Bindibu, the aboriginal people of Australia, at peace with the
desert even into the twentieth century because they know every
crevice where hidden water may linger, which parts of the dry
stream beds may hold moisture within their sands, and what
species of plants can be tapped to yield root sap to sustain a
man's life. Thorny plants are almost nonexistent in the Outback,
perhaps because alone among world deserts this vast region has
never felt the browsing pressure of native hoofed mammals. At
least one theory explains that plants may have developed thorns
as protection against being eaten, and kangaroos and wallabies
simply are not as relentless in their feeding habits as are desert
sheep and burros and antelope, the browsers native to other
deserts.

The Eurasian continent includes the Turkestan Desert, three-
quarters of a million square miles, half again larger than Alaska,
and the Gobi and Taklamakan Deserts of China. Long summer
days at the high latitude of these deserts allow sunshine to pour
onto the land, heating and parching it, and the mountain arc
that swings from the Caucasus to the Himalayas and on into
China effectively blocks the monsoons of Southeast Asia and
denies the interior their moisture. Winters in these deserts are
intensely cold with dry air blowing down from the Arctic.
Throughout the winter night temperatures drop to $-60°F.$,
whereas summer noons experience well above $100°F.$

In South America there are the Patagonian Desert fingering north from the Argentinian tip of the continent and the equally long ribbon of the Atacama Desert along the coasts of Chile and Peru, the driest desert in the world. Rainfall in the Atacama averages half an inch per year and parts go as long as a quarter of a century between showers. Cold ocean currents offshore chill the air to such an extent that it cannot hold much moisture as it moves landward. The sea washes a bone-dry edge of the continent.

In North America desert covers a large part of Mexico and reaches up through the western United States with a discontinuous prong as far north as eastern Oregon and Washington and into British Columbia. Five distinct regions lie within this expanse, their differences great enough so that a person familiar with the land could parachute in blindfolded and know which division he had dropped into. The distinguishing lines of course are not clearcut, for inevitably catagories are sharper in man's mind than in nature; but even so, a Sonoran Mexican would know he was a long way from home if he arrived abruptly in California's Mojave Desert, and a Navajo Indian from Arizona would find little to recognize in the desert of Texas.

The northernmost of the five North American desert regions is the Great Basin, which really is not a single basin but a series of basins, each bounded by mountains and drained internally. Southern Oregon, Idaho, Utah, and Nevada form the heartland of this province. Contrary to stereotype, the dominant vegetation is not cactus and the dominant landscape is not sand. Drive the Great Basin Desert and you find roads shooting arrow-straight for twenty or thirty miles, crossing plains dotted unendingly with sagebrush, blackbrush, or antelope brush. Eventually such a road will angle and then continue for another twenty or thirty miles, climb a mountain range, and drop to the other side onto another plain dotted with sagebrush, blackbrush, or antelope brush. The Great Basin is the largest and most uniform of the North American deserts. It also is the coldest, often whitened by snow in winter.

The red sandstone cliffs and canyons popular for calendar

Great Basin Desert

Death Valley

photographs belong to a different desert: the Colorado Plateau where the four corners of Colorado, Utah, New Mexico, and Arizona adjoin. Here live the Navajo and Hopi Indians, and here slumber the silent cities abandoned hundreds of years ago by the Cliff Dweller Indians. Maps of this desert carry place names famous throughout the world: Grand Canyon, Monument Valley, Mesa Verde, Canyon de Chelly, Petrified Forest. In this desert, too, winters are snowy and summers arrive with raging thunderstorms — "male rains," the Navajos term them. Among the plants of the Plateau, sagebrush, grasses, pinyon pines, and junipers are the dominants.

The Chihuahuan Desert belongs mostly to Mexico, lying between the twin mountain spines of the Sierra Madre Occiden-

tal and the Sierra Madre Oriental. ("Sierra" is a Spanish word for "mountains.") The northern Chihuahuan Desert reaches into Texas, best exemplified at Big Bend National Park, and crosses southern New Mexico into the southeastern corner of Arizona. It is higher and cooler than the desert farther west, and also wetter because it lies close to the warm waters and moist air of the Gulf of Mexico.

The Mojave Desert stretches east of the mountains backing Los Angeles and San Diego, the smallest division of the American desert and a transition between the high desert of Nevada and the low desert of Arizona and Sonora. Winters in the California desert are too cold for the cactus forests found farther south, yet they are warm enough for a much richer flora than the drab brush of the Great Basin. Creosote bush is the prime indicator plant in the Mojave, a lacy plant with shiny olive-green leaves and bright yellow blossoms. It is joined by scores of other bushes according to precise habitat, and by myriad wildflowers in season.

A fifth province of the American Southwest is the Sonoran Desert, embracing southern Arizona as far into Mexico as Guaymas, about 250 miles south of the border, and including most of the Baja California peninsula. Sometimes the Sonoran is subdivided into separate units such as the Vizcaíno, the Arizona Upland, the Gulf Coast, and the Colorado Desert (which lies along the Colorado River, not in the State of Colorado). Sometimes geographers include Death Valley as part of the Sonoran Desert, since its winters are warm, but more often it is included as part of the Mojave or the Great Basin. The classifications do not really matter. They are mental hooks for man's convenience; the desert itself is a whole, and not an assemblage of isolated factors and components. Even so, no matter how its borders are pinpointed, the Sonoran Desert probably rates as what most Americans have in mind for the term "desert." It is the landscape around Phoenix and Tucson. It is saguaro cacti standing like succulent trees, arms stretched heavenward as if in supplication. It is bushes blooming in March and April, painting whole hillsides with the brilliance of their petals. It is jackrabbits leaping to safety when a man presses too close to take a picture, and cactus wrens saluting the noontime heat with their odd, chortling paean to sunshine and wildness.

For all its look of age, this desert (and every other desert in the world except probably the Namib) is a relatively recent feature. In fact, the entire Southwest seems only recently to have been shaped as it now is and become desert. The planet Earth is believed to be nearly five billion years old, the beginning of life reaching back about half that far. To sense this kind of a scale, imagine a time-lapse movie taken as the planet began to form, with one frame exposed every five years (compared to the twenty-four frames per second which is the normal speed of actual motion pictures). To project such a film of the earth's history, even with a full five years represented by each frame, would require a nonstop showing for twelve months. If the movie began at midnight on the first of January, it would be mid-July before the first groping of life appeared on the screen, and man in his earliest form accepted as human would flash into view on New Year's Eve about 9:00 P.M. Just before his arrival the North American desert would appear, somewhere around noon on December 29.

There have been previous American deserts, for traces such as fossilized sand dunes still exist as far northeast as Kansas. But for the present Sonoran Desert about the earliest structural history that can be pieced together dates from the Cretaceous period, 136 to 65 million years ago. At that time the entire Southwest region was an upland with an enormous eroded depression about where the southern base of the Rocky Mountains now is. Then in early Miocene time, perhaps 20 to 25 million years ago, the topography reversed itself. The sandstone country of northern Arizona and southern Utah, which had been low, was instead lifted into a high plateau and began to be cut by the myriad canyons of today. At about the same time the Basin and Range Province started to warp and fault into roughly its present form, which is like a giant washboard with generally parallel mountain ramparts trending north to south

Colorado Plateau: Navajo Indians (top left)
and Delicate Arch

Left, Mojave Desert yuccas

Sonoran Desert

and separated by flat-bottomed valleys. The great trough holding the Gulf of California also started deepening about this time,
part of a major faulting that still is wrenching Baja California
ever farther from the Mexican mainland.

By the time of the Pleistocene ice age, beginning around 3
million years ago, grassland dominated the region that today
is desert, and mammals such as horses and camels and mammoths
grazed its rich pasturage. No ice sheets covered the Southwest,
although a few of the highest mountain peaks held glaciers.
Rains deluged from the skies and filled basins which flooded
one into another, forming lakes as much as 1000 feet deep and
hundreds of miles long. Then perhaps 15 or 20 thousand years
ago a worldwide warming set in. The last of the four great
ice advances began to melt back, and the lakes started drying.
Our present age had begun.

Modern desert flora seems to have already been substantially

Gulf Coast

present even then. During the cool wet Pleistocene time, bur sage, brittlebush, and creosote bush evidently had been restricted to the steep south-facing slopes of the Southwest, the hottest and driest growing sites, but as the climate warmed they moved back down and again clothed the lowlands. Species such as mesquite, paloverde, elephant tree, fan palm, and seepwillow also were present — in fact were already old-timers. Their pollen has been found in the fossil record of Miocene and Pliocene time, dating back more than 20 million years, far older than paleobotanists had believed possible until recent discoveries. The ancestors of most of these plants seem to have slowly colonized northward from the humid tropics beginning about the end of the Cretaceous when the northern climate was relatively moist and warm. Many have present-day counterparts in South America. For instance, creosote bush grows as widespread in Argentinian deserts as in the Mojave and Sonoran Deserts of the United States and Mexico. It is called *jarilla* in Spanish and, although it probably now dominates more square miles of North America than of South America, it basically is of South American origin. Similarly, mesquite is paired with an Argentinian plant called *algarrobo*, and Mormon tea, various acacias, condalia, lycium, and several other plants of the North American desert have South American analogs.

Perhaps 15 thousand years ago, as the climate was warming and the northern glaciers were retreating, the large ice-age mammals disappeared from the Southwest. Why, is not fully known. Camels and horses and mammoths had been present for millennia before the climate change, and they do not seem like species fatally susceptible to warming. Fossils indicate that ground sloths were present at the same time as the larger animals, and they are a species definitely able to thrive in arid, warm lands. Seemingly, elephants should also have successfully endured the warming; they have ranged to the very edge of the Sahara Desert in recent times. Some investigators, Paul Martin of the University of Arizona among them, feel that a factor other than — or in addition to — climate must have been responsible for dooming the large mammals. Professor Martin infers it may have been man. The great herds disappeared at about the same time that Paleo-Indian hunters arrived in the Southwest, roving in bands and relying on the flesh and hides of animals for their own existence. Perhaps it was this hunting that tipped the balance and cleared the land of its largest mammals. Clues are hard to trace but slowly are accumulating.

In an opposite way, certain vertebrates present in today's Sonoran Desert also tell something of the timetable. These are endemic species, creatures that have lived and bred in isolation long enough to become biologically distinct from their nearest relatives, an indication that areas where they dwell have been isolated and unchanged for very long periods. Islands in the Gulf of California are prime strongholds for many of these species. You see the islands from the air. One is forty-two miles long; another is a volcano lifted 1000 feet above the water and cradling a second, smaller, crater at its top. Islets stud the sea by the hundreds, many of them mere jagged rocks pounded by surf. Yet on the islands are animals peculiarly evolved, like lesser prototypes of the Galápagos populations. There are rattlesnakes with no rattles, black chuckwalla lizards far darker than any of their kind elsewhere, and the darkest jackrabbits in all the desert, entirely black except for a buff-color belly and ears. From the air, the islands — and all of the plains and valleys and peaks of the entire Sonoran Desert — look bleak. Yet the story of this desert is of life, a greater variety and abundance of life than is easily found in any of the world's other deserts.

2. Hot and Dry

"THE HEAT'S ALL IN YOUR HEAD," the Chief Ranger used to say the first summer we were stationed in Death Valley, but his face would be flushed as he spoke and sweat would drip from the tip of his nose. At night he, like the rest of us, would throw a mattress in the back of a truck and drive to the mountains 5000 feet above the valley floor and 20 degrees cooler. Or sometimes the Chief would sleep in his fish pool, cooled by its waters throughout the long hot night — a traditional solution to summer nights where *minimum* temperatures sometimes stay in the nineties. We had arrived in March. The thermometer stood at 106°F., and it continued to climb above the 100-degree mark nearly every day from then until mid-October, when there was rain. Paper turned brittle. Cold showers ran hot because the scorching earth heated pipes not buried deeply enough. Dust clung to rugs, held firm by static electricity, and sheets crackled and shot blue sparks at night. Kisses became literally electric.

Yet it was halcyon heat. There is peace in seeing the whole milieu of hundreds of square miles at once and knowing where you stand in relation to everything else. Summer gives endless time for books and talk, and even the most extreme days eventually bring sundown and a chance to sit beneath a mesquite tree and watch the purple-gray haze of evening erase details from the land and turn the mountains into a cardboard stage set. The hard glare of day ends and the softness of night comes as a healing balm to be soaked up by body and mind. Actually,

temperature is difficult to discuss meaningfully: *What* temperature? Out in the open, exposed to the full fire of the sunshine —
the kind of temperature most plants experience and animals
try to escape? Temperature with wind hammering the brassy
heat into you; or with the air calm? Temperature at the level
of your head or of your feet? The two are very different.
Ground-surface temperatures have been recorded as high as
190°F., hot enough to be felt even through thick-soled boots.

Standardized weather bureau temperatures are read from
thermometers set in white louvered boxes placed five feet above
the ground. Nobody and no thing is exposed to these temperatures alone except for the thermometers themselves, yet their
readings have the great value of being standardized. They can
be directly compared. For the low-elevation stations of desert
California and Arizona, and south into Mexico, it can be
generalized that maximums reach at least 120°F., at least every
few years. Also, there may be truly hot weather at nearly any
season. Yuma, Arizona, for example, has recorded 90° or above
at least once during every month of the year except for December.
Nondesert locations only approach these ferocious temperatures.
In Boston the normal July high, based on 30 years of records,
is 82 degrees. For Chicago the figure is 86 degrees, for Houston
92, and for Los Angeles also 92. The maximums at these stations
during the same period have been 105, 104, 108, and 110 degrees
respectively — 10 to 15 degrees below common desert maximums.

In addition to extreme highs, desert heat is recurrent and
prolonged. It is routine. In this sense Death Valley is a kingsized
standard. No desert anywhere is hotter even though the world's
record usually is credited to Libya. In 1922 the weather station
at Aziza reported 136.4°F. This topped the world's previous
single hottest reading of 134.6°F. reported from Death Valley
nine years earlier; but the Libyan reading is questioned by
meteorologists because no nearby station recorded anything
approaching such an extreme. On the other hand, Death Valley's singular high seems in line. "I remember the day very
distinctly," wrote the Superintendent of Furnace Creek Ranch

a few years later. "A man by the name of Busch perished in the Valley north of the ranch that day on account of the heat. It was blowing very hard." The *low* temperature in Death Valley the previous night had been 93°; and on the day of record heat stations surrounding the Valley also reported exceptional maximums. The thermometers of ranch personnel climbed even higher than the official reading (which was taken on a thermometer calibrated only to 135°F.). For nine consecutive days that July the official temperature rose to at least 125°. Out on the salt flats it must have been higher. There were no instruments set there, and no long-range study has been made even yet, although one investigation indicates July temperatures about 12 degrees hotter on the flats than at Furnace Creek. The elevation is lower — as much as 282 feet below sea level compared to Furnace Creek's minus 168 feet — and there is no vegetation to ameliorate heat by the transpiration of water.

Great heat of this sort does not come and go quickly. It bakes the desert for long, relentless hours, a fact of enormous importance for plants and animals and for man. The Quartermaster Corps of the United States Army, experimenting at Furnace Creek in 1950, found that temperatures stay within 5 degrees of the daily maximum for six hours and within 15 degrees for twelve hours. This means that the day of the record high the thermometer probably stood at 119°F. or above from 9:00 A.M. to 9:00 P.M., and from noon until 6:00 at 130° or above. Surprisingly, this kind of heat is noticeable in progressive steps of discomfort. It might seem that hot would be *hot* and a degree or two up or down would go unnoticed; but not so. Every two degrees above 115° are discernible, and above 125° each half degree causes a distinct additional heatload. Simply staying alive until evening becomes accomplishment enough.

Of course heat is only part of the desert story. There is also cold. Even in summer, night may bring low temperatures: there is little moisture to conduct the day's warmth deep within the earth, and since skies normally are clear the desert surface cools quickly once the sun has set. Nighttime temperatures may be

50 degrees below daytime highs, a fact causing someone to point out that the lover who promised to be faithful until the sands of the desert turned cold needed to wait only until about three hours after midnight. In winter, freezing occurs at least once a year throughout the Mojave Desert and the northern Sonoran Desert, although it is rare in the Mexican lowlands from Hermosillo southward. Mountains commonly are snowcapped from November through April, depending on elevation, and snow sometimes blankets the desert floor, piling oddly against the thickset thorns of cholla and prickly pear cactus and sifting among the windward blades of yuccas so that only the pointed tips are left exposed, bristling as if set in a giant pincushion. Usually such blankets of snow last only a few hours.

The low temperatures of the desert are not as cold as the lows common elsewhere. Mathematically average the daily highs and lows of Death Valley for January alone and the resulting mean temperature is 50°F., which is just about the same as the average of year-round temperatures in the midwestern United States. Even so, desert winters are cold enough that one bird species meets them by hibernating: the poor-will, a western relative of the whip-poor-will. These are mottled gray and white birds about the size of a robin, although more chunky, a frequent sight in the car headlights on a back road after dusk. Poor-wills crouch on the ground and make short leaping flights after night-flying insects, gorging themselves, then resting and indulging in a second feeding period just before dawn. When winter settles in, poor-wills sometimes hibernate, although only about thirty instances have been adequately reported. The birds blend against the backgrounds of their chosen resting spots so perfectly as to be all but invisible, and therefore how widespread the practice may be is not really known.

The first hibernating poor-will to be examined scientifically — and the first hibernating bird of any species, anywhere, to be examined — was found in December 1946 by Edmund Jaeger, dean among desert naturalists and at the time head of the zoology department at the University of California's Riverside campus. Jaeger and two students were walking up a canyon in the Chuckawalla Mountains, southeast of Palm Springs. They noticed a poor-will, supremely camouflaged, resting in a rock niche of the canyon wall. For ten minutes they watched and saw no movement. They gently touched the bird, and drew no response. They picked it up, shouted at it, and still drew no response. Then as they put it back in its crypt, an eyelid flickered slightly, the only sign that the bird was alive. During the rest of that winter and through the next three winters Professor Jaeger returned to the little canyon, studying the same "sleeping" bird. Its body temperature was 64.4°F. compared to 106°, which is normal for a poor-will. No heartbeat could be found even with a stethoscope. No breath condensed onto a cold mirror held close to the bird's nostrils, and no movement of its chest was noticeable. Once the poor-will was found with one eye partly open, but a flashlight held just two inches from it produced no reaction. A hailstorm battered several feathers but did not arouse the bird.

A nonhibernating poor-will is estimated to need eight calories' worth of insects per day; but while hibernating it needs only one-tenth of this amount, energy being readily available from the heavy layer of a fat just under the skin. Jaeger's bird remained in hibernation from at least November 26 until February 14, seemingly without stirring (although it was not continually observed). The desert advantage of such behavior is the same as for a bear in Alaska, a successful evasion both of the need to gather food when it is scarce and of the need to stay warm after the mercury has dropped.

Water plays a major role in the desert in spite of its scarcity. But perhaps the fact that there ever is rain constitutes a marvel if not a miracle, not only in the desert but anywhere in the world. Lapse-time photography has shown that out of every one hundred clouds fewer than five are likely to yield rain or snow. Most simply evaporate back into invisible vapor. Precipitation is an exceptional circumstance: unless a cloud holds at least an inch of precipitable moisture, none can fall. The marvel is that aridity does not dominate the entire globe. Significant water seems nonexistent in the rest of the solar system, or the universe. Our planet is unique. In fact even considering the oceans and the circulation patterns of the atmosphere, it still is not clear why precipitation developed instead of merely vaporization. The atmosphere of the infant earth differed greatly from that of today, evidently having formed from gases bubbling free as the molten mass of the new planet cooled. There was little oxygen, but a great deal of carbon dioxide and of water vapor. Somehow, as the cooling continued rain began to fall. It did not bathe the earth because it could not penetrate the enormous heat that swaddled the surface of the entire planet. Instead, the rain at first evaporated and recycled into the atmosphere; then gradually the wet curtain dropped closer to the surface, and at last the earth cooled enough to permit liquid water to linger upon its outer crust. The stage was set for the beginnings of the oceans. Rain fell without ceasing for centuries until the clouds emptied themselves enough to thin and tear apart. This let sunshine through, and readied the stage for the second act of the great drama: life appeared.

Perhaps it is because water is scarce in the desert that when rain clouds do appear they set you to thinking. Each of us lives physically for nine prenatal months as an aquatic being; and, although once we leave the womb water may never again be automatically assured, we never cease to depend upon it. No wonder the Christian religion, desert-born, uses water for its rite of baptism and symbolic entry into new life. Some even argue that man as a social creature developed under the goad of planning around water, or at least that this has been one pattern of his development. Only through cooperation could men along the Nile and Tigris-Euphrates support an expanding population and assure themselves of adequate water for crops. Individuals cannot build dams and operate irrigation networks; organization is imperative. Energies once dissipated outward in an endless struggle against environment instead became directed within the band. Change followed. Social structure began, and once set in motion it acted almost as an organism with a life of its own, capable of growing physically, mentally, and spiritually.

In the Sonoran Desert the pattern of rain divides into two seasons. The wettest storms come as summer monsoons, usually associated with warm moist air that sweeps around the margins of the stable high-pressure area above the Atlantic Ocean and Gulf of Mexico. Such storms often become violent over the desert mountains as ground heat reaches its maximum in the middle of the afternoon and sends winds blowing upslope. In the lowlands full storm intensity comes slightly later in the day, when valley floors have heated above the temperatures of the peaks, which by then are covered with clouds. Some summer rains arrive from the west instead of the east. They originate in disturbances off the coast of Mexico that have grown large and intense enough to move into desert latitudes. These Pacific storms are more general than the thunder showers from the Gulf, and they may occur at any time of day rather than typically in the afternoon.

Prodigious downpours characterize the tropics-born storms, whether from east or west. They prompt the posting of street signs in Tucson which warn BEWARE OF FLOODS, an admonition that strikes the uninitiated as ridiculous. Cactus and floods simply do not seem to go together, but one clap of thunder can be enough to convince even a skeptic. The signs stand guard where streets cross drainage channels, and in summer these dips can change from sun-baked pavement burning the bare feet of playing children into raging rivers of muddy water four feet deep. Sometimes the transformation may even come without prelude. A wall of water, hissing and curling back upon itself, appears, although no cloud has veiled the sun locally: runoff from a storm that emptied itself some distance away.

Winter rains usually fall more gently than summer rains, and they blanket wider areas. Some originate within the general storm belt of the middle latitudes, a hemispheric system of winds and wetness that once in a while works far enough south to bring its gift of rain to the desert. Other storms move in from the Pacific, caught in the flow of upper air. These are the heaviest storms of the winter, and may produce several days of rain or even snow, depending on elevation.

Desert rain has a hypothetical orderliness overall, a pattern. Yet as actually experienced, its one certain aspect is its undependability. The amount of rain that is usual for a whole year may fall in a single July afternoon; or one year may bring many times the rain of the preceding year, then for the next twelve to twenty-four months there may be none. "Hope it rains before the kids grow up" goes the standard desert joke. "They've never seen any." In places the quip is nearly as much truth as joke. When once we stopped for gas at a remote Baja California rancheria during a light rain the family living there said that the rain was the first in five years. Weather records bear out the possibility in that part of the Mexican desert, and for the desert as a whole, rain can repeatedly miss one particular area yet fall nearby. Bagdad, California, has gone two years and one month with no rain, the record drought within the United States.

This erratic sort of pattern was studied through an entire year at the Desert Laboratory at Tucson, a Carnegie Institute research station now defunct but responsible in its day for a wide variety of pioneering desert observations and experimentation. A grid of 24 rain gauges was set out, spaced 110 yards apart. During the year measurable rain fell 48 times, two-thirds of it coming in the summer. The total amount and the seasonal distribution were as had been expected, but there was an astonishing difference in amounts just within the small study plot, which extended across a flat area and partway up a hill. One of the August storms dumped nearly 1½ inches in less than an hour at the uppermost gauge, but catty-cornered half a mile across the grid a mere ¼ of an inch fell. This is a difference of nearly 6 to 1 in what would seem like entirely too small a distance to have such an effect. In contrast to these rains, the winter rains held fairly steady over the grid with a maximum difference of slightly more than ¹/₁₀ of an inch from one gauge to another.

Desert residents sometimes can simultaneously watch both a dust storm and a rain storm and if the paths of the two cross, as occasionally does happen, an actual mud storm will ensue. Lightning, sunshine, and rain regularly commingle. The heating of the ground causes air currents to rise, many of them ascending high enough to chill and form clouds. Part of the sky will be a blue background for puffy white cumulus clouds, and at the same time part will be banked with every possible shade of gray. There will be clouds of a soft, gentle gray like the breast feathers of a Canada jay, clouds of a sullen, smog gray, and clouds of an intense blue-gray. These latter sweep for miles across the desert, torrential rain trailing from their bellies like the snaggled teeth of a gigantic comb. Lightning erupts in brilliant silver flashes during these storms, or moves horizontally like a writhing snake seeking a path to the ground. At night the lightning looks yellow instead of silver. It may merely flicker, glancing from side to side within a cloudbank; or it may be a virtual pounding of light, looking the way a drum sounds. Occasionally lightning will seem to come through a crack, as if clouds were a dam holding back a world of light and letting only one ragged streak spill out. The gleam flashes for a moment; then the crack slams shut and darkness again reigns.

Because rainfall is both meager and variable in the desert, the average annual figures that purport to measure it hold less significance than is true in regions with more moderate climates. The drier the land, the more erratic the precipitation, and also the farther apart the weather stations because there is no one living there to read them. Also, whatever the amount of the statistical mean, it will be higher than the normal rainfall that actually occurs. This is because unusually wet years have a disproportionate effect. Four years with 1 inch of rain each, followed by one year with 6 inches, will average as 2 inches per year.

Still, something of a pattern can be traced by studying the rainfall data available from desert stations. Death Valley is the driest part of the continent, its annual precipitation averaging only 1½ inches per year. This amount steadily increases to the east and south, until at Phoenix precipitation averages 8 inches per year — rain mixed with a little snow — and at Tucson the figure is 10 to 12 inches per year. Records from Baja California indicate slightly more rainfall along the Gulf Coast than on the Pacific side.

The validity of rainfall statistics in relation to desert life is lessened by one additional factor besides the overall scarcity of rain, its extreme variability, and its heavy runoff. This added factor is evaporation. The heat of the ground and the nearly constant desert wind combine to drive moisture back up into the air before much of it can be utilized by plants and animals or stored within the earth as a supply for the future. Soil moisture depends on a race between immediate surface evaporation, downward seepage, and upward capillarity. The outcome is determined largely by the porosity of the soil. Heavy claylike soils rapidly give moisture back to the air. Coarse sands and gravels allow it to soak in.

Runoff scribes the mark of water upon the desert, shaping

Water erosion

the landscape just as water shapes the land of humid regions. Summer outbursts pound the desert earth briefly and set flood-water and rock debris to churning wildly. "In the sierras," W. J. McGee, a pioneering desert geographer, wrote of the mountains, "the storm torrents gather loosened rock masses . . . hurl them down the cliffs and hurry them through the barrancas [canyons], bursting them asunder and knocking loose other masses on the way."

Such floods result as rills and streamlets finger together in mountain catchment basins, gathering runoff from a vast land surface and funneling it through narrow canyon outlets onto alluvial fans and bajadas, the slopes where mountain fronts merge with desert lowlands. At any given spot, decades or even centuries may separate one of these storms from another, but within the whole of the desert there are floods each year. A trip to the grocery store — which can be a hundred miles or more — may last a week if the highway has washed out or has been buried by five feet of rock rubble and mud. Ironically, one of the toughest desert jobs is to maintain roads against summer floods, and because of them certain scenic drives are closed to travel each summer. Titus Canyon, leading into Death Valley, is one of these, a typical hourglass canyon with an enormous catchment basin draining through an outlet so constricted that a carload of people driving through the canyon can touch both walls simply by reaching out of the windows on each side. Water and debris fifteen feet deep roar through these narrows, a force infinitely greater than road or man can withstand, and tragically responsible for the name of the canyon. A young mining engineer from Pennsylvania, Morris Titus, set out on foot during the turn-of-the-century boom days. He and a companion were low on drinking water and in danger of dying from thirst. Instead, Titus drowned somewhere in the canyon, caught in a flashflood.

Established channels cannot always carry the rushes of water that burst from such canyons. A flood may spread out and move as a sheet, affecting areas as great as one hundred square miles.

Cobbles and pebbles swept along by the water begin to drop out near the mouths of the gorges, too heavy to continue as the flood spreads and begins to lose force. Sand and silt may

Left, Titus
Canyon;
right, runoff
patterns

carry long distances. McGee tells of watching a sheetflood
"advancing at race-horse speed at first, but slowing rapidly and
dying out in irregular lobes." The water depth was about eight

to twelve inches and the flow was uniform. The flood spread more than a mile wide at its edge. It lasted only ten minutes, and in half an hour the ground was drying. Except for its steaming and for the new piles of flotsam caught against bushes, there was no sign of anything beyond the ordinary.

Few written accounts of sheetfloods exist because they occur only sporadically and in a land that until recently was far beyond the probing investigations of modern man. However, the Indian peoples of the desert have long known where to expect storm runoff, and there they plant crops. Some locations are close to the mountains; others are far downslope, affected by sheet-floods that originate on the plains rather than among the peaks. Flood farming is a timeless harmony between man and desert, a means of agricultural expecting and receiving that dates back at least two thousand years in the Sonoran Desert and is still practiced by Papago Indians and Mexican rancheros. Successful yields of corn, beans, and squash may be expected six years out of seven from *temporales,* as the flood fields are called in Spanish. With these odds and with farmers hedging their bets by planting in several locations, there seldom is a starving year. Relatively little work is required. The system is mostly plant, wait, and harvest. A fresh supply of water and mineral nutrients is delivered, or withheld, according to the infinite vagaries of the desert. When — if — the flood arrives, man sows his seeds, and the patterns decreed by the gods take care of the rest.

Alluvial fans are another signature of water upon the dry land. These are great wedges of debris carried by floods from mountain peaks and spilled out onto desert plains, one of the distinctive geologic features of the desert. Such fans are particularly nota-ble in California and Nevada, where they spread like voluptuous aprons from the deep notches of each major canyon. Mountain ranges in this part of the desert commonly rise 7000 to 10,000 feet, providing both sources of detritus and ample walls against which the gigantic fans may build. Dynamic processes such as faulting or warping are much in evidence, and some geologists believe that the formation of alluvial fans, or at least those with

Alluvial fans

1765938

steep gradients, require such activity. Throughout much of the southern desert mountains tend to be low and fans often coalesce into a bajada, seeming like a single unit at the base of a range rather than separate deposits poured from individual canyon mouths. Or there may be a pediment of rock edging the mountains, thinly veneered with loose alluvial gravel and looking almost like a bajada.

In a dry climate streams seldom flow, but when they do they easily overload with sediment. Vegetation is sparse, so each raindrop strikes the ground with maximum impact. Loose material gets splattered and churned, every least trickle of water able to pick up debris and move it downslope. Alluvial fans probably reflect past conditions when major rainy periods accounted for a more rapid weathering of rock than occurs today. Debris accumulated in the mountains and washed through the canyons to form the fans. Relatively little new material is added now except in the aftermath of an unusually wild cloudburst.

Two characteristics distinguish the alluvial fans of the desert from the deltas and other alluvial deposits of moist regions. The fans form from a heterogeneous accumulation of material ranging from silt to gravel to cobbles — whatever happens to be worn from the peaks and carried to the lowlands. The term "fanglomerate" designates this rubble mix after it has partially indurated into crumbly rock. Alluvial fans also are distinctive because of isolated boulders scattered far out from the mountains, even where slopes are nearly level. How such boulders moved across gradients of only 3 or 4 percent puzzled geomorphologists until the work of Eliot Blackwelder established an answer: mudflows.

Writing for the Geological Society of America in the late 1920s, Blackwelder quoted the eyewitness account of a rancher:

Some time before the mudflow made its appearance, its dull heavy roar could be heard from up the canyon, quite distinct from and rising above all the other noises of the storm, reminding one of the breakers against a rocky shore. As it issued from the narrow mouth of the side canyon it was accompanied by a cloud of dust, occasioned by the breaking up of huge masses of dry soil from projecting points in its rush down the canyon. Through the dust glimpses could be had of great piles of drift, with an occasional tree turning end over end. After descending about one-half mile from the mouth of the smaller canyon, this wave came to a full stop, only to be succeeded in a few minutes by another wave, larger and swifter than the first. There was no dust with this or any of the succeeding waves, but immense masses of rock, many of which must have weighed several tons, were dancing along on the surface, apparently as light as corks, supported by the earthy mass beneath . . . Each succeeding wave [kept] getting thinner and traveling with greater velocity than the preceding one, until finally, in about half an hour the mass was no longer mud, but a steady rush of yellow, foaming water . . .

As to the distance of the action of this flow and the size of the rocks moved by it, a sandstone boulder carried down by it from a point 7 miles up the canyon has a height of 8 feet, a length of 16 feet, and a width of 12 feet. On the plains about 5 miles east of the mouth of the canyon several masses much larger than this one can be seen. These also were brought down a canyon by cloudbursts.

Such a mudflow ranks somewhere between a flood and a landslide. Effects are akin to the devastation that occurs when tons of volcanic dust get mixed in with thunderstorms, like the flow that buried Herculaneum after Mount Vesuvius erupted in A.D. 79, or the outbursts that rip the sides of glaciated peaks such as Mount Rainier in the State of Washington when ice dams break and unleash impoundments of water onto unconsolidated rock rubble. In all of these situations a thick porridge of mud forms, and boulders ride it easily, the whole mass gliding like viscous batter. Where it becomes thick it temporarily dams. Water then collects, repeatedly damming and breaking through. In the desert, vast and easily erodible catchment slopes plus loose deposits contribute to such flows. Boulders swept along by them will come to rest as soon as the momentum of the flood has ebbed. They may not move again, ever. For decades and centuries they remain on the alluvial fan, until time at last reduces them to debris and rain and winds sweep them away.

Thin fluid flows will of course move more rapidly and travel farther than thick boulder-carrying flows. Water may reach to the floor of a dry desert basin and turn it into an ephemeral lake an inch or two deep, a wondrous sight catching the glow of sunrise or sunset or lined with the silvery path of a moon crossing the barren desert. Once in a great while such lakes gain considerable size. In 1969, heavy rains formed a lake in Death Valley almost sixteen miles long, five miles wide, and deep enough to float a canoe. The Amargosa River ran wet for its entire length, remarkable not only for that particular river but for most desert rivers, which are more nearly potential surface drainage courses than actual ones.

Even without water the myriad drainage sinks of the desert hold dry lakes, or playas, formed of the silt that has washed in by repeated floods. Such "lakes" really are lake beds, fills of fine debris accumulated throughout centuries and sometimes measuring several thousands of feet deep. Their surfaces, cracked into a mosaic of mud curls, are typically so dry and firm that an 1885 United States Geological Survey expedition could report "horses hooves clatter while crossing them," and in current terms the playas serve as raceways and airplane landing fields. If slopes impregnated with salts happen to lie in the path of floodwaters, a playa may stretch as a gleaming, lifeless salt flat. Sodium chloride is the most common salt, but gypsum, potash, and others may also be present. Deposits sometimes are enormous, enough so for long-term mining in the case of ancient lake beds such as Lake Bonneville outside Salt Lake City, Utah, and Searles Lake west of Death Valley.

Channels leading to the playas or draining from one basin into the next are called dry washes, or arroyos. They are the same as the *wadis* in the Sahara, *sand rivers* in East Africa, *omurambas* in South-West Africa, and *sai* in the Gobi. Water may flow once or twice a year, or not for a decade; and even where year-round streams flow they seldom run more than a few miles. The Colorado River and its Arizona tributaries, the Bill Williams and the Gila Rivers, are exceptions; but those rivers are born of high mountains, not of the desert. The same is true of rivers in Sonora such as the Altar and the Yaqui. They begin in the mountains and cross the desert because it lies between the peaks and the ocean. The rivers do not belong to the desert; they simply happen to flow down into it. Maps show desert rivers as drainage lines, but in most cases a man

Anthills in dry wash

comes closer to choking on their dust than to drinking from them. As the saying goes, "Never trust a man who tells you he's drunk from the Hassayampa," a large river in Arizona with no water (except subsurface).

The bed of a wash may be more "desert" than the surrounding country, because the runoff that pours down it will strip vegetation and leave only churned gravel in its wake. Washes curiously reverse usual hydrology. In humid lands streams tend to cut lower than the level of groundwater and are fed by subterranean flow from the water table into the stream. But in the desert the opposite holds: the water in a wash originates in rain storms and percolates from the stream bed into the groundwater.

Wind, as well as water, figures in the shaping of the land — persistent wind. Wind that stirs dust and dims visibility. Wind that forces closure of highways because of danger to vehicles, and that pits windshields and sandblasts paint, leaving bare metal on the windward sides of cars and causing a pileup of insurance forms on city desks. Dry regions typically are windy. Air contacting the ground heats and expands, which lowers its density. Air from higher pressure zones moves in, and winds result. This complicates life for plants and animals. Gusts break twigs off plants and blow sand away from roots. They dry the soil and dissipate the frail envelopes of moisture formed around leaves by transpiration. A wind of 40 miles per hour has 16 times the drying effect of a 10-mile-per-hour breeze, the effect varying with the square of the wind's speed, given a steady humidity. Birds and animals build their nests in the protection of rocks and bushes, in some cases to windward so as to avoid being smothered by sand and debris deposited in the lee of bushes. One species of butterfly, *Philotes speciosa,* has even learned to cope with wind by alighting on the ground and hooking the three legs on one side of its body over the top of a pebble. This lets the wind blow it parallel to the ground, where it waits out the gusts in a streamlined position, offering the least possible resistance and saving its wings from a battering. Natural mosaics of small stones produced and maintained by wind pave many stretches of the desert. They form only one stone deep, with light soil beneath. The finest material continually blows away, and this polishes and abrades the stones to an even closer fit. Such armored surfaces are called desert pavement in the American Southwest, *reg* in the Sahara, *serir* in Libya, and *gibber plain* in Australia.

Winds of enormous force frequently roar across the desert, particularly where topography such as a mountain pass funnels the air and increases its rush, like the stepped-up pressure of water forced through a small garden hose. No example is more striking than the "moving rocks" of the Racetrack Playa in the mountains west of Death Valley. There, rocks from walnut-size to quarter-ton blocks of limestone have scraped tracks into the dry-lake surface. Twigs and the dung of wild burros also slide, leaving marks, and a few tracks end only in piles of playa mud. One of these mud trails measures two inches wide at one end and grows to a low ridge twelve feet across at the other end. The length of the track is only twenty feet.

The playa is level. The rocks do not move by gravity, and in any case their tracks point in all directions of the compass, so simple downhill motion could not account for them. Rolling is not involved. The motion is by sliding, gently gouging and smoothing shallow furrows as the rocks move. The longest tracks zigzag and schuss for 1500 feet and occasionally include complete loops and right-angle jogs. Wind seems the best explanation. When rain or snow has wet the playa surface it becomes so slippery that a car can be pushed across it without the wheels

Moving rocks

turning. Silts from similar playas are used as drilling muds for oil rigs because their coefficient of friction is so low. Given these conditions, wind quite plausibly could skate the rocks. Gusts of hurricane force surely occur, but because of remoteness the actual conditions have not yet been fully documented.

One theory holds that collars or floes of ice help to support the weight of the stones and facilitate their movement as winds from the peaks howl across the playa valley. Winter freezes are not uncommon at the Racetrack, which is located in a 3700-foot mountain valley. Ice unquestionably forms, but it cannot be essential for the rocks to move. Fresh tracks have been reported following a summer rainstorm, which rules out ice, and Robert Sharp, geologist at the California Institute of Technology, has carried the disproof a step farther. As part of a study of the movement he ringed one particular rock with a corral of stakes far enough apart to let the rock escape, although not if encircled with ice. In March the rock slid out, thus establishing the fact that movement does not depend on ice, at least not always.

Similar tracks are known on a few other dry lakes, including Bonnie Clare in the mountains east of Death Valley and on a remote playa in Baja California; but the Racetrack rocks are by far the largest and produce the longest tracks. Winds may be peculiarly strong there and the supply of rock unquestionably is greater than usual, since most playas dot the floors of drainage basins far removed from possible rock sources. The Racetrack Playa happens to abut a bedrock cliff, and it also has an outcropping of rock like an island near one end. Nobody claims actually to have seen the rocks move, but the tracks were reported by early-day prospectors and the rocks must have been skating for centuries before that. Individual tracks remain visible anywhere from a few months to ten or twenty years, depending on their depth. Heavy rocks seem to gouge about three or four inches into the playa. At times evidence of their movement nearly fades from existence; then conditions become right and the rocks slide again.

Occasionally spiraling, local winds set the desert to smoking with dust devils. These are usually too small to cause damage beyond carrying off hats and filling hair and eyes and teeth with sand. Such spinning cones of wind, common throughout the deserts of the world, occur when a mass of air gets heated out of equilibrium with surrounding air. Differential heating of this sort is frequent and substantial. For instance, a ground-surface temperature of 160°F. has been recorded while the air temperature 5 feet above the ground stood at 116° and was 92° at 1000 feet. Under these conditions the passing of a jackrabbit or a car may disturb the superheated air of the ground surface and set it rising. This in turn lowers the pressure of the immediately adjoining air and sucks it in from all directions to feed the rising column. The inflowing streams of air accommodate to each other by spiraling upward, forming the dust devil. The spin may be either clockwise or counterclockwise, seemingly at random. An observer in Egypt reported finding 175 clockwise dust devils and 200 that were counterclockwise during a single investigation. Occasionally a whirlwind would lose part of its force by coming in contact with an obstacle, then reverse its rotation and revive. Usually dust devils zigzag slowly across the desert, their course following the topographic relief of the land, such as along a ridgecrest, but occasionally one stays stationary for hours. Accounts of railroad construction across the Altar Valley of Sonora mention a dust devil that halted work for half a day by stalling above an embankment and sucking up sand at a rate of one cubic yard per hour.

Ronald Ives, who has intently studied the remote wilds of the Sonoran Desert, reports seeing dust devils more than 5000 feet high as measured by triangulation. Such heights can be expected especially where vegetation is sparse and soil surface temperatures are maximum, as in Death Valley or on the delta of the Colorado River. Ives has measured the height and progress of whirlwinds moving across the ground and found that they generally travel 4 or 5 miles per hour. They wander erratically and cover about double their actual straight-line distance. Once he shepherded a dust devil that whirled across the desert for 7

hours, yet traveled a net of only 40 miles from its point of origin. By driving his Jeep into the vortex of this wind, Ives found that the temperature at the spiraling heart registered several degrees lower than at the edges. He also recorded wind speeds of more than 20 miles per hour, which was as high as his portable instruments would register.

Actual speeds of at least 90 miles per hour seem more likely. Fixed anemometers have shown sudden brief accelerations of this magnitude when hit by dust devils, and the readings probably should be even higher. Velocities are hard to measure because in mere seconds dust devils can fill anemometer cups with sand and burn out the bearings, destroying both the instruments and the chance of a complete record. Tornadoes have been recorded at 170 miles an hour, but tornadoes belong

Sand dunes

to humid lands; their air holds moisture and this added factor intensifies the air's instability and increases its velocity. Dust devils, with only dry air, are not likely candidates for such great speeds. Around 30 or 40 miles per hour probably is their common maximum, with brief gusts double or triple this. Ives reports kangaroo rats spun aloft, a situation requiring theoretical speeds of at least 30 miles per hour. ("The animals appeared unhurt after landing," he comments, "although usually very angry!")

Sand dunes build where winds play upon loose earth, and dryness enters in too since damp sand will tend to stick rather than blow. But given enough of the right material, together with strong winds, sand lifts a foot or so above the land surface and blows until the wind stops or an obstacle triggers release of the load. The obstacle may be a bush, the crest of an existing dune, or simply a break in the air current. Some dunes form as long parallel ridges. Others shape into *barchans,* crescents with tapering horns that point downwind. What seems from the ground to be a welter of humps and hollows shows a surprising symmetry seen from an airplane, an exact repetition and geometric order unknown elsewhere in nature on so large a scale.

By world standards the North American deserts are lacking in sand. Along the Egypt-Sudan border sand forms a uniform sheet about one foot thick. In the Sahara, dunes blanket an area larger than the whole of France. (Even so, eight or nine square miles of the Sahara are bare rock for every one square mile of blowing sand). In the Japanese language the word for desert derives from the Chinese characters for *sa,* meaning sand, and *baku,* meaning vast and carrying a feeling of such exceeding vastness that the mind can scarcely grasp an end to it. This concept tends to be the expectation of people unfamiliar with the American desert. They expect nothing but sand and may cross southern Arizona or the whole of Death Valley without feeling that they are in "desert." They see hills and washes and trees and bushes and birds — none of which fit the stereotype of desert as purely sand.

Occasional areas are covered by dunes, but they are far apart and usually only a few square miles in extent. Within them wind ripples a surface that looks sterile. No obvious sign of life beckons the human eye except perhaps overhead, where buzzards soar, black and rhythmic as they wheel watching for carrion. A close look, however, contradicts the first impression: signs of life are plainly marked upon the surface of the sand. Here will be the lace tracery of a beetle's passing; there, the foot and tail marks of a kangaroo rat, or perhaps the curious successive j's that mark the progression of a sidewinder rattlesnake. Sand-dwelling creatures actually are so common in the various deserts of the world that evolution has equipped them with special means of coping with loose sand. The sidewinder of the North American desert has counterparts in the viper of the Sahara and the side-running cobra of the Namib, snakes that are not close relatives but move in the same looping, sideways manner. American kangaroo rats and kit foxes grow tufts of bristly hair between their toes as an aid in traveling across sand, and the same holds for the jerboas and fennecs of the Sahara. The bodies of "horned toads" (which actually are lizards, not toads) are flattened for efficient side-to-side wriggling into sand to escape daytime heat and possible predators; and so are the molock lizards of the Australian desert.

Even insects show specific adaptations. Grasshoppers will crouch close to the surface of sand in the morning when temperatures are low, and then as the sand heats they stiffen their legs into stilts. This raises their bodies a full inch, enough to lift vital organs into an environment six or seven degrees cooler than the sand surface. Digger wasps will burrow furiously for a moment at the surface of a dune, hollowing a hole for egg-laying, then flutter a few inches above the surface to cool off before continuing to work. When the hole is an inch or two deep the wasps are working in cooler sand and can dig more steadily. Such examples of adjustment to life in the hot and dry land of the desert are numerous, but tell only a small part of the story; there is more to this land than its bake-over essence. Adaptations to heat only begin to describe the desert, for above the hot flats stand the peaks, "sky islands" of green blessed with relative coolness.

3. Peaks and Canyons

"IF I WERE TO PICK A PLACE in the Southwest to live . . . where every landscape composes and has color, and where I could always have my fill of birds and plants, mammals, reptiles, insects and all the things that make an artist naturalist happy, I should choose Tucson," writes Roger Tory Peterson, dean of American ornithologists, in his *Birds Over America*. "From there I could have almost everything within reach."

Mountain peaks and canyons are what give the region this special charm — vertical scenery upthrust in a horizontal land, short ranges rising like a rocky archipelago above a sea of gravel and cactus. Here are mountains notably rugged, abounding in precipices and knife-edge ridges, and soaring high enough to partially produce their own weather. Air heats as it passes over the desert, and when it rises to clear the mountains it pulls tongues of moisture from the Gulf of Mexico. This condenses and bathes the heights with as much as thirty-five inches of precipitation per year, a particularly wet legacy compared to the bare ten or fifteen inches typical of the flats below. As might be expected, this moisture makes possible life forms unknown in the rest of the desert. Bird and mammal species that are essentially Mexican have adopted the ranges as a northern outpost, and several plants and animals common in the Rocky Mountains thrive in the Arizona mountains at the southern extreme of their ranges. These latter species, which basically belong to northern latitudes, live at the upper elevations of the desert peaks; whereas the Mexican species hold to the middle elevations, above the drought and heat of the desert but below the alpine conditions of the crests and peaks.

How they all arrived is something of a mystery. The birds, which are the most numerous, may be accidentals; but mice and shrews and salamanders are too small to have crossed the ecological barrier of the lowland desert. They could only have come when conditions were different, most likely during the last ice age. Glaciers were shielding the established territory of these small animals at that time, and survival lay in migration. Fortunately, the ice affected climate ahead of its actual reach, and the Southwest was a mild, readily habitable land. The northern migrants fitted in easily, and millennia later, when the ice age ended and temperatures rose even higher than they are now, these creatures simply moved into the coolness and verdure of the mountains. Their shift, together with the warming conditions, allowed other species from the hot tropics to invade the newly suitable, and unoccupied, lower slopes.

Today the peaks and the great gashes of the canyons hold a mix of life forms that delight desert aficionados, each person extolling his own favorite location yet not disclosing the name lest it be overrun with admirers. The ranges are an unexpected poetry in a generally harsh land: take Sabino Canyon, close to Tucson city limits. You head for the Santa Catalina Mountains, and for four or five miles wend through signs that advertise real estate and boys' schools, then pass houses scattered along one side of the road and creosote bushes on the other. Finally comes a United States Forest Service visitor center, a nature trail, a picnic area — and a sense of peace that floods even through the windshield. The canyon closes to a narrow gorge twisting out of the mountains. Saguaro and cholla and ocotillo stud its walls, which are buttressed with bold beige and pink rock outcrops and enormous balancing boulders. A clear creek alternately rushes toward the thirsty desert below, and slows to form pools where dragonflies and swallowtail butterflies dip, and where humans lie basking on white quartzite beaches. The road remains beautifully antiquated with one-lane swayback bridges that cross and recross the creek, hugging close to the water. Boulders slightly awash invite sitting and staring up into the emerald web of tree branches, or watching a black phoebe or a dipper pick its livelihood from the insect life of the stream. The canyon gives intimacy. The desert with its hot vastness lies somewhere far beyond.

Above Sabino and its sister canyons — (Esperaro, Pima, and Bear) — a road climbs to the top of Mount Lemmon, 9150 feet above the desert floor and about 25 degrees cooler. The drive takes an hour and a half, lifting from teddybear cholla and mesquite up through sotol, sumac, and manzanita into oak woodland. Above that comes a forest of pinyon pines and junipers; then ultimately, ponderosa pine and Douglas-fir. In autumn aspen trees shower the forest floor with gold, here reaching the southern end of their range, which stretches almost from the Arctic Circle. Winter brings skiers to slalom the high slopes, and windstorms to batter the trees and flay them into the classic Krummholz shape characteristic of alpine ridges everywhere. Yet far below, unrolled like a brown carpet, lies the desert. Few places in the world permit traveling ecologically so far, so fast. The vertical journey from Tucson to the summit of Mount Lemmon equals a trip from Mexico to northern Canada as far as plants and animals are concerned.

South of the Santa Catalina Mountains stand the Huachucas, cut by other favorite canyons. Carr Canyon is one, a gorge that heads near Miller Peak, 9500 feet, and debouches onto the desert floor at the base of the range 4000 feet below. Birds so favor the relative succor of this canyon that 107 species flit and soar and sing on the acreage of just one of the ranches near its mouth. Not far from Carr, there is Aravaipa Canyon, classified by the Bureau of Land Management as a Primitive Area ... It has a particularly gemlike portion, purchased by the Nature Conservancy (a private agency that protects threatened wildlands until public funds and means can be arranged, or that may manage the land itself). For seven miles here a swirling, perennial creek splashes between thousand-foot cliffs, typical of a fair number of such mountain-born creeks that once flowed like grace notes on the desert landscape. Somehow Aravaipa has escaped the obliteration or modification dealt by fate to most of the others. Nine of an original eleven species of fish still swim in its waters, a larger percentage of aboriginal fishes than remains in any other Arizona creek or river. Roundtail chubs, nearly lost from the desert, laze in pools close against the cliffs; and where algae streamers wave in the riffles there are speckled and longfin dace and loach minnow, gone from the Southwest except for this creek and the upper Gila River. Sonora and Gila suckers, plus a hybrid cross between the two, remain; there also are spikedace, black bullheads, and green sunfish. Formerly pupfish and topminnows must have been there as well, but they need marshes, which now have disappeared (along with the malaria that cursed early military expeditions and settlers).

Still another favorite canyon is Madera, one of the haunts of the coppery-tailed trogon, exceedingly rare in southeastern Arizona and a prized objective for bird watchers. The trogon is limited in the United States to the Huachuca, Santa Rita, and Chiricahua Mountains, and is not necessarily present every year even in those ranges. The chances of seeing one are about as good as hitting the jackpot in Las Vegas, as the late Weldon Heald, who lived in the Chiricahuas, used to rate the odds. Even so, one year in late May we decided to try.

We started from Nogales on the Arizona-Sonora border, driving toward the small town of Patagonia, skimming across grassy hills with only occasional ocotillo and the saddest, most pockmarked saguaros ever to stand upright and look half alive. In places the chartreuse of seepwillow contrasted brightly against the deeper jade of mesquite, which at this season was past the embryonic green of new leaves, yet not quite into the drab dusty green of full summer. A dry wash served for camp when nighttime came; jerry cans provided water and we gathered dead mesquite as fuel. Dawn brought a dove-gray sky hung with a round moon that stayed brilliant as daylight took over from the night. For perhaps an hour sounds dominated the day's beginning rather than sights. Warbling and trilling and rhapsodizing and plain squawking drifted to our sleeping bags from cottonwoods up the wash, from mesquites on the sidehill, and most especially from where Sonoita Creek wove a thread of green onto the drab tapestry of the desert floor. From the hill the night before, we had seen the avenue of life that the creek produces in this dry land; now we were hearing the life.

Three-hundred-twenty acres held by the Nature Conservancy form a wildlife sanctuary along Sonoita Creek, land that very nearly was lost to a golf course. In the mid-1950s the pioneer owner offered the site to the state or some other public agency as a gift, but nobody was interested. When the owner died his heirs sold to a land speculator — and here the Conservancy stepped in. They raised funds and bought the land. Then they raised more funds and fought against a dam downstream which threatened destruction of the wild character of the creek and its banks. The result is a moist haven preserved for research and delight. Anyone can go.

Walk along the creek banks, and the water seems so rushing and sweet, the cottonwoods so tall and sheltering, that it is hard to remember how essentially dry the overall setting is. Bird watching keeps binoculars and brain busy, and the pages of an identification manual flipping. It was windy, our morning there, which meant trouble for the birds in controlling their flight; also a lessening of insects available for food and a confusion of sounds and glinting light as leaves danced on their stalks. Even so, we counted nineteen species in thirty minutes. Two separate crimson streaks welcomed us as we climbed through the barbed wire fence surrounding the sanctuary: a vermilion flycatcher that launched out from the fence itself and a cardinal that had been perched in a mesquite. Next sighting was a small falcon (sparrow hawk?) crossing overhead with a snake in its talons, diminutive predator and diminutive prey, perfectly scaled one to the other. After that it was whitebreasted nuthatches that we watched. They were exploring a dead cottonwood, one of them hopping along the topside of a branch, the other moving upside-down with equal ease along the underside of the branch. Their advance disturbed a Bewick's wren, which flew from its nest behind a flake of bark on the trunk of the tree. Nearby, bridled titmice were circling the inner reaches of a cottonwood, hunting insects and working upward as if the branches were a spiral staircase. Repeatedly we heard Gila woodpeckers calling, and once we saw an acorn woodpecker in flight, readily identifiable by its white wing and rump patches.

More land birds are said to nest in southeastern Arizona than in any other equal-size area of the United States, and at Sonoita Creek you believe it. Birds of wetlands, of open fields, desert, and mountains all intermix here, and as further enticement there are several Mexican species such as rose-throated becards, Harlequin quail, blue-throated hummingbirds, and — at least formerly — groove-billed anis; a total of a dozen or more essentially Mexican birds. The combination offers more birds of more varied shades, of more hues, than could be expected anywhere, such a plethora that Heald used to tell of an Eastern friend with 407 birds on his life list, who added 57 new ones in less than a week at Sonoita Creek and in the Chiricahua Mountains.

At Madera Canyon, a few hours' drive north of Sonoita Creek, we were to meet Edward Steele, an Englishman turned desert bird watcher, and more informed about Arizona trogons than anyone else. He has poured total being into Madera Canyon. Physical energy, mind, spirit. He has possessed it, and it, him. Walking with Ed, watching him, talking, you understand the peculiar satisfaction that comes from birding: the sharpening of skill with binoculars, learning to recognize species and mentally to retain their distinguishing characteristics, studying the differing habits of various species, and knowing the satisfaction of an intimate, repeated, personal association with a particular stretch of countryside.

For Ed Steele, Madera Canyon is the best of all possible worlds: plunging from Mount Wrightson, its trough is green with junipers and oaks on the sidehills, sycamores and more oaks along the canyon bottom. A few pines tower above the broadleaf trees and shade them, but the true pine forest of the canyon was logged long ago. Leaves crunched underfoot as we started up the canyon. Because it was May the creek's voice was silenced, its water reduced to a slow trickle by the dry foresummer; but bird song more than made up the sound deficit. It cascaded from the treetops and rippled along the cliffs. Ed gave us staccato identifications of each call without need to pause and look or to puzzle.

"That's a Hutton's vireo."

"Painted redstart nest just ahead. You can see the male with a grub in his beak."

"Mexican juncos!" (One of the distinctly Mexican species sought by avid bird watchers.)

"See that stump? Sulphur-bellied flycatchers have nested there the last four years." (Another of the Mexican species.)

"Cooper's hawk nest, here. Thank God it's not active this year." Three times in past years hawks from this particular nest killed trogons, by far the most treasured birds of the canyon. In fact, Cooper's hawks menace the continued existence of Madera Canyon trogons more than any other predator or factor. They sit screened by foliage, watching for prey; then plummet to make a catch. Female trogons are easy kills because they fly and feed low in the trees. Trogon cocks feed high, and safe.

Coppery-tailed trogons, the one kind present in Arizona, are showy birds nearly a foot long with iridescent green and rose body plumage, a red eye ring, a curving yellow bill, and a long, wide, coppery tail. At the time of our visit, a total of six nests had been observed in the canyon during four summers of patient work by volunteers who record behavior and also festoon bushes close to the nests with cherries and grapes for the hens to feed on — then gather in the fruit at night to prevent encouraging a false population of raccoons or rodents.

Trogons belong to a tropical family with about thirty species found in African, Asian, and American jungles. The quetzal, which is the most showy of all trogons and perhaps the most gorgeous bird in the world, is the national bird of Guatemala. The flag and national seal carry its likeness, and the basic unit of currency is called a *quetzal*. In Mexico the colors of the federal flag supposedly came from the red, green, and white of quetzal plumage, and earlier, among the Aztecs, the bird was so valued that rulers wore the feathers as headdresses and decreed death to any commoner who killed one of the birds. When Hernando Cortés furled sail at Vera Cruz in 1519, the Aztec chiefs presented him with a quetzal headdress, welcoming him as a legendary god-king — a tragic error, as events soon proved. In Madera Canyon the coppery-tailed trogons nest only along the creek in a stretch between the 5000- and 6700-foot elevation. They court in late May when the canyon is dry, but by July, while the nests are active, rains of tropical proportion pour from the sky. Keeping watch for ten to twelve hours each day, Ed considers umbrella, helmet, and ski jacket standard equipment for a trogon vigil, and he relies on sight alone for monitoring the birds' comings and goings. The roar of the rain-flooded creek drowns their calling.

The summer downpours bring life popping from twigs and seeds, and this in turn produces sudden swarms of insects. Acorn woodpeckers, red-shafted flickers, Mexican jays, wood pewees, and other birds feed on the wing, utilizing the largess by diving, swooping, and sailing out from perches like flycatchers. This remarkable versatility is reported by ornithologist Joe T. Marshall, Jr., authority on the birds of the pine-oak woodlands of Arizona and Sonora. Hepatic tanagers and black-headed grosbeaks also try on-the-wing captures, but succeed in little more than clumsy leaps and short flights from the tops of oaks.

Theoretically, bird species with the same food and nesting needs have difficulty coexisting within a territory, but desert canyons deny the theory. Species that supposedly compete with each other manage to avoid competition, let alone conflict: one simply retreats to a less desirable site or at least shifts its time or place of foraging. Along canyon bottoms similar to Madera, Marshall has seen both black-chinned hummingbirds and broad-tailed hummingbirds, such notorious warriors that battle would seem certain; yet no strife occurs. The males of each species display in territories separated by elevation, and the female black-chins nest only in creek-bottom sycamores, which female broad-tails avoid as if by pledge. The territories of the two species overlap, but the birds themselves do not really compete. Similarly, Hutton's vireos will feed in the same trees as solitary vireos, but at a lower level; lesser goldfinches and black-headed siskins will claim the same trees but on different days; and sulphur-bellied flycatchers will arrive at a nesting ground after Wied's crested flycatchers have finished raising their young and flown away.

Nesting holes are another matter. They do stir contention. The supply of holes generally falls short of demand, and in Madera Canyon this is a frequent source of trouble for the trogons. In choosing a hole to rest in, a male trogon will inspect a succession of stumps and hollow trees, bobbing in and out, in and out. Finally a hen joins the investigation of a particular hole, enters with him, and thereby assents to a domestic pact. Nesting soon follows, incubation lasting about two and one-half weeks and the young birds staying in the nest for another two or three weeks after they hatch. Then comes a crucial day when impulses and reflexes all have somehow focused onto flight, and the fledgings forsake the nest in favor of the world. In a pouring dawn rain Ed once watched such a departure of two trogons — round, soft little birds with long tails poking up, great eyes, and conspicuous white beaks that would darken to adult yellow within a year or so. The first would-be flier launched itself from the hole and fluttered to the closest possible branch, there teetering and vulnerable, but quickly joined by its mother and coaxed up the hill to the protection of a dense juniper. The second bird appeared on the lip of the hole, fluttered out, and was also coaxed to safety by the adult female.

The year of our trek to Madera Canyon, two trogon nest holes were presumed active, or at least were expected to soon be selected by the birds and made productive. The upthrust

Screech owl

branch of a partially dead oak was the first likely site we came upon as we hiked. A hole gaped darkly near its split end. One year screech owls had arrived at the hole before the trogons had come up from Mexico, Ed told us, and although trogons are much the larger birds, they surrendered the site and moved on to a less desirable hole in a sycamore. This year the trogons had successfully claimed the hole in the oak, which had been theirs for two summers before the owls' preemption. A college-age girl, was sitting under the tree as we approached, binoculars hanging limp from her neck. The hen had just flown, she reported.

We hiked on toward the second expected nest site, a sycamore with a shaded hole in its trunk about fifteen feet above the ground. Ed's instant assessment as we arrived was, "The flickers have got it." For the last two summers trogons had held this hole, although one year they had competed with sulphur-bellied flycatchers that kept entering through a separate opening and trying to use the hole. Confusion reigned for a few days; then the coppery-tails had routed the sulphur-bellies. Now it was flickers that had taken over.

Ed made a guess as to where the evicted trogons might have gone and we climbed on, arriving at a sycamore grove where we stretched out to wait. Watching trogons is like looking at the Sistine Chapel, according to Ed: it's best done flat on your back. The wind died and sunrays burst through the clouds, but the afternoon air still held surprising coolness for early summer. Ed called, imitating the raucous yet melodious notes of a male trogon, variously described as *co-ah co-ah,* or *cor-ee cor-ee,* or *cav-ik cav-ik,* with agreement by all factions that the call is somehow less than worthy of so elegant a bird. From down-canyon a female began answering Ed's call. She seemed far off, yet there quickly was motion, and forty feet from us sat a trogon. We could not see her well even with binoculars — little more than a wide tail hanging down, a curved bill, and a white patch behind the eye that marked this bird as still young. When she flew we caught the flush of rose on her belly.

We lay on the bank watching tall columbine nod their creamy blossoms and oak leaves shake as the last of the day's breezes caught them. We kept watch on the hole in the sycamore and the treetops all around. We listened; we talked. The branch with the hole had lost another foot of its length to the ravages of the past winter, Ed commented. By next year it probably would be gone, this nest site lost. Two summers ago an entire tree had fallen, taking a nestful of trogons with it and ruining hopes for that year. An hour or so passed, and then swooping motion drew our eyes to the tops of the sycamores, and we saw the cock trogon land close above the hole. He stretched his wings, and revealed the brilliant rose of his belly. He was close to us and silhouetted so plainly that we could see the whiskers bristling from his bill, and the swelling of his throat as he sounded the soft mating call, not the hoarse *co-ah* cry. For perhaps ten minutes he called, then the hen answered. At first she was far up-canyon, but slowly her responses came from closer and closer.

When she arrived it was as a gray shadow gliding a bare six feet above the ground, ending with an abrupt lift to where the cock sat waiting. Immediately he entered the hole, and

re-emerged; then the hen went in, and he followed. This would
be it. Here Ed Steele would sit for the next six weeks. If wind
didn't topple the tree, if Cooper's hawks didn't come back to
the canyon after all, if flickers or owls or flycatchers didn't turn
out to have previous claims on this hole: if all went well there
should soon be a trogon nest and renewed hope that the birds
would continue to come to Madera each summer.

For every mile of a watered canyon, Marshall has estimated
that about fifty pairs of birds can find living space and food.
Nearly one-fourth of them will stay in the immediate area of
the stream, species that could not be in a canyon at all except
for the flowing water and the verdant conditions it produces.
Included are birds such as Cooper's hawk, Mexican black hawk,
black-chinned and blue-throated hummingbirds, thick-billed
kingbirds, sulphur-bellied, Wied's crested, and western flycatchers, warbling vireos, brown-headed cowbirds, and western tanagers. All need the leafiness of close-set tall trees and a varied
understory to provide nectar and insects. On canyon walls above
a creek bottom, comparatively dry pine and oak slopes offer
food and cover in less concentrated supply, and there birds
disperse more widely. Their feeding territories need to be larger
than along the streamside, and nests are spaced farther apart.

The Chiricahua Mountains — 40 miles long, 20 miles wide,
and 10,000 feet high — rise above the desert to the east of the
Huachucas. They perhaps outdo all other Arizona ranges in
variety of plant and wildlife unexpected in the desert, and in
number of migrant Mexican species. If you know where to look,
you find springs bubbling up through patches of watercress, and
meadows where wild irises bloom. Rainbow trout swim where
creeks slow their splashing and form quiet pools at the base
of cliffs; occasionally, so Weldon Heald used to speculate, the
debris swept down-canyon by flashflood must chance to bury
a few of these fish, preserving them as fossils to be discovered
someday by posterity. The bird species of the Chiricahuas
number at least 245. Mammals total 75 species and include
mountain lion, ocelot, and gray wolf, which for the most part

have lost the struggle for survival even in the remaining wild places of the West. Reptile, amphibian, and insect species common in habitats as diverse as the Pacific Coast, the Rocky Mountains, and the north Mexican highlands commingle in the Chiricahuas, along with a few species not known beyond these mountains. "The place is a bloomin' Paradise," someone has expressed it.

The orientation of slopes and the altitude at the base of desert ranges both affect vegetation. The Chiricahuas run north and south, true to the pattern of ranges throughout the desert, and canyons consequently cut into their flanks from the east and the west. This makes shady north-facing slopes on one side of a canyon and sunny south-facing slopes on the other side. The difference between the two sides produces such opposite growing conditions that plants belonging to the mountaintops will descend noticeably farther on the cool north-facing slopes than on those facing south, exposed to the full sun. Or in a few exceedingly steep canyons, like Rucker Canyon, there will even be an inversion of vegetation. Cool air from the peaks drains down the canyon, bringing an invisible avenue of lowered temperatures and increased moisture nearly to the base of the mountains. Down these corridors come pine trees and their associates, plants normally characteristic of middle elevations, but here growing in canyon bottoms below the scrub oak and juniper of canyon walls.

Near the summits of the Chiricahuas stand true conifer forests. Douglas-fir, ponderosa pine, and Chihuahua pine form stately groves, their trunks straight, their branches interlaced as a canopy of dark green. At the very highest elevations grow white fir, subalpine fir, and Englemann spruce — true species of the North which reach their southernmost limits in the Chiricahuas. Bobcats and badgers and porcupines roam these high forests and occasionally wander down the canyons onto the desert floor. Among birds, wild turkeys are a stellar sight. Their nesting begins in May, and adults and gawky young poults stay until October, when snow drives them into the protection of the

Bobcat, porcupine, badger
(southeastern Arizona)

canyons. According to early-day newspapers, flocks of turkeys formerly were common in the lowland valleys of southeastern Arizona, as well as in the remote canyons and peaks. However, settlers wiped them out, boasting of shooting forty "gobblers" in an evening by ambushing a roost. In the White Mountains of the Arizona–New Mexico borderlands a few flocks persisted, and finally were granted protection. Their numbers rebuilt rapidly, and from them the Arizona State Fish and Game Department now has moved breeding flocks back into mountain ranges such as the Santa Catalinas, Grahams, Huachucas, and Chiricahuas.

In the book *Bird Watcher's Anthology,* Herbert Brandt tells of waiting at a turkey roost among the yellow pines of Rustlers Peak, a crag 8600 feet high in the central Chiricahuas. At dusk the flock arrived, peacefully feeding on the ground and "talking" as they moved toward the roost, arching their necks to see if all was well before settling for the night. At length they flew into the pines, alighting near the trunks and walking out on the limbs, or jumping up a branch or two. They preened and talked a bit more; then, three or four to a tree, hunched down for sleep, the entire flock an odd silhouette against a star-dotted desert sky.

Flocks of thick-billed parrots were once another avian specialty of the Chiricahuas, chunky green birds sixteen inches long with heavy black bills and red foreheads. Since about 1930 none has been seen in the canyons or flying along the ridgetops, but the watch for them, and the hope, continues. If they come again they will be the United States' only parrots, for those native to the southeastern states were killed long ago. Pine forests in Mexico still ring with what Marshall terms the "ear-splitting obscenities" that parrots exchange among themselves as they fly. Flocks of fifty or sixty birds congregate where pines have set a good crop of seeds, or where some other favored food permits a mass feast. Mated pairs will fly wingtip to wingtip, with a yard or two separating one pair within the flock from the next.

Apparently it was feeding sorties that previously prompted the parrots to cross from Mexico into the Chiricahuas. They seem never to have nested north of the border; they would be seen and heard for only a few days, then would vanish. Roger Peterson tells in *Birds Over America* of talking with an oldtimer who remembered the flocks from before World War I: "He said the big green parrots with the red faces and huge bills appeared suddenly in August. They came by the hundreds and the hurtling flocks made the canyons echo with their noise. He told me he shot fifty-seven of them. They stayed until January when snow blanketed the Apaches' mountains and covered the juniper berries lying on the ground. Once he saw two or three hundred of them swarming over the branches of a tall pine like living ornaments in a gigantic Christmas tree.

" 'Old Lil,' who hung around the cafe in the little mining town of Paradise, kept one of the parrots in a cage for four or five years. It never learned to talk."

An opposite case of increasing numbers, rather than a falling off, marks the arrival of coatis north of the border. In Mexico these relatives of raccoons are fairly common; they are called *chula*, which means both "pretty" and "rogue," an apt name. In recent years reports all along the border from Texas to Arizona have increasingly mentioned coatis, but substantial numbers are found only in the Huachucas and Chiricahuas. They range both

Coatis

high and low, but the best chance of seeing them is at elevations between 4000 and 7000 feet. In bands of a dozen, or up to as many as thirty or more, coatis travel together, snuffling along the ground for toadstools or acorns or lizards or grasshoppers or all manner of other delicacies. They also scramble through overhead trees as if they were monkeys. Indeed they are sometimes mistaken for monkeys because of the way they walk, with hindquarters high and tails held like balancing poles. Their appearance also suggests a fifteen-pound cross between a cat and an anteater, with perhaps a few raccoon genes added — plus the touch of monkey. The nose tapers and is constantly sniffing; the fur is dark and thick; and the forepaws seem constantly to be searching for edible tidbits. Only once have we seen coatis, a small band that was moving swiftly and warily down a dry wash in the Chiricahuas.

Luck has treated us better with peccaries, or javelinas, another of the exotic mammals that roam the Chiricahuas and most of the Sonoran Desert ("exotic" in the sense of special fascination, not in the technical sense of being beyond normal range since peccaries are the native boars of the American desert). Our most satisfying experience with them came at a camp where we had veered off the regular road onto a set of tracks at the base of the Chiricahuas. In the morning we awoke to coyotes taking the lead in the dawn chorus, their wondrous yapping dominating all other voices of the desert. The song roused us from sleep, although as usual the coyotes could be heard but not seen. The only wildlife our binoculars picked up were mule deer grazing in foot-high grass between clumps of juniper. We dressed hastily to follow the deer and try for a photograph, and in tracking them we came on the peccaries. A band of ten was just stirring for the day. They still lay close together, like a careless pile of grizzled lumps; and as the sun hit, they began to rise stiffly, yawning and spraddling their legs to stretch. The bright pink of their mouth and throat membranes showed plainly when they yawned; so did very long, white, curved fangs. Awakened finally and sensing human presence, all began to move away with mincing steps. They would walk a few feet, then stop and sniff, each peccary holding up whatever foot happened to be in the air at the moment. The whole band would peer myopically in our direction, aware of something but uncertain of what, then move on.

Peccaries

That same day we stopped at the Southwestern Research Station, a field study center operated in Cave Creek Canyon by the American Museum of Natural History. Here projects have ranged from tape recording owl calls to collecting solpugids (257 specimens of five species, meticulously measured, cross analyzed, and preserved); from studying the chromosomes of cactus to classifying rattlesnakes by venom and checking the insect population of cactus wren nests. Among bird watchers the research station is renowned for its hummingbirds. Three or four species hover and dip around the feeder at the same time — wild hummers, representative throughout the desert and the mountains of the Southwest, and concentrated in the Chiricahuas by the unique geography. The small size and flashing color of hummingbirds prompt human admiration, but the English names given them remain coldly analytical: black-chinned, broad-billed, broad-tailed, blue-throated, violet-crowned, white-earred, Lucifer, Costa's, Rivoli's, rufous. These ten particular flying rainbows brighten the Arizona desert, a tiny sampling of the hummingbird family, which belongs wholly to the Western Hemisphere and totals 319 species. The smallest of them all (and the smallest bird in the world) is the bee hummingbird of Cuba. It weighs five to seven grams — less than one-quarter ounce, half the weight of an airmail letter sent with a single stamp. The largest hummingbird is about the size of a swallow, a native of the southern Andes; instead of the fast blur of most hummingbird flight, which reaches as high as 4500 beats per minute, this giant hummer flies with ordinary wing-strokes.

A characteristic of hummingbird flight is ability to move backward, rotating their wings at the shoulder and getting power on both the downstroke and the upstroke. They have proportionately the biggest heart of any bird known, and with reason: their outpouring of energy is fantastic. If a man were to spend energy at a rate equivalent to a hummingbird, according to Crawford Greenewalt in his definitive book *Hummingbirds*, he would need to eat almost 300 pounds of meat daily simply to fuel his body. To stay cool he would have to evaporate twelve gallons of sweat per hour. Otherwise his body temperature would rise higher than the boiling point of lead.

In one of the studies made at the Southwestern Research Station, Robert C. and Richard J. Lawiewski of the University of California at Los Angeles recorded the heartbeat of Rivoli's and blue-throated hummingbirds from a low of 36 beats per minute to a high of 1260. The fast rate occurred during normal activity, and the slow rate came when a hummer had dropped into torpor. Such a temporary turning off of the body machine provides a mechanism by which several small creatures survive their own energy demands. In the case of hummingbirds, the long tongue pumps enough nectar into the stomach each day to supply sugar equivalent to half the bird's own weight, and added nourishment comes from occasional gnats, swallowed both incidentally and intentionally. Yet even this huge amount of high-energy food would fall short of supplying these feathered dynamos if it were not for their ability to drop in and out of torpor during the day. This physiological trick has been so long recognized that Jesuit priests pioneering the desert Southwest used to point to it as an illustration when converting Indians to Christianity. As a hummingbird appears dead yet instantly stirs to life, they preached, so Christ arose from the tomb.

The intense iridescence of hummingbird feathers does not come from pigment but from structural color. Light refracts through special platelets so minute that ten thousand of them end-to-end would measure only an inch long. Eight or ten layers of these coat each barbule of each feather, and since every square inch of plumage has a half-million barbules it adds up to billions of platelets and rich, saturated, flashing color. You watch hummingbirds at the research station, seeing the glass feeder of sugar-water surrounded by darting and hovering blue-throats, broad-tails, black-chins, and Rivoli's. This is what the eyes see, but what they are looking at is the double marvel of the birds' physiology and of man's impulse to understand it in such detail.

Dusk comes early to Cave Creek Canyon because the abrupt wall of the mountains shuts off the evening sun. While the sky is still light, poor-wills and whip-poor-wills call from the cliffs and western pipistrels skim the creek for insects, followed later by a dozen or more other bats, including Mexican varieties. Even before blackness gains control of the canyon, spotted owls start to call and occasionally a great horned owl adds its authoritative hoot (although they more often stay in the lower, open desert beyond the canyon). The real night show of Cave Creek belongs to the owls — and to the ears rather than to the eyes, for not only does darkness thwart human vision but in any case the most interesting Chiricahua owls are small and exceedingly difficult to see. All three *Otus* owls rule the night in the canyon — screech owl, whiskered owl, and flammulated owl, a trio found together only in southeastern Arizona, where the whiskered owl reaches its northern limit. Elf owls also join from among the sycamore trees.

Of the four, the screech owl was the first we heard, its wavering, repeated whistle seemingly a means of locating prey, much as bats use ultrasonic cries. Whiskered owls were next. In appearance these are nearly identical with screech owls, but their call is distinctive, a high-pitched series of *boos*. Sometimes it comes in threes with a pause followed by a fourth *boo*, and then repeating; sometimes the series holds steady until the end and runs down like a music box in need of winding. Flammulated owls filled the long middle hours of the night, their double-toned hooting soft and melodious. Elf owls called too, although they don't sound like owls or even like birds. They chatter and yip and cackle in a voice almost like a mammal's, and often unrecognized even by desert residents, despite their being widespread.

The night song of that Chiricahua canyon haunts us still, uncommonly rich because it rang with voices that belong to the Sonoran Desert's great mingling ground of unexpected life forms. Try with your inner ear to hold on to the pitches and timbres and rhythms of such a night, and you can't. But the magic enters the soul and pleases you forever. It brings gentleness in the midst of a thorny land.

4. Tall Cactus

CACTI COME IN ALL SIZES, shapes, and colors. Saguaros stand fifty feet high, proportioned like living candelabras. Barrel cacti sit squat and cylindrical, armor-plated with stout curving thorns the color of rusted iron. The oval pads of prickly pear are a soft green, lightly spined with thorns the color of straw. Night-blooming cereus grows as an umpromising stick half an inch in diameter and a yard long, seeming more dead than alive; then one June night it unfolds long petals of shining white and wafts an exquisite fragrance into the hot darkness. The bloom has an unexpected, almost disproportionate glory, bursting from such singularly plain parentage, although cactus species outdo the rainbow with the color of their flowers. Every possible red, pink, orange, and yellow is represented, and even greens and browns. Petals are luminous and saturated in hue, as though endowed with structural color like that of tropical fishes instead of the pigment of ordinary flowers.

Thorns vary widely. They come as hairs, hooks, and bristles; as short spines, straight spines, curved spines, long spines. As Father Johann Jakob Baegert, one of the early-day desert Jesuits, wrote: "Thorns . . . are surprisingly numerous, and there are many of frightening aspect. It seems as if the curse of the Lord, laid upon the earth after the fall of Adam, fell especially hard on [Baja] California and had its effect." He counted the thorns on a section of organpipe cactus the length of his handspan, and found "no less than 1,680 . . . It is easy to see that, according to my calculation, a single one of these shrubs carries more than a million thorns." The good padre also comments on the usefulness of thorns as toothpicks, "One of them will serve for many years without repointing or resharpening," and he marvels that "the always barefoot and very careless California Indians, especially the children, do not get hurt every day . . . This gives me cause to admire the vigilance of their Guardian Angel."

For the cactus, thorns serve several purposes. In species such as barrel cactus and pincushion, they shade one-quarter of the plant at a time, acting as a built-in lathhouse and preventing overheating. They also reduce the drying effect of wind. You realize this when camped with sleeping bags spread at the base of a saguaro or organpipe cactus. If the night is a usual one with the air astir, wind will whisper among the thorns as a lullaby, or rise to a wild sibilance, its hiss as fierce as the gusts that race along the crest of a mountain ridge. By breaking the force of the air's rush, thorns lessen demand for the moisture hoarded within the plant.

Thorns may possibly also directly affect the water regimen of cactus, although the theory rates as a bizarre one among many botanists. The idea is based on plants' tending to build an electrical charge greater than that of surrounding earth or air — the charge coming from free ions in the water, absorbed by the roots and carried to the branches and leaves. With cacti, thorns act something like reverse lightning rods, discharging the built-up electricity from their tips. This helps raise water within the plant in a sort of pumping action. The concept, if true, may help to explain the lifting of water by giant cacti such as saguaros and cardons, which are so tall that capillarity alone scarcely seems adequate. For most plants the transpiration of leaves creates an enormous suction that roots respond to. But cacti have no leaves and the cuticle encasing trunk and branches is waxy and serves to minimize the loss of moisture. Consequently, the mechanics of lifting water from roots to highest branch tip has been difficult to explain. Thorns may be part of the answer — and any desert traveler who has cursed the bother of

Chain cholla

thorns can take comfort in the possibility of this compensating usefulness.

When it comes to pain, no thorns surpass those of cholla. Desert hikers carry pliers specifically for pulling cholla from boots, elbows, and fingers; and this is all to the good so far as the plant is concerned. The thorns anchor easily into whatever brushes against them, causing whole joints to break off and attach to hides, pantlegs, and rubber tires. Cholla thus propagates itself, for the hitchhiking joints root readily, drawing on stored moisture and nutrients until established. One species of cholla, the size of a small tree, has dangling clusters of spiny joints and fruits which give it the name "chain cholla," but since the joints loosen at the slightest touch it also is called "jumping cholla." Other cholla cacti grow stiffly branched, one of them looking something like deer's antlers, another like oddly jointed pencils, and a third covered with thorns that felt the joints and give a softly napped look, especially when backlit at dawn or sunset. This last is "teddybear cholla," but the name is a hoax, since its stab hurts the most of all.

An obvious purpose of thorns is to protect the plant from undesirable contact. Yet rodents devour cactus seedlings by the hundreds of thousands; peccaries feed heavily on mature prickly pear; and desert range cattle are a common sight with three or four cholla joints bristling from their lips. Once at dawn we watched a jackrabbit sitting with its long pink ears aglow, as if lit from within, calmly gnawing cholla joints fallen onto the ground. The half-inch spines caused no trouble: the jack simply thrust its mouth between the thorns, held the upper jaw stationary, and moved the lower jaw to scrape off the pulp. It could as easily have been eating a cucumber as the cactus.

Many animals find thorns no threat. Ground squirrels climb barrel cactus, drawn by the promise of rich seeds at the top and indifferent to what impresses a human as the hazard of thorns. They climb even chollas, sometimes for no apparent reason other than to bask in the sun, although how their soft footpads withstand the barbs has yet to be explained. Birds are equally at ease. They perch on a cactus without so much as a preliminary hovering to pick a spot; they simply fly full speed and drop their legs and fold their wings, and alight as if on a telephone pole. Saguaros, in fact, are the favorite roosts of hawks and owls and vultures, probably because of their commanding view of surrounding country. Chollas serve a similar purpose for cactus wrens and thrashers.

In spring, birds fly over cactus country competing for nest sites. Thrashers and mourning doves, being fairly large, claim the innermost, thorniest branches of cholla, occasionally usurping a spot already picked by a cactus wren or a verdin. When this happens the smaller bird may simply move to the outer edge of the same cactus, a comparatively exposed position. Nevertheless, it balances out. Wrens and verdins weave great balls of twigs as nests, assuring protection for their young by virtue of architecture, whereas thrashers and doves fashion mere open cups as nests. Their young need the protection and shade of the center branches.

Cactus wrens — the largest wrens in the world — nest almost exclusively in cholla. The bird and the plant are so commonly associated that mentioning one immediately calls to mind the other. Anders and Anne Anderson, who spent several seasons watching wrens near Tucson, report that thorns rarely interfered with the building of a nest, although occasionally they would notice a wren yanking at a particular thorn that was in a key position and in the way. Construction of the nest invariably started with a lattice of stiff dry twigs laid among the cholla branches, and this framework would then grow to the size and shape of a football, built from the inside with layer on layer of grass completely padding the thorns. Feathers would provide a last touch. Outside, such nests look like willy-nilly conglomerations of sticks, but inside they form a neat entry tunnel and a soft bedchamber.

The work must be easy. The wrens make roosting nests and decoy nests as well as brooding nests. A pair typically has five or ten nests, although they use only one for what humans would consider the prime function of a nest, as cradle for the young.

Dove and wren nests

Watching the various types of nests under construction, the Andersons found that male and female wrens work more efficiently alone than as a pair. Roosting nests, to be occupied alone, went together fairly quickly; a wren would average less than one minute between trips for bringing additional materials. But when a mated pair worked together on a brood nest, the time between trips doubled. Materials may need to be more carefully chosen for a brood nest. Certainly there must be time out for interaction between male and female: mere efficiency cannot be enough as two individuals join in the perpetuation of life. The urge to declaim territory and domesticity makes the chortling metallic call of cactus wrens the main music of Southwest cholla hillsides as surely as the lilt of a meadowlark symbolizes the prairie, or the tremolo of winter wrens belongs to the dark forests of the Northwest. Producing the sound swells the throat of the male wren with such a lump that bare skin shows through the quivering feathers of his neck, and his tail vibrates in perfect rhythm with his throat. Trembling courses the bird's whole being, and seems to set every cell within to dancing. No wonder work is slowed.

Sometimes thorn-dwellers get into trouble. Alden Miller, an ornithologist who has spent a great deal of time in the desert, found three separate cases of birds stuck by thorns within a one-month trip, and he confesses a "certain unworthy satisfaction" at finding that he was not alone in repeatedly getting stuck. In one case he had stepped close to a verdin's nest, whereupon the brooding female bolted from the opening and caught a wing on a thorn. Miller reached to help — and frightened the bird into such fluttering that she freed herself. The second case was a juvenile cactus wren impaled at the entrance to its nest, dead and mummified. The third involved thrashers just old enough to leave the nest, and probably extra vulnerable owing to inexperience. The birds saw the man watching them, took fright, and started to run along the limbs of the cactus, only to have their feet catch on thorns and pitch them over. Evidently there is a technique to placing the feet which these young birds had not yet learned. One even got a cactus joint stuck in its side and would have been in serious trouble if Miller had not rescued it, thoroughly sticking himself in the process.

Woodrats, or packrats as they are more commonly called in the West, handle cholla with uncanny ease. Ronn Olsen, working on a Ph.D. dissertation in zoology, found hillsides with nests built 90 percent of teddybear cholla. Mounds two feet high and eight feet across lay piled at the bases of organpipe cacti and paloverde trees, and since cholla joints are little more than thumb size, this represents a prodigious job of gathering, carrying, and arranging. Yet wherever cholla grows abundantly, nests are built of it with inside passageways and chambers padded by grasses and shredded bark. Where there is no cholla, the rats live in rock dens heaped with twigs, stones, cattle dung, raveled bits of cloth, rifle shells, buttons, children's plastic toys, and whatever else they happen to find — on occasion even false teeth left untended by a desert prospector or camper.

Just how packrats handle cholla has long puzzled observers. Using infrared light at night, Dr. Olsen watched a female scurry along carrying a joint of cholla in her mouth, but unfortunately she disappeared before he could see how she would set it down. Zoologists believe the rats manipulate cactus joints with their forepaws, somehow avoiding getting stuck. "But don't ask how," Olsen comments, and goes on to remark that sometimes the animals do get badly stuck. "I have released them from live traps only to see them run headlong into cholla joints littering the ground," he says. "No panic accompanies this ordeal. Experience seems to have taught packrats that panic only makes matters worse, and they stop and slowly disengage the spines by use of mouth and forepaws."

Occasionally some must cope with thorns by nipping them off, for another researcher reports seeing a packrat climb a cholla and seem to bite off spine tips as it went. This was at night, too dark to see well, but investigation the next morning confirmed the observation. A route of neatly blunted thorns led into the upper branches of the cactus.

Cacti are native only in the New World, although they have thrived when transplanted abroad, enough so to have become serious pests in Australia. In the Americas, the natural range is from Patagonia nearly to the Arctic Circle. Cactus thrives in low hot deserts and in cold high deserts, in windy prairies and tropical jungles, and at foggy seashores. At least one species grows native and wild in each state of the United States except Maine, New Hampshire, Vermont, Alaska, and Hawaii (where it has been introduced). Every province of Canada has native cactus except the Maritimes. Twelve hundred species belong naturally to North America, 300 of them found only in the United States. Arizona alone has about 80 species.

Botanists consider cactus one of the youngest of the world's plant families, although its origin is imperfectly known. Probably it once was related to violets and begonias, evolving through the ages as environment changed. Possibly earth movements around the West Indies tilted the islands and blocked the prevailing sea winds, which lessened rainfall and caused lakes and rivers to dry. Many plants must have died; but a few changed form and survived. One of these — the briar *Pereskia* — developed thickened leaves and fleshy stems with chlorophyl in the bark, a prototype of today's widely varied cacti. Change continued. Cuticle became heavy and waxy to minimize the loss of water. Leaves were dispensed with or converted to scales (although each spring chollas and a few other cacti bear small soft leaves that soon wither and fall). Stems took over photosynthesis, and thorns evolved from what had been the growing tips of twigs. To safeguard further against aridity, spongy water-storage tissue developed, and moisture entering the roots became transformed into a mucilaginous sap that can resist the pull of hot, dry air.

Cacti are defined botanically as perennials with no persistent leaves (except in the case of pereskias, the ancestral cactus, which still grow in Mexico and South America). The ovary of the cactus flower is borne below the petals and sepals, and the fruit is a one-celled berry with no divisions between the seeds. Spines, branches, flowers, and roots generally develop from special organs called areoles. Belonging only to cactus, these organs look like small depressions heavily felted with hairs to reduce water loss. Any plant that does not meet all of these specifications is not a cactus. Thorny, whiplike ocotillo is not cactus, although widely mistaken for it. Neither are bristling yuccas with their sharp-pointed, swordlike leaves. However, true cacti grow in a great variety of forms: solitary or in clumps; hugging the ground or standing as tall as shrubs and even trees.

Tall cacti are the symbol of the Sonoran Desert, with two general types among them, those with a central trunk that branches well above ground, and those with many branches springing from a common base at ground level. Saguaros are the best known. They belong to the first type and are as much

Cardon

as fifty feet high and with two to six uplifted branches. Cardons reach about the same height and look much like saguaros except for being coarser and more branched. They grow only in Mexico, whereas saguaros are familiar on both sides of the international line (and in fact are so abundant and beloved in Arizona that the saguaro blossom is the state flower). A third, also found only in Mexico, looks about halfway between a saguaro and a cardon, and bears odd spiny fruit the size of a baseball. Yaqui and Mayo Indians used the fruits as brushes, hence the name of the plant, "hairbrush cactus," or *Pachycereus pectenaboriginum* in Latin, literally "Indian comb."

Four other species of giant cactus are found in the Sonoran Desert, all of them the type that branches profusely at the ground. Organpipe and senita grow in Arizona, Sonora, and Baja California; agria and sina belong only in Mexico. These four grow with as many as twenty or thirty clumped upright arms, which give the plant the look of a strangely massive shrub ten or fifteen feet high. Actually, Arizona can barely claim this form of cactus. If the boundary were five miles farther north there would be no senita in the United States; eighty miles north, and there would be no organpipe.

Woody ribs support all of the giant cacti; and within the wood, xylem and phloem transport water and nutrients between roots and stems, the same as in other woody plants. The ribs come in two styles. Saguaro, cardon, and hairbrush cactus have circlets of twelve to twenty slender rods that run the length of the trunk and branches. In organpipe, senita, agria, and sina a woody core like a three-inch pipe supports each branch. Both the circlets of individual ribs and the pipelike cores are filled with pith and are surrounded by cortex in the living plants. When the cacti die both stand like gaunt wooden skeletons. Desert peoples prize them as building material: long, straight, and lightweight, the rods and cores become fences and roofs. They are greatly valued in this dry land where there is little to choose from other than the crooked branches of mesquite and ironwood trees, or pines too far distant in the mountains to be practicable.

Like all plants, cacti need water. Some botanists feel that they may even need proportionately more water than other types of plants in spite of their ability to live on inner reserves alone. The succulence of cactus equalizes desert conditions, bridging from those rare times of abundant water to the far more common and prolonged periods of drought. Succulence hoards water; but it does not produce water. Wherever succulence occurs — and it is not limited to cactus — its effect is an emergency extension of the plant's capacity for life. The stored moisture may provide the margin needed for new shoots, and for blossoming and setting fruit to start the next generation on its way to life. Sedum, a noncactus succulent, has flowers that will set seed even after they have been severed from the plant and placed in a collector's press to dry. A stem from another kind of succulent, *Ibervillea sonorae*, stored in a museum cupboard for eight years, formed new growth each summer while its weight slowly shrank to half of what it was when brought in from the field. Applied on the scale of a saguaro or a cardon, succulence involves a considerable volume of water. Cardons weigh twelve to fifteen tons; saguaros, with fewer arms, weigh about eight tons. Close to 90 percent of this is water; it is a reservoir that for each cactus about equals the moisture supplied by two years of desert rain.

Saguaro
cross section

The ways cacti obtain and keep moisture reveal remarkable specializations. With saguaros and other giants in the genus *Cereus*, fleshy roots radiate near the soil surface, assuring the best possible chance to soak up rainwater before it can run off, evaporate, or percolate beyond reach. Even so, according to studies by the Atmospheric Sciences Department of the University of Arizona, saguaros do not absorb water from rain showers of less than 0.20 inches. Below this amount the rain is wasted so far as saguaros (and most other desert plants) are concerned. It evaporates before it can seep into the soil, although temperature, humidity, wind, soil conditions, and other factors of course determine exactly what happens. To speed absorption, special "rain roots" grow out immediately after a rain, whether a gentle shower or a torrential downpour. The new moisture stimulates their growth, and so long as it lasts these lengthy hairlike roots suck it up thirstily. When the soil dries, they drop off and the root system returns to the minimum network needed to hold a topheavy cactus upright.

Aboveground, the accordion-pleat structure of trunks and branches allows swelling and contracting, according to actual moisture supply. In fact, the diameters of the cacti are a fair gauge of current conditions. If the pleats are deeply folded you can know that it has been a long time since rain last fell, and that the plant is slowly spending its inner reserves. But let there be a thunderstorm, and cacti quickly become plump, their pleats expanded to accommodate the fresh swelling of the water-storage tissue. Once in a while the roots of a saguaro will draw up more water than the cells can hold, and a cactus will burst. Usually the ruptures heal without serious injury, although sometimes infection sets in.

Once moisture has been taken up, the next need is to safeguard it. All plants lose water to the air by transpiration. The process is for them like breathing for animals: a gas exchange absolutely necessary, no matter what the cost in moisture. Cacti have evolved various means of regulating the loss, thereby suiting themselves to life in the desert. One of the chollas has minute moisture-proof tubes that channel the flow of carbon dioxide and oxygen from the atmosphere into the plant and back out again, a system that minimizes water loss. The tubes are present in mature joints, but not in new joints. On the contrary, water is transpired flagrantly from the new joints of these chollas and also from the half-inch, cylindrical leaves that appear at the onset of the first summer rains. Experiments show that the leaves give off water at triple the rate of mature stems, and their presence coincides with the fleeting days of abundant water. When the rainy period passes, the leaves wither and fall. Their only purpose seems to be to step up transpiration; to squander water and thereby stimulate growth. Prickly pear cactus also sprouts short-lived leaves that stud the edges of the pads for a time then dry and fall.

In saguaros, as in all dicot plants, growth takes place at the tip of trunks and branches, the most water-saturated part of the plant. The growing period begins as soon as the summer rains arrive in mid-July, and it continues until they taper off a month or six weeks later — the wettest time of the desert year, and also the hottest. The combination works well. Water is readily available and the high temperatures reduce the viscosity of both soil moisture and plant juices, providing optimum flow. Furthermore, the warmth steps up the metabolic activity of the cactus, helping to fit needed growth into the briefly favorable time available.

The densest stands of saguaros often are on the hottest slopes, which face south and southwest and catch the full force of the sun. The position is not a matter of needing maximum heat, despite the link between optimum growth and summer; the comparatively moderate temperatures of other slopes would be hot enough and their greater moisture would be an advantage. The largest known individual saguaros are found in moist canyon bottoms. It is winter cold that augurs against slopes facing north. Saguaros also are essentially nonexistent west of the Colorado River or north of the Gila; the California desert is too dry and northern Arizona is too cold.

Organpipe

The range of organpipe and senita is similarly restricted by low winter temperatures. Marginal conditions north of Mexico commonly mark Arizona organpipes with curious pinched-in constrictions where tips have been frosted and stopped growing, then resumed when hot weather returned. Both organpipes and senitas have thicker stems and fewer flutings the farther north they grow. Along the Arizona-Sonora border at Sonoyta, Mexico, these cacti actually look like a different species from those at Guaymas, 250 miles to the south, where mean winter temperatures hold about seven degrees warmer. All columnar cacti develop thickened stems toward their northern range, regardless of the latitude where that northern extreme happens to fall. All reduce their fluting. Both devices increase volume in proportion to surface; this slows the loss of heat to the atmosphere and prevents freezing. Thus, stems from Sonoyta cacti typically have five ridges, and in cross section look like fat five-pointed stars; but those from Guaymas may have as many as eleven ridges, and look like gears with sharply protruding teeth.

Various aspects of cold affect plants differently. Some arctic species survive even when ice forms in their cells, providing they can thaw slowly. If the thaw comes suddenly they die. For other plants the crucial factor may be the minimum temperature reached in winter, or the length of winter from first frost to last. It may be how long individual freezes last without relief;

Senita

or the cumulative total of frost regardless of how many consecutive hours there are. For saguaro, which is more cold-tolerant than any other giant cactus, the deciding factor seems to be how long a freeze lasts. Forrest Shreve, a pioneer in desert botany, studied this by potting young saguaros and subjecting them to mild freezing. They survived readily if given only six to fifteen hours of freezing at a time, but with an increase to thirty hours or more wholesale fatalities ensued.

By inserting thermometers into mature saguaros growing near the Carnegie Desert Laboratory, Shreve found a remarkable response to changes in air temperature. The temperature of the outside inch or two of cactus tissue consistently fluctuated more widely than that of the surrounding air, often warming above air temperature by day and dropping lower at night. Heat absorbed from sunshine during the day would be lost by reradiation at night, and transpiration would add to the nighttime chilling. From his data, Shreve realized that weather alone does not tell the story of the temperatures a cactus actually is experiencing. In winter the outer layers of tissue may be subjected to more hours of freezing than a weather-station reading indicates; or conversely, since the sun nearly always breaks through the clouds at least briefly even on cold days, the warmth of its rays may raise cactus-skin temperatures above freezing while ice still crusts in rain puddles and thermometers register 32°F.

As might be expected, internal temperatures vitally affect plant function, such as flowering. Saguaros bloom in Arizona from late April through June, with as many as two or three hundred buds ringing the tips of main trunks and crowning branches. Some stems produce a series of ten to fifteen concentric rings of buds, rising one after another from the areoles. However, the number of buds does not accurately indicate the number of flowers there will be, for less than one-third open. Some years, a full half of the buds are killed by larvae of the beetle *Carpophilus longiventris*. Attacks come while the buds are still marble-sized, causing them to shrivel and turn to blackened nubs. Cactus wrens and other birds also destroy buds when seeking insects to feed on (although buds infected enough to attract birds might be doomed in any case).

Insects and birds of course are not the complete explanation of flowers that fail to open: many buds wither without discernible reason. Investigating, Duncan Johnson, an early-day ecologist, noticed that flowering success followed a definite pattern around the stem, beginning with buds on the east and southeast. Why? Temperature. Morning sun warms the east side of the cactus three or four degrees above the rest of the plant, and gives buds there a headstart. By late afternoon the sun swings around and heats the stem's west side, but little time is left before sundown and the cooling of night. As a result, west-side buds may never open, and those on the north may stay mere nubbins.

With flowering so uneven because of temperature, it can fairly be asked how stems stay symmetrical. The answer seems to be that saguaro tips receive equal sunshine on all sides. The tips are blunt and slightly cupped, and this shape allows the entire rim of growing tissue to receive the sun. The temperature within the cup is effectively averaged and a matting of cottony hair helps to hold the warmth. Thus saguaro tips do not actually experience the erratic temperatures of the rest of the cactus, and the stems retain symmetry.

Saguaro flowers

On a typical saguaro about one hundred flowers succeed in getting beyond the bud stage, spreading their bloom over a four-week period. Petals open between sunset and midnight, and close the following afternoon. During these few hours pollination must take place, and it must be cross pollination not only from one blossom to another but at least from one branch to another. Three thousand stamens stud each blossom, producing an enormous amount of pollen. The grains are too large to be carried by the wind, and this indicates that other means of fertilization must take place. Honey bees are attracted to saguaro flowers in great numbers, for good reason. Each individual blossom produces about 125 bee-loads of nectar, an exceptionally rich supply that totals a sixth of an ounce per flower. Even so, honey bees cannot account for saguaro pollination. They were not introduced into the Southwest until 1872, and consequently cannot explain the earlier growth of the cactus forest, whatever their effect is currently. Furthermore, bees tend to visit one flower repeatedly without stopping at adjoining ones, or at those on other arms or on other saguaros, and this pattern would not be conducive to cross pollination. One investigator watched an easily recognized dark bee for three hours as it made trips back and forth between a certain blossom and the hive. He clocked it at seven minutes per trip, and it never varied this time or sampled another blossom. A test then was set up using flowering saguaros in mesh cages where potential pollinators could be introduced and checked, one kind at a time. Bees proved effective cross pollinators in spite of their habit of visiting single flowers, perhaps because hive-living involves a great amount of body contact and inadvertent exchange of particles. In any case, about half the flowers in the cage set fruit, which is the same proportion as under natural conditions.

Even so, there remained the historical impossibility of domestic bees being responsible for saguaro reproduction. There had to be other pollinators, and S. E. McGregor and Stanley M. Alcorn of the United States Department of Agriculture desert experiment station decided to continue the cage experiments, testing doves and bats as candidates for the role. They collected forty branches with buds, largely from windthrown saguaros (working under special permit, since the species is protected by law on state, Indian, and federal land). They knew from previous work that by cutting stems one to three feet long, normal blossoming would continue, drawing on stored moisture and nutrients.

White-winged doves were tested first. Several saguaro arms were placed in the cage, which measured 12 × 24 × 9 feet and had its bottom edges well buried to keep out mice and rabbits and peccaries. The doves were thought to be likely pollinators because their range from near the Mayo River in Mexico northward to the Arizona borderlands coincides with that of saguaro. Furthermore, the spring migration pattern of white-wings duplicates the progression of saguaros' blooming. They arrive in the Tucson region just as the flowers are beginning to open, and are a common sight as they dip into the blossoms and emerge with their foreheads powdered. In the cage the doves went readily to the flowers and perched for ten seconds at a time with their heads inside the petals. Evidently they were drinking nectar, or at least their throat motions were the same as when drinking at a waterhole. Toward the end of their feeding period, which is at sunrise, the doves seemed to feed also on the lower, nectar-soaked anthers or on other flower parts. In this test there had been forty-two flowers; in time, half of them set fruit. This equaled the pollination rate of the bees.

Yet doves could not be the prime pollinators of saguaro because they are active only by day, and substantial pollinating was known to occur at night. McGregor and Alcorn had previously experimented with controlling the precise hours that flowers are available for pollination. They fitted drinking straws over the styles of blossoms and folded the ends shut, then opened them on a controlled basis to provide access. The hours between midnight and sunrise proved the most productive time for pollination, the same period that the style is at its longest, lifted well above the stamen. Such an arrangement prevents accidental self-pollination and simultaneously allows the style to receive a brush of pollen as visitors first arrive. Later the style shrinks. These predawn hours are therefore the flowers' most receptive time.

For a nighttime pollinator, long nose bats seemed the likeliest. Different from most bats, which feed on insects, this species has a diet of nectar; and, like the doves, it arrives in Arizona from Mexico at the time saguaros are starting to bloom. Small and brown, with short round ears and a long nose, these bats are well suited to life among the flowers. They have bristly tongues about a quarter as long as their entire body, ideal for lapping nectar. Nine female bats and four young were released into the test cage. They alternately hovered at a blossom and fed quickly, then clambered like clumsy mice among blooms ringing a stem. Nearly two-thirds of the flowers tested with the bats set fruit, more than in the tests with doves or bees.

The three species investigated were picked because they seemed the easiest to work with. Others may contribute to pollination as significantly. Gila woodpeckers alight in the tops of blooming saguaros as commonly as white-winged doves, and they dip slowly and delicately into the blossoms like tomboys remembering teatime manners — drastic contrast to their usual raucous chasing of one another. Thrashers, cactus wrens, and gilded flickers also are probable major pollinators in the Tucson region. So are various native bees, moths, and hognose bats, relatives of longnose bats and similarly equipped with long tongues.

On an average 37 days pass from the time a saguaro flower opens until the figlike fruit ripens, its pulp a spectacular scarlet studded with nearly 2000 shiny black pinhead seeds. The seeds are the object of mystery: What happens to them? Around 15 to 20 mature saguaros per acre are the average in the cactus forests near Tucson. Each of these produces about 4 flowers per day for 30 days, or 120 flowers per plant. Now, botanists reason, if half of these blossoms were to set fruit, as experiments indicate is usual, there would be 2 million seeds per acre per year. If a single seedling from this vast production established itself every 5 years a saguaro forest could maintain itself — a regeneration that is occurring in most locations, although not in the case of the widely publicized population decline in the lowlands of Saguaro National Monument.

The other seeds disappear by the millions into the gullets of insects, birds, rodents, and man. Papago Indians relied on saguaro fruits so much in the old days that they began their calendar year with *Navaita*, the time of the saguaro harvest. They utilized juice, pulp, and seeds. Susie Wilson, a Shoshone Indian woman who taught me basketry in Death Valley, spoke of traveling to the Colorado River to trade for ripe saguaro fruit and join in the harvest. It was a trip she had made only a time or two, and one that possibly dated no farther back than the transportation convenience of automobiles; yet her experience indicates the widespread importance attached to saguaro fruit by the aboriginal people of the desert. Among wildlife, birds gorge on fruit still clinging to saguaro branches and packrats, coyotes, and a host of other species scurry to feed on it after it falls. Harvester ants may deplete the supply of seeds most of all. Seeds swallowed by birds and animals tend to pass through their digestive tracts unharmed and are given a second chance at germination; but ants gather millions of seeds and take them into their labyrinthine nest chambers, far too deep underground to sprout successfully.

Warren Steenbergh, a research biologist at Saguaro National Monument, decided to find out exactly what happens to the seeds. He patiently separated 50,000 from the sticky pulp of a basketful of saguaro fruits and scattered them onto test plots, 1000 seeds per plot. In just an hour's time, harvester ants had carried off every seed from one plot. Other plots failed to germinate for different reasons. Sprouting requires a precise combination of light, moisture, and temperature; and seeds will hold over for years until these conditions occur if necessary. Steenbergh found that rain has to fall twice within five days if seeds are to germinate, and must be enough to let the seeds directly contact free water. Mere moisture won't do. Light also is crucial. In a separate test more than 8000 seeds were supplied with every condition known to be necessary for germination except that they were kept in darkness. Only thirteen sprouted. The experiment was repeated using daylight, and the seeds grew.

In nature, saguaro seeds probably germinate best lying at the surface of the soil or in a crevice well exposed to light. Temperatures should be in the seventies or eighties. In reality, temperatures at the soil's surface swing far above and below this optimum, but the fluctuation seems of no consequence so long as the seeds receive enough cumulative hours at an ideal temperature. If highs stay persistently below 60°F., or if they climb above 95° for several consecutive days, few seedlings will appear. Conversely, brief exposures at extremes as great as from several degrees below freezing to 180°F. seem to cause no harm, at least under laboratory conditions. Rocky soils are a boon. They trap moisture, and their coarseness helps to anchor saguaro roots. They provide camouflage, which hides seeds from the eyes of rodents and protects against pulverization beneath the feet of grazing cattle. The roughness of the soil also breaks the force of wind and creates eddies of calm air that pose less of a threat to the frail moisture supply of tiny seedlings.

"Nurse" trees are a help too. More than a century ago men on the Border Survey along the Arizona-Sonora line commented in reports that young saguaros inevitably seemed to be growing beneath mesquite or paloverde trees, although nobody then knew why. The effect of the trees is now understood: they act like parasols. Daytime shading may be crucial during practically the first decade of a saguaro's life. In fact, decreasing nurse vegetation in the eastern unit of Saguaro National Monument is believed to be the main cause of the saguaro loss there — a loss so marked that all saguaros will be gone from that particular area by the year 2000 unless something reverses the present trend.

In addition to guarding young saguaros against excess heat, the nurse trees act as a shield against frost. This was shown a few years ago when a hard freeze gripped the foothills above Tucson. Of the saguaros growing there, nearly one-third of those

Young saguaro overtopping nurse bush

eleven feet tall or over were killed, by bacterial rot that set into frost-damaged tissue, if not directly by the cold. Saguaros less than eleven feet high fared much better. The reason for the difference was that these shorter cacti were still within the protection of nurse trees and bushes.

Little seems to go right for saguaro seedlings, all factors considered. If the number of germinations seems minute in view of the prodigious quantity of seeds produced, the ratio shrinks still further when it comes to establishment among those that do sprout. Here results often approach zero. Eight hundred seedlings set out in unfenced plots in one test had only 14 still alive after six months. In another year and a half, those particular 14 were dead and so were 770 seedlings from a second planting of 800. Rodents destroyed practically all of the plants that were lost. Probably it was packrats. Cacti provide nearly half of the food eaten by these animals the year round, and in May the amount jumps to 90 percent. In the laboratory packrats live indefinitely on nothing more than saguaro seedlings and water, whereas the same diet is quickly spurned by kangaroo rats and other common rodent species. In this regard, too, man's war against coyotes and other predators has often been blamed for allowing rodent populations to increase, thereby in turn hampering saguaro regeneration. However, this assumption cannot be substantiated. There is no real indication that rodent populations have increased in cactus forests; more likely the number of predators is controlled by the rodent population available as food, and not the reverse.

Desert weather is another factor affecting saguaro seedlings — not just heat and dryness and cold but also rain. Rain of course supplies needed moisture; and it also offsets summer soil temperatures that otherwise might climb disastrously high. The mid-July onset of the rains coincides with the period of greatest heat, and their cooling effect has been measured as deep as twelve inches beneath the surface of the soil. The importance of this is apparent from the high death rate among seedlings that survive their first summer but perish during the hot foresummer of the following year, before the rains bring their cooling. These tiny cacti have inherently small water-storage capacities and large evaporative surfaces; they are exceedingly vulnerable and may be saved only by rain. A few may also be lost because of it, for rain has a detrimental effect as well as a beneficial one. Saguaros have no protection against washing out in a rainstorm. Their roots are shallow to permit a quick absorption of moisture but success in this direction at times proves fatal in another direction. Storm waters rip young plants from their holds and sweep them to destruction, and even mature saguaros fall victim to torrential rains, their roots undercut and loosened and unable to support the plant if wind accompanies the rain. They crash to earth, the victims of rain.

Survival is further complicated by an unusually prolonged period of vulnerability. Saguaros are extraordinarily slow growing. After 2 years a seedling will stand only a ¼ inch high; in 15 years, it barely reaches 1 foot, and by 40 years it won't measure more than 10 feet. Not until it is 60 or 70 years old, and two or three times the height of a man, will the cactus finally have passed most of the dangers likely to befall it. About this time, prickly balls will begin to appear near the top of the plant, the first buds of branches. By 150 years of age, saguaros reach full size, standing 35 to 50 feet tall and with branches that commonly number from 2 to 7 or 8. Another 50 or 60 years of life will remain for these mature specimens — and perhaps this longevity is a pivotal factor in the case of stricken saguaro populations such as that of Saguaro National Monument. It may be perfectly normal for several decades to pass in a particular locality without producing conditions ideal for saguaro germination. A marked decline may appear within a saguaro forest and continue for a period that seems long to man but is actually of little real consequence. Such declines do not necessarily doom the future of even that particular forest, let alone the species, since abundant seeds will still be available so long as a single saguaro continues to flower and set fruit. Sites reported sixty years ago by Shreve as lacking young saguaros now support healthy stands, despite his bleak remark that "plants less than one decimeter in height are so rare, or inconspicuous, that nine botanists who have had excellent opportunities to find them report they have never done so." Man's patience and perspective is often out of step with nature's, and the dilemma of threatened saguaro forests may belong at least partially in this category.

Perhaps one saguaro out of every thousand will develop an odd crested growth called a cristate. Nobody really knows the cause of these. They may be genetic; or possibly a response to injury, such as insect damage. Maybe they result from

Cristate

radioactivity in the soil, or from a cancerlike multiplication of cells. Whatever the reason, cristates seem benign: they bring no harm to saguaros, or to organpipes on which they also sometimes form.

In the case of necrosis, a disease similar to the common rot of carrots or to fireblight in peas and apples, the story is different. There may be very real harm. Necrosis was first noticed and identified in saguaros in 1899, but nobody even yet knows what to do about it. Some investigators believe the disease directly explains saguaro die-off; others feel that the disease merely starts the decomposition of tissue already fatally damaged by other causes. A bacillus carried in the digestive tract of the larvae of a drab nocturnal moth *(Cactobrosis fernaldialis)* is the cause of the trouble. Adult moths live only three nights, just long enough to mate and lay eggs and thereby affect the future of the particular saguaros in which their larvae will feed. Sometimes a cactus will manage to wall off an infected area with a corklike seal; if this fails the rot may spread even to the roots and once that far the cactus is likely to topple in the next wind. Several species of cactus are affected by the necrosis, which is carried by fruit flies as well as the moths; but no other is as damaged as saguaro. Decay from the disease ruptures saguaro skin and sends a suppurating black ooze trickling down the trunk, darkening the soil for a five- or six-foot radius. This contamination ends the life of any cactus seedlings near the parent plant, and it spreads the disease to other mature saguaros. Windblown dust carrying bacilli may also infect open wounds, and root injuries provide avenues of infection within the soil.

No field control seems possible. At one time the National Park Service tried experimentally to control the disease by destroying infected plants in Saguaro National Monument. Men used tractors to pull down cacti that showed telltale discoloration; next they cut them into sections and hauled them to a pit. There they drenched the whole pile with insecticide, sealed it in a tarp for twenty-four hours, and then covered it with dirt. Unfortunately the work proved to be slow and costly and was abandoned. About the same time, Professors James Brown and Alice Boyle of the University of Arizona began treating the disease with penicillin. The "miracle drug" was still new and scarce at the time, and they had to make their own. It successfully killed the bacillus in laboratory cultures, so the two researchers carried hypodermic needles and ladders into the saguaro forests and set about giving injections. Results were spectacular. Sixty-seven out of seventy treated cacti lived. But the method was laborious and had to be abandoned.

Gila woodpeckers and gilded flickers are perhaps the saguaros' best vigilante committee. They tunnel after cactrobrosis moths in the saguaro forests of the desert as readily as their relatives work over the pine and fir forests of the rest of the world. Sometimes they also seem to peck open a saguaro trunk to "drink" from the watery pulp, an action that may be incidental to searching out insects but often seems intentional. Either way, the habit rids the cactus of at least some future trouble and at the same time benefits other birds unable to pierce the rough outer covering of a saguaro for themselves. Juices soon coagulate and seal the wound, although before they do the cactus offers accessible moisture and may be visited by several species. While studying birds at Organ Pipe Cactus National Monument, Max Hensley noticed a Gila woodpecker chipping vigorously at the top of an eighteen-foot saguaro and showering the ground with green chunks of cactus, a sure indication that it had dug beneath the outer skin to the moist pulp within. When the woodpecker flew off, a thrasher quickly replaced it and began to make characteristic drinking motions, dipping in its bill, then raising its head and swallowing.

More common by far than "drinking holes" are cavities deliberately excavated in saguaros and cardons as nest sites. A few minutes in any part of the giant cactus forest easily reveals several of these — round holes three or four inches in diameter, gaping black and inviting. Woodpeckers and flickers chisel them out, usually about the size and shape of a football, and a surprising variety of desert creatures use them. The excavators themselves use a hole only one year, pecking a new one each spring. The cactus secretes callus tissue a quarter- to a half-inch thick to wall off the holes, a process that remains a puzzle. One researcher cut an imitation woodpecker cavity into a saguaro and found after sixty days that it had a shell only three sixty-fourths of an inch thick. This rate suggests that the linings may continue to form for at least a year, and ties in with observations of woodpeckers hollowing out cavities several months ahead of nesting time. Chemically, however, the callus is still a puzzle, for although it contains a considerable proportion of lignin (the woody substance found in cactus ribs and in the wood of all trees) none of this substance is present in cortex tissue, which is where the wound occurs. So far there is no explanation.

Many features enhance the value of saguaro holes as nests, with evaporative cooling perhaps the most important of all, since nesting in the desert often depends more on keeping eggs cool than on warming them. A hole deep within a living cactus solves this. The temperature of the desert air may hover around 110° or 115°F., yet be only 90° inside a nest hole because of the evaporation of moisture, according to work by Richard Krizman of the University of Arizona. At night the situation is conveniently reversed, with the inner part of cactus as much as 12 degrees warmer than the air. Nest holes have a further advantage in holding relative humidity 5 or 10 percent higher than that of the outside air. This significantly lessens the drain on birds' body moisture and is a particular advantage for nestlings.

There are other effects as well. For example, among birds nesting in the open eggs usually are camouflaged by color and a speckled pattern, but those of hole-nesters tend to be nearly white. This difference probably developed through long centuries of evolution as the need of camouflage disappeared for eggs laid inside holes. Or it may be that the light color of nest-cavity eggs is not so much a loss of camouflage as a means of guiding adults settling into the darkness of the hole: white eggs show up better, and the parent birds are more sure to find them immediately and sit on them. This matter of seeing within the dim light of the cavities also affects feeding. The beak nodes of hole-nesting infants generally are white, an advantage since hatchlings tend to wait until an adult taps them on the node before they open their mouths for food. After the first few days this gaping pattern becomes triggered simply by the darkening of the nest entryway instead of by a tap on the beak; the young open their mouths and stretch their rubbery necks even before the parent bird has clawed down inside the hole to reach them.

Nesting in a hole affects courtship, too — drastically so. In locations where the branches of one tree or bush are about as acceptable as those of another for a nest, birds will first claim their territory and after that will select a building site. Where a hole is needed for nesting, the priorities are reversed. The nest site itself must be found first and then the territory can be worked out. This is because an area with adequate food cannot necessarily be counted on also to have a hole available, but the chances are that any place where a male bird with rising hormones finds a tempting hole he can also find food. (Studies of fish corroborate this order of selection: those with definite nesting requirements pick that site first and then secure a territory

Nest holes

around it, whereas species not choosy about nest requirements pick a general territory first and then decide where to lay.)

Nest holes are so much in demand that beginning in April competition for them becomes keen. A male bird finding a hole does not dare stray far from it. Rather than go in search of a mate and risk losing the hole, he may use a special "advertising" song to lure a female into range, as in the case of the trogons. When a female responds and comes close, the hopeful bachelor will pop in and out of his prized hole, hoping to stimulate her urges to the same pitch as his. For some species the number of available nest cavities almost surely limits population more than the availability of food does, and in various locations springtime fights over holes cause a higher mortality than comes from predators or any other cause. Yet the value of a hole is great enough to warrant struggle. Polygamy is much more common among species that nest in holes than among those that nest in the open: with the young relatively safe inside a nest cavity, the male can leave the major responsibility of defense and feeding to the female and devote part of his attention to seeking a second mate and starting a second brood. Providing well initially allows him simultaneous families, and thereby benefits the species.

A much higher percentage of young birds survive in nest holes than in open nests — and this affects the number of eggs laid. Some sparrows increase clutch size by 50 percent. Birds that nest in the open have a pressing need to get their young fledged and on their own as quickly as possible; consequently they lay few eggs. Fewer mouths to fill means a faster development of each individual nestling. In contrast, among birds using holes prolonged vulnerability is relatively safe. These species can afford more gaping mouths and the added days it takes to bring insects and lizards and fruit enough for the transformation into feathers and wings and functioning nervous systems. At least sixteen species of birds are known to use saguaro holes abandoned, or left unguarded, by their original makers. These sixteen are the elf owl, screech owl, pigmy owl, sparrow hawk, Bendire's thrasher, cactus wren, ash-throated flycatcher, Wied's crested flycatcher, western kingbird, Lucy's warbler, purple martin, bluebird, house finch, English sparrow, lark bunting, and starling. Without the cool moist microclimate within cactus it is doubtful whether these species could endure desert conditions. Their presence depends directly on holes in saguaros.

Working on a master's thesis at the University of Arizona, Oscar Soule found that of the sixteen, only starlings and house finches carry nesting materials into the holes; the other species nest on the bare floor. Probably evolution explains this difference, since starlings and finches have only recently started to use saguaro holes. The finches normally build rather compact nests in brush or cholla, and evidently they carry over the urge when they nest in saguaros, because they will nearly fill a hole with grass and twigs, then settle into a depression scooped into the top of the pile. The approach offsets much of the advantage of the hole's moderate temperature and deep concealment, and persistence of the habit suggests that these finches have not yet had time to develop complete efficiency as hole-nesters. A saguaro cavity is a finished nest in itself; no additional lining is needed. Starlings, on the other hand, come closer to utilizing the full advantage of the holes. They first appeared in the desert only about 1950 but already have adapted so fully that they take only token strands of grass into a nest hole — vestigial behavior left over from other conditions and already an urge they barely heed. The starlings are a surprising sight in the desert however at home they now have become. The species was unknown in America until 1890 when a flock of 80 was brought from Europe and set free in Central Park, New York. An additional 40 starlings were imported the following year. Now the descendants of these original 120 birds range corner to corner across the continent, from Hudson Bay to Mexico, adapted even to the theoretically difficult habitat of the desert.

Mammals also use saguaro holes. Brown bats frequently roost within them throughout the summer, and packrats and cactus mice occasionally take over holes as much as twenty feet above the ground. They gnaw spiral corridors up to such nests, feeding on saguaro pulp as they go. Or, if they choose, they can climb by the thorns and ribs alone without fashioning a special passageway. As for smaller creatures, Soule found thirteen species of insects in saguaro holes, one nematode, three spiders, and a pseudo-scorpion. One of the insects, a mosquito, apparently is limited only to saguaro holes (a fairly typical sort of restriction for mosquitoes, since some of them belong specifically to the tiny pools of water that collect against the internodes of tropical bamboo and others only to the pools held by pitcher plants in northern bogs). Even so, a "saguaro mosquito" seems incongruous: a dryland plant as host to a wet-habitat insect. It is possible, given suitable angle and exposure, because rainwater runs readily into saguaro holes and provides the pools needed by mosquito larvae.

Few detailed observations have been made on such water sources, a saguaro near Gates Pass, west of Tucson, was found with nearly four inches of water in a hole even though two months had passed since the last rain, and it had been little more than a light shower. A sample of the water from the hole quickly filmed over in the laboratory, covered by oily scum plus bits of callus tissue, bird feathers, insect wings, and animal debris. Such films probably help to reduce evaporation and underwrite the chance for mosquitoes to complete their cycles and perpetuate their kind.

According to work by Anthony Ross at the University of Arizona, the mosquitoes lay eggs within the tissue of the cactus during the winter and these stay dormant until summer rains and rising temperatures initiate hatching. Larvae then progress into adulthood with exceptional rapidity, as if aware of the essentially fragile quality of aquatic life inside desert cactus. Some of the pools that the mosquitoes use must last nearly year round since they serve as water sources for birds. It is not unusual to see a flicker or woodpecker fly from hole to hole looking in, ultimately find one with water, and drink.

Various wasps and bees also are among the parade of species that rely on saguaro holes. Sometimes a saguaro can actually be heard buzzing from a distance of twenty feet, so active are the bees swarming within. Flies breed in saguaros too, probably feeding on springtails, small primitive insects that abound in the holes; grasshoppers and katydids often retreat into cactus holes to escape daytime heat and radiation.

Saguaros have long been the symbol of the Sonoran Desert, and appropriately so. They stand as romantic sentinels for humans, and as refuge and entire world for various desert creatures. Perhaps nowhere else is the dependence of the animal kingdom on the plant kingdom more dramatically evident. Saguaros and other tall cacti first win the battle against desert drought; then birds and animals and insects dependent on them also can claim victory.

5. In Search of Boojums

INTERMIXED WITH THE CACTUS of the Sonoran Desert are other
plant forms equally successful in adaptation and even more
startling to the human eye and mind. Boojum trees illustrate
the point.

Twice we have sought out these curiosities (and there are just
two places in all the world to look for them: near Puerto Libertad
on the Sonoran mainland of Mexico and in the midsection of
the Baja California peninsula). Boojum "trees" rise from their
chosen hillsides like upside-down parsnips as much as 70 feet
tall, their branches a snaggle of mere pencil-like twigs and their
tops crowned in summer by a burst of sulfur-yellow flowers.
With such an appearance, a stand of boojums is worth seeking —
like Mount Everest — simply "because it is there." No plant
anywhere looks more peculiar, and none in the desert can match
the boojum for age. Bristlecone pines live longer, reaching ages
as great as 5000 years, more venerable even than sequoia trees;
but bristlecones are desert plants only in a map sense. Go to
their strongholds in the White Mountains of California (east
of the Sierras), or the Panamint Mountains edging Death Valley,
or the Wheeler Peak area in Nevada, and you find yourself
thousands of feet above the desert. Your eye looks out across
desert, its barrenness painting the landscape a brown earth color
all the way to the horizon; yet close at hand the scene is alpine,
at Wheeler Peak replete even to a glacier. The pines are *in*
the desert but not *of* it; they grow high above the heat and

drought. Not so with boojums, which thrive where rainfall scarcely equals four inches a year and temperatures stay well above 100° for weeks at a time. In spite of such conditions boojums live to be 700 or 800 years old.

Our first search for these desert Loreleis took us south of Tucson and into Mexico at Sásabe, a village of squat adobe houses, some the color of the earth from which they are made and others whitewashed to dazzling brilliance. The road leads quickly over the hillocks of town and into the desert beyond, the car wallowing from side to side and necessitating repeated stops for selecting a course among chuckholes. Beer cans tied in mesquite trees mark infrequent junctions with tracks that angle off to unseen waterholes and rancherias. Occasional stretches are graded and there speed picks up to thirty or thirty-five miles an hour, but for the most part the road south makes and maintains itself simply by the rolling of wheels upon its surface, and how passable it is depends on the circumstances of the day. Too dry, and you may not succeed in crossing a sandy stretch; too wet and you will certainly be stopped in the muddy places. But let conditions approach "right" and such a road gives a leisurely closeness to the land akin to riding horseback or paddling a canoe. A jackrabbit barely paused in its browsing to watch our approach, then ran off, its hindquarters and forequarters held on the comfortable, even plane of a trot rather than pumping furiously to power great leaps. Its ears, shell pink and as long as its legs, stayed erect, hardly even vibrating with the easy motion. Quail fled ahead of us on foot, not wanting to take wing or to forsake the relative smoothness of the roadway, and when at length they did fly it was low to the ground, their topknots streaming backward. A roadrunner disdained our intrusion and kept right on turning over crusts of dry mud in an evaporated rain puddle as we passed, evidently looking for crickets and scorpions that had retreated into the relatively damp shade of the cracks between the crusts.

The desert wore its annual corsage of flowers, brittlebush the most showy of all. Mile after mile its yellow blooms floated on almost invisible stalks. There were scores of flowers per bush and so many bushes that our pantlegs grew yellow with pollen in just a few steps off the road. Spring also was showing itself in the series of minuscule Mexican villages we drove through. Hay had been cut and stacked in the fields of Pitiquito and Bámori, and fields of barley were beginning to head. At Las Molinas, a village of eight or ten houses, we passed a tiny cubicle of a church freshly whitewashed outside and glowing with candlelight on the inside. A girl perhaps twelve years old rose from her lone kneeling and lounged in the door to watch us pass, curious because so few outsiders wander this road. She wore a pink dress and a pink veil, for this was Good Friday, a day cherished in the hearts of the desert people, who hold both to the teaching of the pioneer padres and to their own Indian beliefs. The two streams long ago blended into a unique theology known as Sonoran Catholicism, neither fully approved nor outrightly rejected by the established Church.

We had driven nearly all day when there appeared ahead a sudden streak of blue, a line marking where sky meets water: the Gulf of California. We knew that somewhere nearby were the boojums, and even without these most exotic of plants yet in sight the scene was a world apart. A huge cardon cactus towered above our truck; hunched in its topmost branches were two ospreys, the fish hawks of the Sierra Nevada and the Rockies,

Ospreys

the great birds that hover above evergreen forests and plunge into foaming streams to catch fish. Here they sat in cactus. We counted eleven nests, all in cardons. The thorny arms of each nest-cactus were white with droppings, and occasional fish skeletons littered the desert floor. Once we heard the clear whistle of an osprey cutting through the hot silence, and watched it wing in carrying a stick in its talons. The bird worked the stick into the general nest tangle and then sat so close and still that its white breast, black eye stripe, and hooked bill showed plainly in our binoculars.

Sunset continued the feeling of the unexpected, a perfect prelude for a boojum hunt. On a rock shelf barely above reach of the lapping tide, small hollows held pools of water splashed by the day's highest waves. There we washed our desert-hot feet and watched the glowing ball of the sun slide silently into the Gulf. Seven brown pelicans flew by in single file so close to the water that their reflected wingtips touched their actual wingtips. They were soaring even though flying so low, not flapping. At length the leader did begin to stroke with its wings, and one by one each pelican followed suit and crossed in front of the sun's sinking disk. Still in line, they rose and disappeared. A tern plunged into the purple ocean and reappeared with a fish.

Darkness enfolded us and for the present hid the meeting of desert and sea. We turned to our camp, up a gully away from the water and the chill of the ocean wind. A great horned owl was calling, and bats swooped overhead squeaking their sonars as we cooked dinner. Soon the moon climbed above the rim of the mountains, a round silver moon due to eclipse that night. The odd blend made a memorable camp: we were surrounded by elephant trees with their strange, swollen, sprawling trunks, and the moon would enter total eclipse in just a few hours. We hoped for boojums in the morning. At eight-thirty a shadow began to spread from the lower left of the moon, and the whole orb took on an eerie red-brown glow and looked as if lit from behind like a candled egg. The shadow worked upward for an hour and a half, and reduced the moon to the merest rim of light. Then, having reached climax, the effect immediately began to reverse: darkness ebbed, seas and craters regained their familiar appearance — and we gladly surrendered the night to sleep.

At five the next morning the dawn chorus began with a mockingbird as featured soloist, a bird that had practiced its songs at midnight and again at two. Quail, doves, a gilded flicker, a cactus wren, and a flock of a full 100 lark sparrows joined the chorus species by species. The latter put up a great buzzing and twittering, turning the desert into what seemed like a poultry yard with miniature fowl noisily scratching out seeds and insects. The sparrows' mottled brown backs blended against the stony ground, and only their incessant calling and the bobbing of their chestnut-and-white striped heads betrayed their whereabouts. I counted 20 sparrows in the field of the binoculars at once; at the same time, a roundtail ground squirrel crossed my vision and 6 mourning doves flew through and settled to feed in the background, out of focus. This was Saturday, but it was worthy of Easter morning itself. Certainly resurrection prevailed: here was the yearly resurgence of desert life, pollen blowing yellow from brittlebush, ospreys nesting in cactus, and somewhere close at hand, the boojums that through centuries of desert life had witnessed countless rebirths.

Puerto Libertad is Seri Indian country, a tribe superbly adapted to life in the desert and on the sea. Their homeland formerly reached almost to the Arizona line, and southward nearly to Guaymas. The Spanish repeatedly sought to "tame" them and resettle them at inland missions for transformation from fishermen and desert hunters to farmers of corn and squash. They failed. Nor could the Mexicans who succeeded the Spanish as rulers manage to subdue the Seris. As late as the 1940s the government of Mexico acknowledged that the tribe still controlled about 1000 square miles, determining their own lives and thinking their own thoughts, frontier Indians holding their culture intact and dealing with modern realities only on their own terms. The Seris fished and sold the catch; they hunted sea turtles with spears, and deer with bows and arrows. They painted their faces and sang their songs and lived their lives. Only a combination of earnest Protestant missionaries in the 1950s plus overpowering competition from Mexican fishing fleets in the 1960s conspired to break the Seris' ancient hold on themselves. A final blow came in 1965 when Tiburón Island, the largest island in Mexican waters and the most beloved stronghold of the Seri Indians, was decreed as a preserve for wildlife and closed to hunting. The measure is the only conceivable hope of saving the wild creatures that belong to this desert-sea region; but the cost is high in terms of people torn from their traditional moorage and loosed on a sea of twentieth-century confusion.

By luck we chanced on a small group of Indian women and children selling carvings and fish vertebrae strung into necklaces. We dickered for a beautifully proportioned, satiny black porpoise carved from ironwood — a creature of the sea exquisitely rendered in hard, close-grained "desert" wood. Forty pesos, $3.20, was the final agreed price — and I have felt ashamed ever since. We have bested the Seris as a people, our modern society against their ancient society, and there should have been no urge to repeat the conquest on an individual basis by sharp bargaining. Nonetheless, the exchange back and forth in Spanish led to a chance to ask about the boojums, using the name *cirio,* the same word used by the Mexicans for the tall wax tapers of their church altars. At first the women simply pointed to the south. Then they discussed the question in Seri, a language full of glottal stops and sounds made far back in the throat, a flow of conversation indiscernible as separate words to the uninitiated Caucasian ear.

At length the woman with whom we had bargained squatted on the ground and drew a map in the sand with her finger. She traced a line for the bay where we were huddled and another for the mountains we could see on the southern skyline. Then she made a dot with her fingertip, a spot between the bay and the mountains and below the crest of the range. That is where we found the boojums. We first spotted them while still distant, but because you don't have to have ever before seen a boojum in order to recognize one we knew immediately that our quest was succeeding. Nothing else has such a shape. A boojum looks like a boojum, and nothing except a boojum even faintly suggests one. Our binoculars picked up poles bristling from a low ridge perhaps four or five miles away — tall poles unlike anything else, some of them silhouetted against the skyline and therefore particularly discernible.

The botanical name, *Idria columnaris,* comes from the tall water jars used by the early Greeks, a word most commonly written as *hydria* but in this case as *idria.* The shape of a young boojum suggests the water jar, its bottom swollen and rounded and its sides tapering gently upward. Furthermore, as in the case of saguaros and other cacti, succulence is the main secret of survival for these plants. The name "boojum" is pure Lewis Carroll from *The Hunting of the Snark.* Boojums are mysterious Things, as Carroll tells it, neither wholly animal nor fully plant, but simply boojum. They might also belong to the bottom of the rabbit hole, ready to greet Alice on arrival in Wonderland. They are "mimsy," or so thought Geoffrey Sykes, a British-born botanist, when he first saw them in 1922. Sykes was leading an expedition into the Libertad region and had focused his telescope on the same ridges that we were rejoicing over with our binoculars. As his son reported the occasion, Sykes let out a whoop of delight and loudly proclaimed, "Oh-ho, a boojum! Definitely a boojum." And so the trees have been known ever since in the world beyond the Mexican border, at least by those few persons who know the plant at all.

Why boojums should be restricted only to Baja California and Puerto Libertad nobody can say. Nor does any one know when or how the one isolated colony established itself on mainland Mexico, directly across the Gulf from the rest of the boojums. Is it critical pollination requirements that so severely limit the range, or matters of germination, or seedling establishment? Why don't boojums spread into the surrounding desert? Are they relicts left from a previous era and headed toward extinction? Or did they evolve this oddness right where they are now and simply never spread themselves beyond their present, limited territory? Answers are nonexistent — so far.

The first outsider to heed boojums, at least in writing, was Father Francisco Clavijero, an eighteenth-century Italian missionary in Baja California. In his account of the region, under a section titled "Noxious and Grotesque Plants," he notes this: "Much more curious is another tree . . . [which] has not been seen by missionaries before the year 1751 because they had not gone into the interior of the country, nor do I believe that it has been known until now by naturalists . . . It is so large that it grows to a height of 70 feet. Its trunk, thick in proportion, is not woody but soft and succulent like the branches of the Pitahaya [organpipe] and the cardon, two large common cacti. Its branches are certain little twigs about a foot and a half long, covered with small leaves and protected by a thorn at the end. There is no use for this great tree; it is neither dry nor good for firewood, but at the Mission of San Francisco de Borja they burn it because of the lack of Fuel."

The padre's description fits boojums

Boojums

well, although, true individualists of the plant kingdom, they come in a far greater variety of forms than he indicated. Most grow straight and deserving of their Mexican name, *cirio;* their trunks taper evenly from bulbous base to pointed tip. But other boojums follow no rules. They sag into arches, yet continue to grow; or they start to sag, recover midway, and grow as gigantic S's. Some fork near the top and stand with arms eternally supplicating heaven; the arms of others intertwine, or droop wearily. There may be any number of arms, of any size, at any angle. A few boojums grow as twins or triplets. Their trunks fork from the base and each follows its own inclination as to position and branches. If nursery-school children could be introduced to boojums and given the chance to draw them, no criticizing adult could call the resulting pictures unreal, for with boojums anything goes.

On the hills near Libertad, boojums are fairly sedate compared with those of Baja California. Branching is minimal and heights average 34 feet, little more than half the height of the record Baja boojum, which stands 76 feet 6 inches. This giant, growing about 10 miles inland from the Gulf, near Bahía de Los Angeles, has a diameter of over 25 inches at a point 3 feet above ground level. It may be that scanty moisture accounts for the difference, since the yearly rainfall at Libertad averages only two and one-half inches, about half of what is characteristic of the boojum's Baja range. At the Libertad site boojums grow only on north-facing slopes, where soil moisture is at its optimum. This leads Robert Humphrey of the University of Arizona, a leading authority on boojums, to believe that a hairline water balance may be a crucial factor in the growth of the Sonoran boojums. The 70-foot-plus specimens that he has measured belong to two areas where soils are particularly deep and coarse, ideal for water infiltration and storage. Most years these locations receive no more than three to five inches of rain, but their soil conditions are so ideal that a substantial amount of moisture is available even so. Given this advantage, boojums are at their best. On drier slopes, such as Libertad's, they fare less well,

Base of
boojum tree

and most stunted of all are the boojums close to the Pacific, where fog and salt-laden winds dominate the desert. There growth is dwarfed and contorted, and boojums may be only two or three feet high even when fully mature and centuries old.

Baja boojums have an additional distinction beyond their veritable forest growth and bizarre individual shapes — a surprise on our second boojum hunt. We had driven south from Tijuana following the road that at the outset is paved and lined with the beach cottages and resorts of escapees from San Diego and Los Angeles. Farther on it becomes graded and unbelievably rutted as it passes through newly developing agricultural land, and finally it wanders gently up the broad drainage channel behind El Rosario. The region is about a quarter of the way down the Pacific side of the Baja peninsula. We had reached there after sunset and turned up a sloping bajada. With nothing more than headlights and stars to help us see, we knew we were back in boojum country, although in the darkness we missed the added touch of these particular boojums. Morning light revealed the usual unusual shape; and added to the silhouette was a sight readily acceptable in the tropics or the soggy evergreen forests of the Pacific Northwest, though unexpected in the supposedly bleak heart of a notoriously arid desert. The boojum forest here is draped with epiphytes, plants that grow on other plants. They use the hosts as toeholds and survive not parasitically but on whatever nutrients and moisture happen to reach them via the air currents.

Pale green lichen *(Usnea)* hung from the twigs of these boojums, forming wispy draperies two feet long, stirring in the gentle dawn breeze. Farther on we found another epiphyte, *Tillandsia recurvata,* a relative of Spanish moss. The late Joseph Wood Krutch, veteran Baja California observer, admirer, and reporter, wrote of it: "I had not supposed that anything could make a boojum look queerer than it does already, but these outdid themselves." Instead of hanging in draperies, this oddity forms tight balls strung on the twigs and arms of its host like a series of bird nests. Tillandsia grows on ocotillos and elephant trees as well as on boojums, and it gives a knobby look to the already peculiar appearance of them all. Seen up close the plant is a cluster of flat, leathery, gray blades curled and tangled in upon themselves, the empty capsules of fruiting bodies raised on strawlike stalks and remaining. The overall impression is of the bromeliads of tropical jungles, except on a small scale. Sources of moisture for the epiphytes are no mystery. Rainfall throughout the boojum forests is skimpy, but as anyone who has shivered down the Pacific side of Baja California can attest, there can be more to moisture than rain. Morning after morning, sunrise comes veiled by fog even far inland from the ocean. The desert world stays muffled and gray and walled in upon itself until noon, and a thick sweater feels welcome even though theoretically the season is hot.

Boojums seemingly do not absorb the wetness of this fog, no matter how much it benefits the epiphytes. For boojums the desert is dry, and they solve the problem by storing water against future need: they grow with a woody, cylindrical framework filled by a spongy, wet, potato-like pith. The outer cores are strong enough so that ranchers split them lengthwise to use as fencing for corrals. The wood is about half an inch thick and the core measures nearly ten inches in diameter, poor enough by usual standards but one of the better building materials of central Baja, along with the weak wood of dried agave flower stalks (century plants) and the fibrous trunks of datilillo (giant yuccas much like Joshua trees). A further use of boojums is their succulence. Occasionally during extreme drought, ranchers hack through the woody exterior of living trees with machetes, exposing the moist inner pulp for cattle to feed on. Father

Lichen draperies   Tillandsia

Clavijero thus was wrong: there is use for boojums beyond their role as captor of the imagination.

The main trunk of boojums is covered with bark so smooth it almost seems like skin. Twigs bristle out directly from it, woody and stiff, totally lacking succulence. Their one purpose seems to be to produce leathery half-inch leaves much like the leaves of ocotillo, which is the only relative of boojums. This burst of greenness generally follows the arrival of summer rains, although if July fails to deliver its usual quota of moisture the leaves may wait for winter rains. Either way, they drop off by April or May, which is "autumn," not because of impending cold but of the long dry weeks leading up to summer. The physiology is perfectly in order. Nonetheless it is startling to come on boojums shining with autumn gold while lupine and poppies and iceplants at their bases have just begun spring bloom.

Boojum trees sprout and shed leaves only once a year, unlike ocotillos, which respond to each passing drought by shedding leaves, then regrowing them whenever the next rain wets the desert. Boojums have inner tissue as moist as that of a cactus and they consequently can afford leaves all year with or without rain, except during the foresummer drought from April through June. Both ocotillos and boojums combine leaves and spines in a way completely unknown in any other plant family. As a branch of either plant lengthens, it sprouts its first set of leaves, each one growing from the tip of what looks like an ordinary leaf petiole but is actually a spine. The leaf flourishes through the growing season, then falls; the spine remains intact. Subsequent leaves grow from the axil (where the spine joins the stem) instead of from the tip of the spine. Invariably these leaves are sessile; they grow tight against the stem without any petiole.

The flowering of boojums coincides with summer rains. Special twigs flare out from the high tip of the plant like a frizzled blond coiffure — evidently a highly perfumed one. Bees, wasps, and hummingbirds swarm about the aerial bouquets and they must perform well as pollinators since young boojums abound.

There seems to be no spreading beyond the existing range, however, not even onto land that seems equally suitable. A few horticultural gardens have *Idria,* but so far none has been favored with the regeneration that is common in the wild. Seeds germinate, only to have something thwart establishment of the seedlings. Growing conditions may not be optimum, no matter how they look to a human eye, or perhaps none of the transplanted boojums are yet old enough to provide their seeds with some particular enzyme needed for successful propagation. In the wild, flowers tip the plants by July even in years when soil moisture is scant and the production of leaves is put off until the winter rains arrive. Yet despite this hardihood, boojums are not expanding their range. Data on growth rates are just beginning to come in, the best evidence suggesting an inch and a half of added height per year or perhaps slightly more for young boojums. Age is difficult to assess, since the woody core and inner pulp of the trees form no annual rings. Furthermore, the region of the boojums is far too isolated for years of systematic observations to have accumulated. The indication of great age is based on new knowledge worked out by Robert Humphrey and his wife, who are continuing their studies.

The longevity somehow prompts affection. You look at a boojum, alive before the Magna Carta was signed and before the lure of Eastern spices led to discovery of America, and you think of how often and how intently the tree has undergone trial by fiery heat; how often and for how many months its moisture has been limited solely to whatever it has stored within its own tissue. You think of the winds it has withstood, including the lashing, howling, swirling *chubasco* hurricanes that rage inland from the Gulf, and the chilling, foggy winds ripping up the valleys and over the ridges of the Pacific side of the peninsula. Yet the tree thrives in its peculiar boojum way, as at home as an oak in New England or a spruce in Oregon.

6. Plant Survival

MEN INSULT THE PLANTS OF THE DESERT as readily as they laud those of a forest. Redwood and pine and spruce stand "stately" in "cathedral groves," but creosote bush and mesquite and ocotillo grow as "worthless scrub," "weird," "drab." It is as if desert vegetation were an offense, a lowly order somehow inadequate in its service to mankind.

Or desert plants may be dismissed as nonexistent. As late as 1922 a writer usually careful with observation and words spoke of Death Valley as "destitute of all vegetation," whereas actually more than 600 species of plants grow within the boundaries of the National Monument and only the salt flats and the sand dunes lie nude. Twenty-one plant species belong exclusively to the valley and adjoining mountain slopes. They are endemic, growing nowhere else on earth. Watercress chokes certain streams in the mountains — delightful places for hiking, green and cool (or at least cool*er*). There are 2 species of orchids in Death Valley, and 6 lilies, 10 ferns, and 30 grasses. Diversity, not destitution, characterizes desert flora if a one-word description is needed.

Few species have economic value and perhaps it is at this point that man's favor and interest get lost before they have really begun. The juice of rabbitbrush can produce rubber of a high grade. Wax in the seeds of jojoba offers qualities similar to sperm oil and has been suggested as suitable for making candles, salad dressings, and high-temperature lubricants. Mes-

Left, joshua-tree buds; right, agave

quite serves as forage for desert cattle, valuable because it is dependable even in drought years when grass turns to dust. The flower buds of Joshua trees were roasted and eaten by desert Indians and those of wild agave still furnish food for Mexican ranchers in Baja California. Other species of agave are cultivated by mainland Mexicans for fiber and for juice to be fermented into pulque and tequila. Of these various desert products, only the liquor has hit the economic bigtime — and it comes not from the wild, but from agave plantations grown on semidesert uplands.

The vital alchemy of all life depends ultimately on plants. Plants complicated in their physiology are dependent on simple plants, and animal flesh is but a reincarnation of leaves and twigs and seeds. This dependence is as true in the sparsely vegetated desert realm as anywhere else. In the Namib Desert of Africa, Wilbur Mayhew, a biologist from the University of California at Riverside found places where constantly shifting sand precluded plants; yet he noticed insects, reptiles, and birds. Investigating, Mayhew found tiny shreds of plant debris blown into the dunes as far as twenty-five miles, coming to rest in the lee of hillocks. Here was the key. Minuscule as the plant supply was, beetles could find food enough to live on. With beetles present, lizards could live too, feeding on the insects. Snakes could feed on the lizards. And hawks on the snakes.

In the American desert the chain of life is more simply based. It is provided with a more certain reservoir of plant life because very few areas lie naked to sun and wind as is common in Africa. In America, saltgrass and pickleweed rim to the very edges of salt flats, and salicornia even grows out into the deadly whiteness, its stems crusted with salt. Plants totally lose the battle against salt only when concentrations become extreme, such as in the Devils Golfcourse of Death Valley, where salt pinnacles stand a foot high. The green march halts also where fine alluvial silt collects in the low points of drainage basins, the dry lakes of the desert which stretch as pale expanses of cracked mud. Probably the most recurrent surface difficult for plants to pioneer is loose sand. In America such dunes are wide-scattered and inconsequential compared to African dunes, yet the largest of them spread sand over an area 40 miles long and 5 wide, forming peaks as much as 300 feet high. These are the Algodones Dunes just west of Yuma, a wind-patterned expanse too hot, too dry, and too shifting for plants to gain hold and grow.

However, walk along the edge of the dunes and you find plants faring very well. Where sand spills abruptly onto the desert plain, bushes push up green and vigorous even when eddying winds half smother them with sand. Creosote bush and bur sage grow taller than a few yards away, beyond reach of the sand; and burrobush, Mormon tea, and four-wing saltbush flourish at the dune edge but are absent out on the desert plain. Flowers spread thick following rains and add extra weeks to their time of glory. It is a vegetative exuberance that depends on rain runoff dammed by the sand and hoarded within its porous layers.

Even in midsummer, hollows between the dunes feel moist to the touch just a few inches below the surface. How far down this wetness lies is governed overall by the physics of capillary tension. The rule is that water falling on dry sand will sink in for a distance directly proportionate to how heavy the rainfall is. A shower that measures one-quarter of an inch will wet about the top two inches of sand; a half-inch shower will double this; an inch will moisten eight inches of sand. When enough rain falls to sink ten or fifteen inches beneath the surface, the moisture may last for decades, forming a saturated zone within the dunes. It will be blanketed above and below by layers of dry sand and held in place by capillarity. Plants growing in sand that appears dry are often actually rooted in this wet sand. If the hollows remain, bushes may grow as high as a man's head and leafy enough to do credit to a city garden. Trees such as mesquite and paloverde may join the saltbushes and creosote bushes; kangaroo rats will burrow among the root fortresses of the subsurface realm; and the birds will nest in the tangled branches of the aerial realm.

If — when — the dunes shift position, the persistence of these

Sand dunes

communities will depend on how rapidly the choking takes place. If sand sifts in slowly around a plant, growth may be able to keep pace. The plant will simply add height, and thereby stay steadily ahead of the dunes' deepening. Creosote bushes topping thirty-foot dunes can keep their tips alive and green above the sand; they seem to the casual glance more like three-inch seedlings than like the tops of mature, buried bushes. We once counted dozens of such tips while walking through the Algodones Dunes, and also found the next chapter in the story. Creosote bushes left bare when the fickle sands had blown on now sprawled branches eight feet long and green for only a few inches at the end across what was left of a dune. A few had new shoots beginning to rise from them, growth that was only an inch or two high but in time would root and dot the sand with new

bushes. Meanwhile the parent roots furnished both nourishment and an anchor against renewed onslaught by wind.

A similar survival plan accounts for the common buckwheat of the Algodones Dunes. It normally grows mere inches high, but if it is buried it can elongate the central stem six, ten, fifteen *feet* — whatever is needed to stay ahead of the sand piling around it. Then, if blown free, the stems will spiral across the dunes like discarded lengths of wire, each one tipped only by the leaves it bore while choked with sand. Other species also cope successfully with sand. Four-wing saltbush, mesquite, and paloverde all may be blasted and debarked by blowing sand, yet callus over and continue life. Bur sage bushes occasionally have dunes pass completely over them, burying them in the lee as the dune advances, then releasing them at the windward edge when it moves on. They emerge leafless and dead-looking; but if rain comes soon enough it brings the miracle of resurrection, and leaf buds again swell and burst.

Plants sometimes are responsible for the formation of a dune and also for its eventual dissolution. Bushes catch blowing sand. A vee of it may trail downwind from a one-foot bush for as much as three or four yards, and as more sand drops from the air currents eddying around the bush, a dune may form. If a plant is already tall, or if it successfully stays ahead of the deepening sand, the dune will continue to build; if not, it will blow on. The rate of creep has been measured as great as thirty-five feet in a single month for small dunes. Large dunes move more slowly.

Humus is hard to come by in the desert. The plant cover is thin and what scanty falling and decaying twigs and leaves there are tend to blow and wash away. Forrest Shreve measured the humus of soil near Tucson as a mere 0.25 to 0.65 percent, a tenth to a twentieth of what is common in the soil of a humid region. Sometimes directly beneath trees and bushes in the desert leaf-fall may be substantial, and even at the base of cacti there may be a reasonable organic level because the branches catch the wind and force it to drop its load. The bodies of insects using the plants for shelter or food also add to the enrichment, and so do the droppings of birds. The amounts of such enrichment are exceedingly small, but proportionately they contribute a great deal since the organic levels of desert soil are so meager at best.

Opposite, creosote bush in dunes; right, buckwheat

Add moisture to this soil, and poor though it may be plants soon appear. The amount of rain need not be much; a little can be a lot in the desert, and in fact a light shower tends to bestow a greater gift of life than a downpour does. What matters is not the water that falls from the sky but what soaks into the ground — a factor that makes the rainfall statistics of the desert almost meaningless from a botanical standpoint. Five rains on successive days each trailing a quarter of an inch of rain may bring back green life to dry stalks, whereas a single inch-and-a-quarter rain will simply run off, carrying soil and sprouting seeds with it. The figures mean little, too, because desert rains often pour onto one area without lessening overall drought. One study found that 97 summer storms out of 100 affected less than 8 square miles of desert. Shreve ran tests on effective moisture and reported that even when rain falls on a given area it must amount to between 0.15 and 0.75 inches if it is to contribute significantly to soil moisture. Below that range it fails to soak in unless the surface happens already to be damp; above that amount runoff is certain for the stony desert as a whole, although sand will soak up whatever falls.

Researchers in Arizona and New Mexico recently recorded eight out of ten summer storms pounding the earth with rain at rates of more than two inches per hour for at least a brief peak period. Equivalents of up to 10 inches per hour were frequent during these peaks, and one storm deluged for a few minutes at a rate equivalent to 24.5 inches of rain per hour. Such cloudbursts, even the more modest of them, swell dry washes into instant flooding. Stream beds that usually serve as smooth avenues for coyotes and cottontails suddenly churn with thousands of cubic feet of runoff per second. Yet an hour later only a freshly scoured channel and sand steaming in the sun will remain as signatures of the storm. Animals will return and again track the floor of the wash and plants will briefly glisten and drip but still have no water for their deep roots.

Rain is not the only source of moisture in a desert. There are fog deserts such as the Namib of South-West Africa and coastal Chile and the Pacific side of Baja California, although these are rare situations, in all the world known only in these three locations. Dew, however, is common even on the hottest deserts. The total cumulative volume of its water amounts to scarcely more than an inch of water per year at the most, according to work in Israel; yet this tiny amount apparently is enough to hold the moisture deficit of some plants within safe limits. It restores tissue to normal turgor at night and allows leaf pores to stay open briefly after dawn, thereby permitting vital functions such as transpiration and photosynthesis. Maximum dew occurs on clear nights, a fact known by anyone who has slept out on a desert floor and next morning found clothes and shoes thoroughly damp. Beginning at sundown, soil, rocks, plants — and campers' gear — give off heat to the cool night sky. As their surfaces chill, moisture condenses onto them, and since cold air cannot hold as much vapor as hot air, the heaviest dewfalls come on cold nights. This is especially true when a cold night follows a hot day, when the air will have held a large volume of moisture. A few plants can absorb dew through their leaves, adding it to the water drawn up from the soil by the roots. Pygmy cedar is one such plant in the American desert, a low shrub that brightens wash bottoms with perennial green. The caper plant of the Sahara and the tumbleweeds and lyciums of the Negev are others.

Bedouin tribesmen centuries ago recognized the value of dew. They realized that stone collects a particularly heavy dewfall, and that since the sun's heat does not sink deeply into stone, the day's warmth is quickly lost as dusk fades into darkness. This chilling forms dew. To utilize it, Bedouins piled large, fairly smooth stones three or four feet high to form traps for catching as much dew as possible. The system netted enough trickles to ease the people's chronic water crisis. Similar dew traps in the Negev Desert date back to 1000 B.C. Piled close to the trunks of fig and olive trees, the stones supplied water for the roots of the trees. Even today French vineyards terracing the hot Mediterranean slopes are watered by such devices.

Hollow pyramids built with an inner core of limestone and an outer facing of concrete are placed among the vines. Pores in the concrete allow air to circulate to the limestone and deposit its moisture. Dew forms and runs down to pans set at the base of each pyramid. As much as half a gallon of water per night is captured in this way following a truly hot day.

Of course no amount of dew, or rain soaked into sand, turns the desert from dry to moist. Plants have problems of survival and their solutions vary endlessly, although with one generality threading the diversity: wide spacing. To the eye each desert plant, with few exceptions, appears wholly separate from all others. Creosote bushes dot a plain and paloverde trees a hillside as if set out by an orchardist, even spacing between each plant. Grass forms tussocks, not turf, and the twigs of mesquite or ironwood or elephant tree do not interlace with neighboring trees. There is no canopy and no competition to reach sunlight. In lands favored by more optimum growing conditions a single form of plant usually dominates, but in the desert forms totaling perhaps fifteen or twenty species commonly share dominance

Wide spacing

even in a restricted locale. Competition is minimized because the roots of each type draw moisture from different levels within the soil, and seasonal activity also varies. One species will be flowering and setting seed while another is dormant and drawing only negligible moisture from the supply available to all. The pattern is very different from that of prairies, where grass dominates, or of a tropical forest, where broadleaf trees dominate, or of a cool northern forest with its conifers.

Creosote bush plains are a conspicuous exception to the general rule of desert variety. They stretch unvaried for scores of miles, each bush repeating the height of each other bush and keeping the same spacing from one to another. Brittlebush and bur sage (often wrongly called burrobush in the Mojave Desert) commonly grow mixed in with creosote bush on such plains. Soils are uniform — the same flat surface, the same soil texture, the same moisture content. The plains offer a single set of growing conditions that are acceptable essentially to only one hardy life form, hence the monotony. An outstanding example is El Gran Desierto, a creosote-bush plain south of Yuma, at the head of the Gulf of California. Surely the most featureless, desolate expanse of land in all of North America, this portion of the desert lies sere and brown, reaching to the horizon without a bump or a tree to break its flatness. Creosote bushes here grow scarcely a foot and a half high, a quarter or less of their potential; and they are so wide apart that you can walk straight for a long way without so much as brushing against one. This kind of spacing is the only way bushes of the same species, with identical needs and growing under identical conditions, can successfully minimize competition. They divide the soil evenly among them, equally "sharing" the available opportunity for life. Conditions are too uniform and harsh for a more dense or varied flora. You can drive the highway by the half-hour without seeing plants other than creosote bush, although such unbroken stands of one species are rare in the American desert. For every square mile of pure creosote bush there are ten square miles of varied vegetation.

The richest variety of all belongs to the bajadas and lower mountain slopes of southern Arizona, northern Sonora, and parts of Baja California. An accessible sample of this remarkable diversity lies north of Wickenburg, Arizona, where plants typical of the Great Basin, Mojave, and Sonoran Deserts briefly overlap. Blackbrush merges with creosote bush, and Joshua trees — the symbol of the Mojave — mingle with saguaro, the mascot of the Sonoran Desert. Blooming paloverde trees paint the hillsides yellow in season, and seepwillow turns roadsides to an emerald green wherever there is water. Beavertail cacti tuft the dry hillsides like chenile on a bedspread. Even a quick look from a speeding car discloses the variety. With conscious attention, thirty or forty species can be tallied in a few minutes.

Among the diverse forms are plants somehow unexpected as part of a desert flora. Puffballs will push through the blacktop of Death Valley roadways, their tissues as watery as the fungus of any dank forest, and on the cactus hills near Tucson's Arizona-Sonora Desert Museum clubmoss forms mats in rocky crevices, shriveled brown and quiescent but capable of a quick resurgence into activity as soon as rain restores moisture. Liverworts form dry nubbins on those same slopes, their black scales curled apart from one another although clinging to a common pad. Let there be rain, and in less than an hour the scales uncurl, overlap, regain greenness, and resume life's active processes. Other unexpected plants, impossible to see without magnification, are soil algae and molds. Their tiny interlacing filaments and mycelia crust the surface of desert soil and help to hold it against wind and rain. Their carbon and nitrogen enhance growing conditions for other plants.

At the opposite extreme in size are trees. Dozens of species are common in the Sonoran Desert, a feature that distinguishes the Sonoran from other North American deserts. The number and kinds of trees increase toward the south as desert merges into the Mexican thorn forest, many of them eye-catching. Beginning around Hermosillo, 175 miles below the Arizona line, are morning-glory trees in full bloom at Christmastime, an improbable sight both because of the winter season and of the overall dormancy of the desert (including the utter leaflessness of the trees themselves). This species solves difficult growing conditions by reserving the season of the most favorable, summer rains for vegetative growth and capitalizing on the light winter rains to get flowering out of the way. The trees stand about the height and shape of twiggy neglected old apple trees, and when in blossom they look as if somebody had attached three-inch round white paper flowers to their bare twigs.

Palosanto trees stand on hillsides close to the first of the morning-glory trees, and they become more frequent farther to the south. The slopes look so rocky that there seems no hope of either soil or ground water, and rain certainly must run off instantly. Yet there the trees are, wispy and graceful and conspicuous because of their peeling white bark, much like that of paper birch. The leaves are pinhead size and present only on new spring growth; photosynthetic responsibility belongs to phyllode-like petioles, special appendages that dangle conspicuously from twigs. These look like green wires about four inches long; and in fact they are fibrous, which helps prevent their squandering moisture the way tender leaf tissues do. No other native American acacias have these organs, although they are common among Australian acacias.

Probably the most publicized of the desert's odd trees is the elephant tree. There are two kinds: *Bursera microphylla,* occasionally found in California and Arizona, and common in Baja California and Sonora, also *Pachycormus discolor,* which belongs to the midsection of Baja California. Both are called elephant trees. Both grow with swollen elephantine trunks and branches and have smooth, light-colored bark. Leaves are small and drop off the twigs during dry periods, thereby rendering the trees naked and emphasizing their odd silhouettes, no two alike. Whole hillsides become galleries of living sculpture. The *Bursera* is related to the gumbo-limbo tree of the tropics. It bleeds with a pungent red sap that smells a little like turpentine and is used as a base for varnish in Mexico — and also as an ointment,

Elephant tree

a dye, a tanning agent, and an adhesive. The *Pachycormus* gets its Greek name from *pachy,* thick or stout, and *cormus,* stump or log. *Discolor,* the species name, refers to the tree's unusual capacity to produce two colors of flowers, pink and white, although with only one color to an individual tree. One time we drove into a veritable forest of elephant trees in full flower, each tree foaming with bloom and the total effect like a peach orchard. Even more striking are elephant trees with dodder, a leafless parasite that grows like a mass of coarse orange hair, soft and moist-feeling and tangled. For the most part the dodder scatters through elephant tree branches in showy disarray, although sometimes it lightly veils an entire tree. On this particular afternoon in the "peach orchard" we noticed three elephant trees so completely covered that they looked like glowing orange haystacks twenty feet high.

Desert vegetation, as forest or meadow or prairie or city-park vegetation, consists of perennials and annuals, and for the desert annuals the chances of continued life depend on successfully using fleeting weeks of seasonal moisture. If a prize could be awarded for recognizing opportunity and turning it to good account, these plants should be the recipients. They spring from seeds to sprouts to bushes to flowers to seeds, in mere weeks. Their precise timing of germination holds the key, the seeds themselves being capable of a remarkably fine degree of control, according to field and laboratory studies (although conclusions from some of these studies are criticized as tending toward overgeneralization from the evidence actually in hand). Much of the better-known work has been done by Frits Went, at the time a botanist at Caltech. Went isolated chemical inhibitors that must leach out of seeds before germination can begin. Furthermore, he found that the inhibitors act as astonishingly accurate weather gauges: it took a certain amount of rain combined with a narrow range of temperature to trigger the right chemical action and let life begin.

The wetting must be *rain;* moisture lingering within the soil from a past storm has no effect. There needs to be a downward movement of water molecules, a dissolving and flushing of the growth inhibitors. Only downward seepage gives assurance that the water supply of the soil is rebuilding and can be counted on. An upward movement could foretell desiccation as soil moisture evaporated back into the desert air. Also, the rain must be gentle, not hard. Seeds "judge" this by the rate at which their inhibitors wash out. Some species need the gentle coaxing of prolonged rain or the cumulative effect of repeated showers. That way, chemicals finish flushing from the seeds at about the same time soil moisture has rebuilt enough to underwrite survival. Only then does sprouting become worthwhile. Other kinds of seeds achieve the same protection by a different means. They re-form their entire amount of inhibitor if even a trace remains after a shower. These species don't respond to a light rainfall; it might only partway do the job and leave the seed vulnerable to germination after the next rain, which might also be inadequate for growth.

The mechanisms are not fully known or agreed upon, and many botanists now feel that the early studies oversimplified the true situation. Not enough heed was paid to variables and interactions. Regardless, the unarguable fact is that there are years when a calico quilt of flowers graces the desert sands and gravels. Some blooming can be found, somewhere, during any month of the year; it depends on exact local circumstances, and the composition of the show will vary according to which species have had their particular needs satisfied. In years of mass flowering, seedlings as dense as 5000 per square yard may upholster washes and hillsides. Life reigns. Death is vanquished. California poppies and gold-poppies are particularly colorful — gleaming yellow, sometimes interspersed with purple lupine or scarlet penstemon, sometimes growing in an uninterrupted blanket of gold. Lavender sand verbena and drifts of white dune primrose are probably the most photographed desert flowers, their massed petals proclaiming "spring" on countless postcards and color calendars. If moisture is abundant and temperatures warm, the primrose will grow so riotously that individual plants coalesce and all contending species are crowded out beneath the drift of their soft gray-green leaves and large round flowers. Or, in poor years, the individual plants stay stunted, practically hidden beneath the three or four blossoms that they produce. Sometimes primrose seedlings burst from the soil in tight clusters, the result of seeds cached and forgotten by kangaroo rats; other times they appear in curious rows that tend to converge. This is because some seed capsules on mature plants burst and scatter their contents but others do not split completely open. Instead, they stay on the woody skeleton of the expended plant, and when it becomes blown over with sand the trapped seeds germinate and outline the skeleton of the parent primrose. The system is an advantage for the species, which needs well-drained, sandy soil in order to grow. Wide dispersal of seeds could be wasteful, since a high proportion would end up in unfavorable sites; but where a parent plant has found life possible, progeny are better assured a chance for life. Some seeds therefore stay with the old plant at the old place. Others are thrown out to test new possibilities.

Every person who has wandered the desert has favorites in the garden show of annuals. Probably it depends as much on particular experiences as on the flowers themselves. Storksbill, an exceedingly humble flower, and phacelia are special favorites of ours; and also, one particular year, a patch of seedlings in Mexico too immature for identification. The storksbill carpeted a saguaro forest at the base of the Superstition Mountains near Phoenix where we walked one March dawn, lured by sunrise light faceting the peaks and by birds flitting and calling from cacti and bushes. Our feet got thoroughly cold. They were wet through from dew held by lush mats of the storksbill, plants no more than two inches high blooming with quarter-inch flowers like miniature pale purple daisies. This very smallness and simplicity formed a perfect counterpoint for the magnificent stereotyped desert of peaks and cactus. The phacelia had a similar haunting quality of the unexpected. The flowers are pretty, an intense purple accented by graceful pollen-tipped stamens. Normally the plants grow a foot high and bear one cluster of flowers after another, new buds opening as the petals of preceding blossoms grow limp and start to shrivel. But if times are tough, phacelias adjust. The one particularly etched in my mind was a lone plant struggling from the stony soil of an exposed hillside in Death Valley. It stood a bare two inches high and only three blossoms brightened its frail stalk. It had stopped its own growth and channeled all resources toward the future, the production of seed.

The patch of seedlings in Mexico represented an opposite, luxuriant flowering still to come. It was Christmas week and we were driving the road just south of the Arizona line, camping for the night in the sand of a wash no more than six inches deep, a mere wrinkle on the face of the desert. Even so, in the morning the wash remained heavily dewed while the sun's rays streaked across the desert and dried vegetation elsewhere, and the air stayed perceptibly cooler those few inches below the level of the surrounding desert. The moisture and temperature difference was repeated in the decided green of plants misting the wash, whereas the adjoining land was barely dotted with seedlings.

Shreve applied the term "ephemerals" to desert annuals such as those we slept among in the wash; they appear briefly, then disappear. Most of the year, or for several years if need be, these plants wait in dormancy as seeds. Then when the right time comes they may sprout within a day after a rain shower, and set their own seed little more than a month later. The system allows a whole set of plants to escape the most stringent of the desert conditions. They need no particular adaptation beyond the remarkable one of compressing active life into a few favorable weeks whenever such a time happens to come along. The plant community as a whole benefits from the system, because with billions of plants vanishing at the end of a rainy season, or failing to appear if the year is dry, the savings in water are enormous.

In the Sonoran Desert two distinct types of annuals soften the bare browns of the plains and slopes. Winter ephemerals produce "spring" anytime from December to February. They require daytime air temperatures of 60° to 65°F. and nighttime temperatures generally above freezing, combined with rainfall of at least an inch. Summer ephemerals begin their germination when the first of the flat-bellied gray clouds dump their torrents in mid-July. Optimum temperatures run 80° to 90°F. for these species. Each type of seed — winter annual or summer annual — holds out for its own needed set of conditions. In one test, soil samples were gathered from the desert floor, including whatever seeds happened to be present naturally. In the laboratory, half of the sample was put in a warm room and sprinkled liberally, and summer annuals emerged. The other half was treated in a cool room, and produced winter annuals. The random mix of seeds probably was about the same; the conditions, and results, varied.

The survival chances of individual seedlings rate differently according to the evidence of various test plots. An early investigator reported that once seeds had committed the life within them and begun wholesale sprouting, half of the seedlings would live and mature. If crowding and moisture were problems each plant might stand only a half-inch high and produce just one flower, but that flower would mature and produce its seed. At least that degree of success seemed built into the whole process of germinating. Another investigator working at another place in another year found an entirely different mortality on the plots he observed. Out of 189 plantain seedlings, 162 died without ripening seeds. Half of these succumbed to withering and sand-blasting; half to rodents and jackrabbits that ate the tender shoots. Ironically it was the succulent, vigorous plants that attracted the heaviest, deadliest browsing. Excellence was their undoing; scraggly plants were untouched and left to set seed and perpetuate the species. Instead of survival of the fittest, this was survival of the weakest.

Certain species of annuals grow in the open spaces between shrubs, often forming the great mats of color that give the desert its spring fame. Verbena and poppy and primrose and phacelia are among these. Other annuals follow a different pattern. They grow close to shrubs, forming a ring around them; and if they happen to germinate at a distance from a nurse shrub they stay poorly developed. In one study desert chicory averaged 6 inches high with only 1.7 flowers per plant when growing isolated from a shrub, while chicories associated with shrubs grew twice as tall and had many more flowers. However, a curious variation was noticed according to the kind of bush the heavily flowering chicories were near. Those circling brittlebushes averaged 4.5 flowers per plant and those around bur sages had 9.5 flowers per plant. The microclimate beneath shrubs may be part of the explanation. Even a sparse plant like ocotillo, which is no more than a cluster of coachwhip stems, casts 10 percent shade, and compact bushes like bur sage and brittlebush far exceed this. Leaf litter may also be part of the story, since it builds to its meager desert optimum beneath shrubs. Another factor might be that windblown seeds catch and hold beneath bushes, and so the basic potential of relatively dense germination is greater there than out in the open.

Nonetheless, all of these factors combined still cannot explain the whole story. If the tie between bushes and seedlings rested purely on the effects of shade, litter, and the number of seeds available, bushes of different species but similar size and density should harbor an equal range of annuals — and this does not happen. Toxins have been studied as a possible answer, a sort of vegetative birth control. Various experiments — many of them sharply disputed — indicate that some seeds seem to be supplied with chemicals which leach into the soil and produce a small zone suitable only for the germination of those particular seeds; others are inhibited from sprouting. Also, toxins were found to ooze from the roots of perennials such as creosote bush, and these toxins seemed to prevent competition within the territory of an individual, established bush. Sages and sagebrushes were found to accomplish the same result by releasing an inhibitor into the air, picked up by dew and dropped to the soil beneath the bushes. Brittlebushes and bur sages produce an inhibitor in their decaying leaves. Some of the published research concludes that such toxins affect only the seeds of the plant's own species. The reasoning is that these would most seriously threaten as competitors because their roots ultimately would seek the same level as those of the parent bush and would draw on the same water supply. According to the studies, other species remain unaffected by these chemicals, or may be stimulated by them. Extracts were prepared from the leaves of brittlebush and sprinkled onto seedling tomato plants (a convenient species for lab experiments) and even in dilute solution the extract stunted the seedlings' growth; at medium concentration it killed them.

Fog swaddles boojum trees as day begins on the Baja California peninsula.

Sunlight rims saguaro cactus, setting thorns aglow, and the Arizona desert stirs to life.

Roadrunners, geckos, coatis, and pinacate beetles set out across the morning-cool land in search of food.

The sun climbs high, and animals retreat. A great horned owl and a cottontail rabbit huddle in shadow, waiting for the heat to pass.

Flowers blaze with color: brittlebush, hedgehog, paintbrush, penstemon and poppies.

Afternoon fades and shadows grow long.
Wild burros and a bobcat head for the
waterhole, the one ending the day, the
other beginning the night.

The sun drops — an ending, and also a prelude for tomorrow's dawn.

Extracts from the leaves of desert rue, greasewood, mesquite, and bur sage proved slightly more poisonous.

Other researchers have found no growth effect attributable to similarly prepared extracts, and consequently conclusive statements cannot be made. Test results are too conflicting, possibilities too complex.

Approaching the matter in a different way Cornelius Muller noticed that bushes with supposedly death-dealing leaves nonetheless had abundant annuals at their bases. He set out to discover why. He picked an area where about one brittlebush in ten was ringed with annuals, and these exceptions were the ones he went after. Digging at their bases disclosed the dead stump of an additional bush in each case, sometimes a brittlebush stump, sometimes another species. Muller then switched to bur sages and checked an area where thick mats of annuals brightened the soil mounds of practically all the bushes. This meant they had pushed up through leaf litter that tested in the laboratory as more poisonous than that of brittlebush. Here was paradox: the species serving as nurse bush for most seedlings in the field was also the greatest killer in the laboratory.

The explanation rested with the presence or absence of buried woody debris. The bur sage had no additional stumps buried beneath the bushes, but it is a species that by itself produces a great deal of organic debris. New shoots are continually sent out from a subsurface crown. These root and produce offspring shoots of their own, thereby perpetuating the individual shrub into virtual immortality — forever the same bush yet constantly new. Consequently plant debris collects around an individual bur sage for decades, and in time a considerable mound of litter and loose soil forms. Brittlebushes, on the other hand, live and die. They branch entirely aboveground and have no way to perpetuate themselves as individual clumps. They reproduce by seed, each bush living only a few years and not piling significant plant litter around itself. This difference in organic accumulation explains why bur sage offers a better site for seedlings than brittlebush, although it is not the direct effect of the organic debris but its capacity of being host to bacteria. By volume, the leaves and twigs under a bur sage (and the stumps buried beneath an occasional brittlebush) amount to very little; nonetheless they are enough to provide a stable medium for soil bacteria. These, in turn, seem needed to break down whatever toxic effect the leaves might otherwise have.

This complicated interaction fits the field actualities of bur sage and brittlebush better than the earlier explanation of toxins as the prime direct agent controlling plant distribution and competition. The only time that these bushes would suffer from competition is during the period of their own establishment, and at this stage they do not have enough leaves to canopy a significant area of soil. No matter how potent their toxins might be they could not affect a large enough area to really benefit the plant, and by the time the bushes are established their roots easily out-compete the roots of seedlings. Consequently there can't be survival value in poisoning the soil.

In time an explanation of the toxins and the other factors that determine the distribution of desert plants will be found. When it is, Dr. Muller concludes in the report of his study, "it will be at least as intricate as the situation it seeks to describe." Sweeping answers are convenient for the human mind; but nature is a web of interactions responsive to myriad balances, not to a single law.

Some plant population controls do seem clear, their implications at least partially understood. For example, saltbushes play the survival odds by producing two kinds of seeds: one that germinates quickly and the other (on the same bush) that needs an additional ripening after shaking free of the pod. These second seeds require bacterial action, which necessitates a series of wettings. A full year may be required before some are capable of sprouting. The two opposite processes, quick germination and delayed germination, increase the chances of life by spreading onset across a broad spectrum of time. Some seedlings are almost sure to come forth when conditions are truly favorable, and not merely full of false promise.

Smoketrees and paloverdes develop hard seed coats as one of their keys to survival. The seeds must be scratched and ground by churning gravel before they can crack and permit germination to begin. This happens only when there is a cloudburst, which of course also furnishes a guarantee of enough water to be worth the plants' risking active life. There may be no additional moisture for months or years, but none is needed; ample seedlings will succeed for the species to survive. Roots will push out rapidly and strike deep for water, thereby preparing immediately for the drought that is sure to come. A smoketree seedling barely an inch and a half aboveground may have a root two feet long. The species' need for fairly dependable water limits its growth to drainage courses, and this puts smoketrees in the one possible desert location where the hard seed coats are sure to get cracked. Ironically, it also writes the death warrant for most of the seedlings. The same churning that frees life within the seeds also breaks and smothers the tender sprouts as successive floods roar downslope. Only the toughest, or luckiest, will survive.

Once established, desert perennials persist. Drought does not easily affect them or competition threaten them. The population of a given species holds steady, and replacement bushes or trees must wait for a vacancy in the life community. Shreve once surveyed and charted an area around the Carnegie laboratory near Tucson, pinpointing the location of every brittlebush and counting a total of 72 individuals. That was in 1906. Four years later he rechecked the area and located each of the same 72 bushes and found only one additional brittlebush, a seedling that was struggling toward establishment (but which died a month later). The established bushes he had first counted were all healthy; no replacements were needed and none was succeeding.

Checking on paloverdes, Shreve counted 8 mature trees and 542 seedlings on a 640-square-meter plot. A little over a year later only 62 of the seedlings were still alive (11 percent) and after 10 years there were none. The eight parent trees continued in health and vigor. This set Shreve to wondering. He tallied hundreds of paloverdes within a 75-mile radius of Tucson and found only 2 dead ones. He cored the trunks of 146 of the living trees and by counting growth rings found the age distribution remarkably steady. One tree was more than 400 years old, 15 were between 300 and 400 years old, 11 were about 200 years old, 18 about 150 years old, 13 about 100 years old, and so on — a steady proportion right up to 10 trees that were no more than 50 years old.

Around the year, hot or cold, the fate of desert perennials is to endure what each day brings, and "endure" is the word that fits. During drought bushes cease growth and go into wilt or shed their leaves as the sky stretches cloudless to the horizon day after day. They survive; but brittle, leafless twigs are not resistant to drought in the sense of being unaffected. They are enduring. They hang on, waiting for raindrops to come again, every cell deeply affected. It is a desiccated wait, with death what they resist and drought what they endure. Even so the entire life of desert shrubs and trees does not center around water economy, because the desert is not one great bake oven. Its climate and situations vary enormously from area to area, and season to season, and noon to night.

The remarkable quality of the vegetation is its ability to put favorable times to use and wait out unfavorable times. Perennials start up and shut down, and switch quickly from one to the other. In short, they are opportunists — even more so than the annuals. Far from hoarding water, most desert bushes actually spend it lavishly. They transpire at prodigious rates given the chance, holding down their internal temperature by evaporating one hundred times as much water per unit of weight as mammals do through sweating and panting. Under experimental drought conditions, desert plants invariably increase the number of their leaf pores, or stomata (Greek word for "mouths"). This speeds the rate at which carbon dioxide can enter the leaf for photosynthesis, but since open stomata are two-way portals the increase also steps up the loss of water from the leaves. As CO_2 enters, H_2O exits. For survival there must be a balance between the two, and by speeding the needed photosynthesis the bushes reduce their period of vulnerability. For desert plants, as for all plants, stomata open as the cells surrounding them swell with water and pull apart, causing minute slits to form. They close when the leaf dries and the cells lose their turgor. Thus, control of the stomata represents a perfect coupling between a need and an automatic action to satisfy it; however, some moisture continues to be lost even after the stomata close, and it is at this point that desert plants need special ways of adjusting.

Xerophytes, plants growing exposed to the full rigors of heat and drought as opposed to those at oases or in mild climates, minimize accidental water loss by several means. While their stomata are open they are water spendthrifts, photosynthesizing rapidly; but once their stomata close, they become water misers, hanging on to every drop and drawing every possible benefit from it. The leaves of some xerophytes carry stomata sunken or recessed into grooves and therefore less exposed to the atmosphere than is true for the stomata of nonxerophytes. Special, gummy, polysaccharid compounds capable of water storage build within the leaves of several species and woody substances strengthen the cellulose framework of tissues, staving off collapse during wilt. A waxy or resinous outer coating forms a watertight seal on some leaves; on others, mats of hair reduce surface

Hairy leaves

Ocotillo

transpiration by cutting solar radiation and lessening the drying of the wind. Experimentally removing just these woolly mats can shoot up water loss as high as 20 to 50 percent, a crucial life-or-death percentage during drought.

Plants as diverse as saltgrass and mesquite reduce exposure to the sun by curling or folding their leaves. Another solution is to get rid of leaves altogether and wait out the dry season naked. Ocotillos are a prime example. They may sprout and shed as many as six or eight crops of leaves per year — able to grow the new sets quickly because ocotillo constantly keeps moisture and nutrients available specifically for the purpose. A special network of storage strands is on standby within the bark, and the nodes of these coincide exactly with the nodes of the stems. The system assures an on-site reservoir for the new leaves to draw upon. Furthermore, cell walls at these points are thin and never waxy, so sugar as well as moisture can move easily and help build the new leaf tissue. Only two or three days after a rain every thorny brown stalk of a drought-blighted ocotillo will be upholstered with green — tender, succulent leaves, vulnerable to the next drought but capable meanwhile of exceedingly efficient photosynthesis.

Other leaf-shedding plants follow other patterns. Some reduce leaves to mere stipules at the onset of drought. A few photosynthesize in winter with large leaves crowded close at the base of the plant, then let these shrivel and drop when summer comes, replacing them with small, dry-season leaves. In the case of creosote bush there are three distinct types of leaves, each specialized for a different environmental condition. This ability to meet nearly any eventuality suits these bushes to habitats from below sea level in Death Valley to around 7500 feet in the mountains of Zacatecas, Mexico, and from regions rainless for a year at a time to grassland-oak communities where rains average fifteen to twenty inches yearly. Deep alluvial soils, rocky volcanic hillsides, sandy plains, alkaline flats — creosote bush is not particular. It rates as the most tolerant and widespread plant of the Sonoran Desert. Roots reach deep into the soil and also radiate widely just below the surface; yet even tapping this double set of water possibilities they cannot always keep pace with the thirst of the leaves. When this happens the first set of leaves is shed. These are soft green ones, typical in structure and function to any ordinary nondesert leaf, except perhaps for a "varnished" cuticle. Olive-green leaves remain on the plant, a little harder and drier than the set of fallen leaves and protected by a thicker cuticle. If drought continues, this second type of leaf also is dropped and only the third type remains.

The last leaves are small and brown and able to continue functioning in a drier state than is possible for any other kind of leaf in the world, so far as known. These creosote bush leaves endure a water loss of up to half their dry weight. They can dry to 77 percent below saturation yet continue to photosynthesize. From the time they first unfold they have this special capability. In fact, diminishing moisture as drought sets in seems to serve as a chemical forewarning and directly stimulate the production of this third type of leaf. They are only about half the size of the other creosote bush leaves (which themselves are no more than a quarter-inch long); and the individual cells of these special leaves are exceptionally small. This aspect more than anything else gives them their endurance. With ordinary leaves, cells are forced to continually shrink and expand as dehydration alternates with restored moisture. Eventually this breaks down the cells and harms the protoplasm. But the cells of the drought-enduring leaves of creosote bush are too small to be forced into great mechanical distortion. Consequently they escape harm.

Satisfying the needs of branches and leaves aboveground calls for remarkable feats by the roots underground. As astonishing as any is the root action of desert oaks reported from Israel by H. R. Oppenheimer. He has found that roots can absorb water directly from stone. The oaks grow where no lichens or mosses have pioneered the way, as is usual in the green conquest of the mineral world. There is no soil, and no cracks to serve as invitation for probing rootlets. Instead, the roots of these trees excrete concentrated acids that allow them to penetrate directly into stone and draw from it the nutrients and moisture needed for life. According to report, stone can absorb water during the wet season and release it in the dry season; thus it offers a suitable substrate for plants that are able to thrust their roots into it.

The basic adaptation of desert perennials centers around this ability of roots to pursue water. Patterns of success vary widely. If rain is light and wets only the uppermost soil, rootlets reach there; if it sinks deep they follow. The roots of some kinds of bushes exude mucus, which picks up soil particles and forms a mineral tubercule that protects against drying. Other species develop not only the corky root sheaths common in the desert and out of it, but also a spongy water-storage layer that forms around the inner, active root. Saltbush, pickleweed, and other plants that tolerate salty soil maintain exceptionally high osmotic pressure in their root sap. This lets them draw moisture from the soil. Otherwise, by the simple laws of physics, the direction of flow would be the opposite and the plant would lose water to the soil instead of gaining from it. Death would be quick.

The underground portion of many plants is spectacularly larger than the aboveground portion. Mesquite roots commonly reach 50 or 100 feet into the earth before striking a water table, and there is one documented instance of their going twice that deep. Roots happened to be uncovered in a gravel bed 175 feet below ground level during an open-pit-mining operation near Tucson. A botanist called from the University of Arizona to investigate found the roots limber and damp to the touch, seemingly alive. There appeared to be no reasonable possibility that they were old roots buried by chance at this depth, an assumption borne out later by laboratory study. Cell analysis suggested mesquite, although positive identification was not possible. No other roots anywhere, ever, are known to have pushed to so great a depth as these.

The whole process of drawing moisture from the soil through the roots, up the branches, out the leaves, and into the air circulates a surprising volume of water. For a plant the size of an apple tree the total amounts to somewhere around 2000 gallons during a normal six-month growing season. Multiply this by the total green mantle of even a small area, and the magnitude of vegetation's role in the water cycle becomes both obvious and impressive. Granted the sparseness of desert vegetation, the volume of water transpired is tremendous. Studies since World War II have measured and evaluated the "useless" dissipation of this water into the air by desert plants. Enormous amounts are involved, and concern grows as man increasingly lays claim to arid-land water for his own purposes. Trees in just one desert canyon give off one and a half million gallons of water per acre during the warm half of the year, and on the floodplain of the Gila River in Arizona saltcedar trees in one month transpire moisture equivalent to a year's rainfall — as much as fifteen inches every four weeks throughout the summer. United States Geological Survey figures show thirty-one billion cubic meters of water per year squandered by phreatophytes in the dry lands of the West. These are trees and bushes whose roots reach to groundwater. Their name comes from the Greek *phrear*, meaning "well," and *phyte*, meaning "plant"; hence, plants that act as wells, drawing water from underground tables.

Mesquite, willow, cottonwood, arrowweed, seepwillow, and other native species are among the spendthrifts of the desert, but the chief culprit today is saltcedar, or tamarisk, a species introduced into the United States from the Mediterranean long ago. A *Treatise and Catalog of Fruit and Ornamental Trees, Shrubs, Etc.,* printed in 1823 by the Old American Nursery of Flushing Landing (near New York City), recommends tamarisk as a hardy shrub with ornamental foliage. Soft, lacy, somewhat pinelike "needles" hang thick, a beautiful, soothing silvery green. The trees cast deep and dependable shade that forms a haven of relief from the desert's glare, partly because of sheltering branches overhead and partly because of evaporative cooling by transpiration. At night even a gentle stirring of air sets saltcedar needles to soughing, and the mind of a camper or a desert resident is lulled off to sleep with memory of mountain winds blowing through evergreen forests. The tree was, and is, encouraged in desert communities as windbreak, as shade for poultry and stock, and as a source of firewood. Wherever water is available, tamarisk grows quickly, and so long as a portion of the trunk remains intact new branches will shoot out. The trees can be cut and yet will regrow. Such a vigorous species naturally has a weedlike ability to escape man's plantings and establish itself widely. A million acres of the Southwest now are choked by it; 2000 acres on the Gila River floodplain alone are a saltcedar jungle.

Beginning in 1950 various federal agencies started working together to control and eradicate phreatophytes, both native shrubs and trees and the introduced tamarisk. The Army Corps of Engineers is concerned with stream channels and reservoir areas overrun with tangled growths of these plants. The Geological Survey recognizes the effect on water tables. The Department of Agriculture is experimenting with bulldozing and deep plowing and spraying, particularly to clear tamarisk stands. The Fish and Wildlife Service is concerned with the fate of white-winged doves that nest by the thousands in the tamarisk, and is concerned also about fish, which are critically dependent on water temperature. Shaded streams are measurably cooler than unshaded ones; also, the insects that fish depend upon are themselves dependent on streamside vegetation. The presence or absence of the trees may therefore determine the future of the fish. As a final touch, the United States and Mexico are wrestling over whose responsibility it is to control phreatophytes and who should profit from any resultant water savings. Whatever local jurisdictions happen to lie side by side argue the same issue. States, counties, water districts, private owners — all are contending their own versions of who should pay, who should profit, and how much.

Complicated court rulings try to stipulate the amount of water each user may draw, but answers are not easy. Say that Arizona controls phreatophytes along the Gila River: Is the salvaged water to be shared with California? Or allowed to flow on to Mexico? Or should Arizona keep it, since all of the work and cost was theirs? And what if a user claims new water rights along a stream that is already allocated, taking on the work of removing phreatophytes. Is he entitled to claim water proportionate to however much his efforts increase the water flow? If so, saltcedar thickets might become the fastest seller in a land speculator's portfolio. What of the doves and fish that are lost, the interrelationships that are thrown out of balance?

Such complexities typify the interweaving of the land with the realms of plant and animal life, a relation that far predates modern man's battle against tamarisk. No individual organism can live truly alone, not even a plant. Its roots might supply water and its leaves produce sugar, but water and sugar alone are not enough for life. There must be nitrogen too, supplied only by certain bacteria and soil algae able to utilize free nitrogen from the atmosphere. These minute plants in turn depend on the decay and recycling of other plants for the carbon and phosphorus that they need to live and produce the nitrogen.

Desert, as a land type, exemplifies as rich a set of plant-animal relationships as those of any other landscape. In fact the story is uncommonly plain in the desert because there are fewer participants.

Crossing the Sonoran and Mojave Deserts you may see an antelope ground squirrel rustling among the dry pods fallen from a mesquite, harvesting the rich seeds to convert into flesh. Or perhaps it will be a chuckwalla that you chance upon, stretched out in the tangled branches of a desert bush feeding on flowers. These foot-long lizards prize the flowers of one species so much that its common name is "chuckwalla's delight." Maybe harvester ants will catch your eye, marching single file to their nest, each with a yellow paloverde petal held aloft like the heraldic banner of a crusading knight. The petals become mulch for the ants' subterranean fungus gardens, which are grown as crops to supply the colony with food.

Birds in the desert set their nesting to coincide with the moist green period that closes winter, the only weeks likely to provide enough food for their young. They breed earlier than the birds of regions surrounding the desert. Or if they happen to breed late, the number of eggs per clutch and of broods per female will be less than for the same species in a more favorable habitat. Heat reduces the area a bird can feasibly hunt, and it forces additional time out for rest at noon. The entire timing of the desert's young coordinates with the period of maximum plant growth. This is true for creatures from birds to bighorn sheep to pinacate beetles. Gestation periods vary with the life forms and species represented, but each creature breeds as far in advance of the yearly resurgence of plant life as is necessary to assure food for its newborn. Herbivores breed the earliest; insectivores next. Carnivores breed slightly later, setting the arrival of their young to meet the peak abundance of species whose own emergence was tied to maximum vegetative lushness. Among some insect-eaters this timing may depend on whether they utilize insects that feed on annual plants or on perennials. A study of lizards showed that those relying on insects associated with annuals vary their breeding from year to year; it is geared to the amount of rainfall during the winter, which in turn controls the spring germination of the ephemerals the insects feed upon. On the other hand, lizards relying on insects that feed on perennials show no such correlation between time of reproduction and rainfall. Their food supply is not critically matched to season and therefore their breeding has no crucial seasonal pattern.

Sometimes the timing between rains and reproduction is related although out of phase. It is said that the women of desert African tribes become sterile during times of prolonged drought, unable to conceive until the clouds again bestow greenness upon the land. This is held to be one reason that Bushman families are small. Another reason is that if the correspondence between drought and birth is out of balance and a woman who has conceived during plenty gives birth during drought her baby is taken from her and killed "before it cries in her heart." In animal populations simple competition and mass die-offs usually correct imbalances. Working with kangaroo rats at Joshua Tree National Monument, Robert Chew and Bernard Butterworth found that reproduction correlated with winter rains and the subsequent development of vegetation, but there were critical lags. By the time kangaroo rats had responded to the abundance of vegetation and bred the population up to great numbers, drought had set in. Worsening conditions quickly lowered the amount of food available, which lowered the population; and the number of kangaroo rats stayed low for as long as a year after rains returned to normal and vegetation had recovered. Conditions were ideal, but rodent reproduction had not caught up. It was off phase.

The links between plant world and animal world are many, perhaps none in the desert more dramatic than that of the yucca family. These are giant lilies, some growing thirty to forty feet high. All are characterized by tough, fibrous, succulent leaves similar to the swordlike blades of century plants or the Old World aloes (which also are lilies). All bear heavy spikes of creamy-white flowers, and these serve as the stage for a classic drama in plant-animal interdependence. Pollination depends on the services of one particular species of moth, a drab little insect scarcely half an inch long, powdery white and effectively camouflaged as it rests or works among the flower stamens.

Hunger is not what draws the moths to the fragrant yucca blooms, at least not their own hunger. Instead, females come to lay eggs in the ovules of the flowers, the one place that will assure their hatchlings a supply of the tender developing seeds they need to feast upon. The highly selective choice of an egg-laying site is usual insect behavior, but some added impulse prompts yucca moths to go one step further. They gather balls of pollen (of no use to them individually) and deliberately stuff these into the pistils of the flowers, thrusting them really deep and tamping them down. The whole process is painstaking. The mouthparts of the moths seem to be modified specifically for the task. Instead of the usual coiled tube for sucking nectar, this species has what looks like a pair of scrapers for gathering pollen, augmented by a sort of toothed rack for carrying the cargo, and pedipalps for pushing it into position. A female yucca moth may collect a pollen ball three times the size of her own head. Packing it into the pistil of a flower where she has laid eggs will require a prolonged and energetic raising and lowering of the head, ramming in the full load. This is because the pistil is funnel-shaped, its constricted tube precluding any pollination other than of this deliberate sort. Windborne pollen could never make its way down the pistil, nor could pollen accidentally brushed onto petals or style by a nectar-feeder. The moths' role is vital in the perpetuation of the yuccas. And the yuccas' perpetuation is vital in the survival of the moths.

Another moth, a yucca borer, affects propagation negatively in the case of Joshua trees (the tall bristly yuccas named by Mormon pioneers because the upright branches supposedly pointed to the Promised Land). The trees grow slowly but vigorously, reproducing by seed and also by subterranean runners that eventually sprout and root as separate plants (much as bamboo does). Somehow yucca borers distinguish the young Joshua trees connected to runners from those that began as seedlings, and they lay their eggs only on the plants associated with runners. When the grubs hatch they eat their way down the plant and into the ground, consuming the lifeline to the parent Joshua tree and often causing the death of the young plant.

A full twenty-five species of birds nest in Joshua trees, packrats gnaw off spiny leaf blades to use in building their dens, and shy little lizards called night lizards know the shaggy bark and rotted-out pockets of wind-toppled Joshua trees as their entire world. They feed on termites and ants and larvae, and never venture into the open desert. In the past man, too, counted heavily on Joshua trees. Indians roasted the massive flower buds in fire pits as a sweet delicacy, and they used the seedpods as a crisp green vegetable or brewed into liquor. Fiber from the leaves provided material for rope, sandals, mats, and cloth. Roots gave tough, satiny-red strands useful in basketry; and also a frothy liquid that could be swallowed as a laxative or used as a shampoo.

The range of Joshua trees is in desert foothills and upland plains where summers are hot and winters drop to freezing. For this reason the Mojave Desert is dotted with absolute forests of Joshua trees, whereas the Sonoran Desert has practically none. The giant yuccas are an indicator plant of the Mojave, as saguaros are for the Sonoran Desert. Both plants are host to myriad forms of animal life utterly dependent on them. Both exemplify the interdependencies of desert life. Without the cactus where would desert woodpeckers and flickers carve their nest cavities, and without the holes what would happen to elf owls and flycatchers and titmice and bluebirds? Where would yucca moths lay their eggs without yuccas, and without the moths how could the plants be pollinated?

7. Oasis

For most people the word oasis stirs a mental image of palm trees, and classic native palm oases do exist in the American desert. California fan palms grow tucked in remote canyons in the Indio-Palm Springs region and on open slopes where seeps provide permanent water; and a single oasis with about sixty palms jumps the state line into Arizona, near Yuma. In Baja California the fan palms are joined by the rare blue palm, known nowhere else in the world. The fronds of this species are a blend of soft green and gray with just enough blue to let you know that here, indeed, is the tree you have journeyed to find.

Sometimes a lone palm marks an oasis, but more often there will be a cluster of trees, their fronds spraying from the trunks like green fountains. Dry fronds hang in skirts, persisting throughout the years and giving each tree a rustling thatch that lengthens layer on layer as the trunk grows. Often these skirts are charred, set afire by men who presumably thrill to a brief torch effect and feel no concern about having turned beauty into ugliness. Happily, however, the burning seldom kills palms. They may well be the most fire-resistant tree in existence. We once passed a blackened palm oasis in Mexico in December, then found ourselves there again the following May. The setting, near Guaymas, is fairytale-perfect. Cave-pocked vermilion cliffs guard a twisting canyon that runs from a desert plain with cardon cactus and jackrabbits and roundtailed ground squirrels, down to a saltwater lagoon replete with mangrove trees and snowy egrets and kiskadee flycatchers. Where the cliffs of the canyon stand their highest, the cluster of palms dots the scene — a different species from the fan palms and blue palms of the two Californias, but equally wild and romantic. Water channeled by folds of bedrock rises to the surface and reflects the verdure of the oasis in its quiet pool. On our Christmas trip the palms stood naked and black, but five months later new fronds were pushing up from the tops of the charred trunks and seedling palms had sprung from the soil. Around a bend, an outrider palm less burned than the others was in full bloom. Its five-foot lemon-yellow flowerstalks had lifted above new green fronds, still tightly folded. Life had returned. Not this year or next, but in time orioles would again hang their nests within the cool curtain of dry fronds and mule deer would come to drink from the clear pool.

Such oases bring enchantment to the desert. The California fan palms are relics dating back to Miocene or even Eocene time, somewhere between ten and fifty million years ago. The species, now limited to the desert, ranged north as far as Oregon in that long-ago time; then climatic and geologic changes reduced their numbers to the few hundred holdout oases of today. Those in the California desert are strung along a major geologic fault where pressures within the earth grind rock into clay and thereby form underground dams that store year-round water. Perpetuation of the trees may depend on periodic burning. Archeological evidence points to man having lived at the palm oases of the desert for 10,000 years, repeatedly setting them afire to facilitate hunting animals that came to drink, and probably also to destroy the hiding places of evil spirits within the rustling skirts of the dry fronds. Lightning must set some oases ablaze, and it also may be that spontaneous combustion within the rich litter of an oasis occasionally ignites the tinder-dry fronds. Whatever the cause, the effect of fire is to temporarily eliminate the competition of trees such as mesquite and cottonwood and to burn out bushes like arrowweed and seepwillow, all of them thirsty plants and some of them able to push their roots much

deeper in search of water than palms can. The burning also
opens the oasis floor to sunlight, which seedling palms need.
Seemingly, desert palms are a subclimax stage at an oasis, and
if it were not for fire setting the clock back every few decades,
other species would choke them out and take over. This evidently
is happening at oases in Joshua Tree National Monument,
California; the palms have very nearly been protected to death.

To know the desert you must summer and winter in it, as
Mary Austin points out in her book *Land of Little Rain;* and
although she does not mention it, there also is need to go to
an oasis and there define the desert in terms that are the precise
opposite of its usual, hot, dry hostility. At an oasis your eyes
feast on greenness — and simultaneously squint against the glare
of the barrenness beyond, where shrubs and cacti re-form their
parched ranks. Your whole being rejoices in moisture and
shade — yet also remembers the crucible of desert air, so dry
that it sucks sweat from you and evaporates it without so much
as wetting the skin. Instead it leaves a faint saltiness: *your* salt,
drawn from your pores and left as a light dusting. If you have
come to the oasis thirsty, so much the better. You will truly
find the meaning of desert. Every cell will take measure of both
the overall harshness of the land and the remarkable green grace
of the oasis, and your whole being will fairly shout the contrast.

An oasis celebrates life. It forms a microhabitat of the possible,
set in an infinity of the difficult. At any oasis one life all but
trips over another in a wondrous, shifting kaleidoscope of activity.
For instance, my journal entry for one late March afternoon
at Saratoga Springs, in the extreme southern end of Death Valley,
records: "I had just focused on a distant green-winged teal to
admire his brilliant wing patch, when a red-winged blackbird
flashed across the field of my binoculars, and I turned to follow
it. Next, I picked up a shorebird and was trying to decide
between snipe and dowitcher, when a swallow zoomed across
the field. A black phoebe perched on an arrowweed across the
pond; and a scaup flew in and landed, spraddle-legged and
spattering a brief shower into the air before it regained dignity

and swam off. The shadow of a raven passed overhead and I turned the binoculars up: then coming back to the scaup caught the yellow flash of an Audubon's warbler."

The joy of such an afternoon is that other persons sitting at other desert oases must have been making the same sort of notes, for Saratoga is a representative miracle. It nestles as a fifteen-acre wet dot at the base of the Black Mountains, particularly bleak crags that lift from the sink of Death Valley. One pool is dependably deep and clear. Another, much larger and quite shallow, was crosshatched that particular afternoon by the paddling of teal and coots. Reeds ringed the water with a garland of fresh green, like a verdant stage incongruously set down in the midst of creosote bush. From my position at the edge of the water I could hear a roundtail ground squirrel calling from beneath a desert bush with its single, thin, high note. It stood 30 feet away, its small body and tail jerking reflexively with each shrill bark. At the same time a marsh wren was singing so close that the faint yellow of its trembling lower mandible showed plainly, and its tail was as linked to its voice as the squirrel's had been. The stiff cocked feathers vibrated in exact rhythm with the trilling.

For two hours we watched that wren and listened to his movement through the dry reeds, a loud enough rustling to herald a creature ten times his size. We admired the trim brown form, especially as he perched low and reflected in the still pond. We also taped his outpouring of song and then played the tape back with the recorder discreetly hidden among the reeds. Evidently the season was at the peak of courting when male wrens advertise for females by the half-hour, warbling their hopes over and over. The first two or three songs from the electronic rival went ignored, but as the notes persisted the wren began to look in the direction of the song first with one eye, then the other; and he changed from singing to a troubled *chit*. In a few minutes he flew across the pond, perched close to the black case of the recorder, and began singing again. Soon he launched into a full-blown contest, reed by reed hopping closer to where our device lay. Then the tape ran out. The wren sang on, no longer rivaled and doubtless triumphant at having successfully defended his territory.

By that time sunset was claiming the western sky and we turned from the narrow focus of the one bird to the broad scene, walking around the uppermost end of the pond. Marsh wrens by the half-dozen were singing. Along the far shore a pair of cinnamon teal were swimming sedately, and near to us a coot preened. The sun had left the valley floor but was still searing the mountains, casting the reflection of the range onto the pond like a crimson sawtooth, and on this background the coot made a double appearance. It was preening in reflection as well as in reality, a delicate mirrored ballet as "both" coots dipped their bills and tossed water that danced and rolled from the freshly

Saratoga Springs

oiled feathers like droplets of silver. Farther along a male shoveler duck was rhythmically tipping to feed, and paddling furiously to hold himself upended. White underparts, orange legs, and black tail would be all we could see; then up would come the glossy green-black head with sedge trailing from his broad spoon bill. A lesser yellowlegs stood in still water at the end of a narrow neck of white salt-laden mud. It squawked and plunged beneath the water with its wings stretched up as if it was being pulled from below; but it simply was bathing. Repeatedly it wallowed and splashed and squawked and shoved itself under the water, emerging each time with an additional cry, maximizing its fuss in some lone ritual known only to yellowlegs.

Darkness was fast enfolding day. A coyote began its night rounds, starting with a lengthy howl, sobbing and rejoicing at the same time and flooding the world with sound that came in ten keys at once. Swallows — barn, violet-green, and rough-winged — skimmed the water for insects, and before we got back to the car a lesser nighthawk added its slim wings and flashing bars of white to the aerial dance. Climbing, dipping, swooping, the nighthawk was silent, but it expressed physically the evensong vocalized by the others.

The population of birds in the world is estimated at 100 billion individuals of about 8600 species according to James Fisher, the late British ornithologist. Yet for each species at present alive, 195 others are believed to have had their day and passed into extinction. Universal laws govern such disappearances and the replacement of individuals and species by others. Most bygone birds have succumbed according to these inexorable dictates, but their rate of disappearance has accelerated shamefully since man's rise to dominance, and especially since the advent of technological man. According to the best evidence, it was reptiles that sired birds in the early chapters of evolution back about 180 million years ago. Triassic reptiles with long hind legs learned to hop through the treetops from branch to branch. In time they added the ability to glide, upheld by membranes stretched from their short forelimbs. Eventually scales along the edges of these membranes started to fray and form feathers, thereby increasing the sailing surface of the wings-to-be.

The new aerial behavior prospered and so did accompanying structural changes. Breeding brought additional changes into the evolutionary mix. Feathers became the overall body-covering, lightweight yet strong. Heavy teeth and jaws were eliminated, and a gizzard was substituted along with a changed diet. Bones thinned and became hollow. The intestine shortened, reducing weight still more. The large muscles of locomotion moved to the central body and limbs became controlled by lightweight tendons. Heartbeat quickened. Blood carried more oxygen. Breathing grew synchronized to the motions of flight. Vision became acute. And life on the wing passed its test; it had come to stay.

When you step into the small moist realm of an oasis you realize how well birds have fared, how adaptable they are, how able to endure by utilizing the small favor of scattered places and times. In Death Valley coots and an occasional pied-billed grebe use the Park Service swimming pool as an oasis, both species able to land and take off on that short stretch of water. More extreme, a great blue heron one summer claimed the overflow puddle of the cooler at the Stove Pipe Wells Hotel. It was a forlorn sight, standing at the corner of the veranda with hot brown desert showing between its stilt legs — forlorn, off-course, and ridiculous. But alive.

That same summer a killdeer established itself in the dank coolness of the communal showerhouse at the Wildrose Canyon summer headquarters for Death Valley personnel. Showering from June to September began with chasing the bird from the shack. It never accepted our presence or even stayed within sight of the building while we showered; once we had left, back it would come. Water was too precious for us to allow a dripping faucet, but since eight families shared the one shower there was moisture enough for the killdeer and it survived the summer.

Some oases are even more modest. Researchers recording

Collared lizard

water sources available to wildlife in Death Valley and its surrounding mountains found goldfinches plummeting to earth in their camp where drips from waterbags formed two-inch puddles, and lizards coming to lick damp towels thrown over cameras to keep them cool. In tinajas (rock pools that hold rain runoff) they noticed fairy shrimp, primitive cousins of the familiar ocean shrimp. These were scarcely more than a quarter-inch long, translucent, and with a fringe of swimmerets used for propulsion through the water, and also for gathering microorganisms and windblown debris as food to be stored in a body groove and drawn to the mouth by a string of mucilage. The system seems awkward, but the stomach is located in the head efficiently close to the mouth, and the basic merit of the design is evident in the short time needed from hatching to maturing and laying eggs. It takes only three weeks. The water of an oasis as undependable as a tinaja cannot be expected to last longer than that, although the time of course varies with the individual basin and the amount of rain that has happened to fill it. As further safeguard, fairy shrimp eggs settle immediately to the bottom and may be picked up on the feet and mouthparts of birds or animals that have come to drink. Or when the water evaporates, they may blow away to other suitable locations; or simply stay and bake in the dry bottom of the erstwhile pool.

Red-spotted
toad

Eggs as much as twenty-five years old have been known to hatch
when conditions again became favorable.

Brief active life during wet periods followed by long dormancy
during drought is also the life pattern of desert frogs and toads,
species for the most part not limited to desert lands but
thoroughly at home there. Males by the hundred line the edges
of waterholes in season, blink their eyes, swell out their throats
like bobbing ping-pong balls, and fill the night with explosive
barks and trills and whines. Their chorus rises and throbs, music
with many beats and many melodies. Each member sings his
own song, and does so *fortissimo*. The bleat of a male bullfrog
will carry for two miles, probably one reason the species can
survive in the harshness of the desert; though widely scattered.
How else could a male summon a bride to the right puddle
on the right night? For it is not only the established, year-round
oases that resound with mating serenades. Let there be rain
and the whole earth of the Sonoran Desert pops open with
spadefoot toads hastening to whatever puddle provides a temporary oasis, there to copulate and perpetuate their kind. Father
Baegert wrote of them in his account of Baja California, describ-
ing how a river formed by rain runoff quickly vanishes and
adding that "in a few hours nothing is left but the former drought,
innumerable toads, and a few scattered mud puddles." Indians

recognized that toads follow rain and incorporated the observation into a dance of hope, according to a white settler born in Sand Papago country near the mouth of the Colorado River in 1870. As a boy he watched men wearing gourd masks dance a "whooping and hollering" supplication for rain. They would work into a frenzy and then "an old man would come out hopping like a toad," a symbol of the gods' favor and their promise that rain would come.

Desert conditions and the needs of toads seem poorly paired at first thought. In the dim past three major phyla slithered from water to land: vertebrates, arthropods, and mollusks. Of these, the vertebrates have undergone by far the greatest changes, starting with lungs as replacement for gills (which were the prototype breathing apparatus). Amphibians developed early in the terrestrial experiment and they stopped short of evolving a fully efficient lung. Part of amphibians' oxygen still comes from uptake through the skin, which means that they must keep the body surface moist, since all gaseous exchange requires a moist membrane. This alone would seem so impractical in the desert as to bar amphibians from its dry lands; but toads and frogs also depend on water for reproduction. In nearly all species females can lay eggs and males fertilize them only in water, and only there can the young develop. As a final disadvantage for desert life, adult amphibians cannot drink but must instead meet internal needs for water as well as for oxygen by absorption through the skin. After a light shower that has barely wet desert plants and rocks, toads emerge from hiding and flatten against moist canyon walls to rehydrate. At least one species (red-spotted toads) have a special seat patch of thin skin that speeds the soaking up of water and helps suit them to desert life.

Unfortunately, what goes in also goes out, and the permeability of a toad's skin works both ways. A few insects transmit water inward more readily than outward, allowing a replenishment of body tissues when surroundings are moist without paying the price of a commensurate evaporation loss when conditions are dry. But amphibians do not have this capacity. Their skin absorbs moisture quickly, and loses it just as fast. In fact, evaporation through a toad's skin is as rapid as from the surface of freestanding water, or perhaps even more so since tubercules act as conduits. A spadefoot toad loses water four times faster than a kangaroo rat or pocket mouse, and forty times faster than a rattlesnake.

Yet the chorus that follows July thunderstorms gives no hint of difficulty, and in truth much of the reconcilement to desert life is simple, albeit remarkable. The flattened form of a toad lets it penetrate crevices to escape heat, and its low center of gravity helps in climbing steep canyon walls to find sanctuary. For spadefoot toads a special spur on the hind foot eases digging into sand or wash banks, where they usually can find moisture; and if need be they can dry out with no particular harm. Vital organs and muscles stay miraculously moist by the slow expenditure of body water specially stored for the purpose. The water or urine held in the bladder like a reservoir can be reused, and fluid horded in lymph spaces can also be drawn upon. These supplies are generous. The bladder alone may furnish water equal to half the body weight of the toad, and essentially all of it can be used for body hydration; the formation of true urine will cease as the withdrawal from the bladder begins, and body wastes will instead be stored as urea for excretion later, after the animal has returned to a pool. Meanwhile the urea may even increase the body moisture balance of a buried toad, because it raises the osmotic pressure of body fluids above that of the soil's moisture and renders the direction of flow at least theoretically into the body instead of out of it.

Spadefoots spend ten months at a time buried. The outer layer of their skin darkens and grows horny, forming an all-encasing cocoon. Even eyes, mouth, and cloaca are covered. The only breaks are minute openings at the nostrils. The wrapping holds moisture within the body and permits an opting out from activity, thereby making survival possible. When rain comes the zombi existence ends, but it must be heavy rain. Mere showers or winter drizzle leave spadefoots unaffected, for their need is puddles that will last long enough to let eggs hatch and tadpoles change into toads.

The hatching is incredibly swift. In one species eggs laid at midnight can hatch by nine o'clock the next morning; for another species a record of twelve hours is documented. A day and a half from laying to hatching is common, and in ten days tadpoles will have their legs and soon hop onto land. Furthermore, puddles invariably hold large tadpoles and small ones, and if the two sizes are separated in the laboratory some of the small ones grow as large as the large ones, overnight. Separate them again and the same thing happens. The chemistry is unknown, although the evident effect is to assure food for the big tadpoles, which eat the tails of the little tadpoles. The system ignores the individual, yet maximizes the survival chances of the species.

Often tadpoles cluster into masses as they swim. They seethe and turn as one, swirling against the soft bottom of their puddle, and this too seems to help in the odds race between maturation and evaporation. Probe gently into such a mass to break it up, and it immediately re-forms, although perhaps as two or three separate aggregations instead of the single large one. Such masses are believed to absorb more radiant heat than isolated individual tadpoles could. This warms the water, which steps up metabolism; it thereby hastens metamorphosis and betters the chances for living to adulthood. It also may be that the rotation deepens the puddle and staves off evaporation for a few additional minutes or hours, a timing that can determine life or death for spadefoot toads and other amphibians.

Despite what would seem all but impossible conditions, a host of amphibians dating back to the last ice age, fifteen or twenty thousand years ago, still thrive in land that has now become desert. They live in isolated, cutoff populations but fare so well that the Sonoran Desert is regarded as having one of the great amphibian populations of the world. Among the unexpected species represented are a recently discovered Mexican leaf frog and a desert slender salamander, a creature new to science. The leaf frog, a member of the large and varied Hylidae family, was found on the extreme southern fringe of the Sonoran Desert in the hills near Alamos, Sonora. This is a species with the unfroglike habit of attaching eggs to the leaves of shrubs close to a pond instead of laying them in water. A gelatinous mass sheathes the eggs and developing embryos and seems to provide cooling by evaporation. When the tadpoles hatch they fall directly into the pond, or if the female has not properly calculated the trajectory they land on the ground, usually within range of being able to flip their way to water. Most can survive for two hours, moving three or four inches at a jump. Any that fail to reach water in that time die. Rain or dew probably prolongs the period, and most hatchings seem to occur at night or in the early morning when temperatures are cool and humidity relatively high. However, leaf frogs belong basically to the tropics, not the desert; their tadpoles need five weeks to mature and at the northern, essentially desert extreme of their range many cook to death in the sun-heated water as their puddles dwindle and disappear. The species persists at the edge of the desert, either having slowly evolved and expanded into it, or else never having been forced fully out of it when the climate began its most recent overall warming about 4000 years ago.

Desert slender salamanders apparently have lingered since the ice age, although no one can yet be sure. They are known at only one small location in a mountain canyon near Palm Springs, California — a surprise because salamanders as a life form seem particularly ill suited to a region of cholla cactus and creosote bush. Yet there they were discovered, a whole writhing cluster of four-inch, pink-brown salamanders uncovered beneath a limestone slab by a wildlife warden who had stopped to scoop a small drinking hole into the moist sand of the canyon bottom. Little detail is known, but evidently these salamanders live under the limestone in summer, pressed against the wetness of the sand, and in winter they wobble on their weak legs to the talus slope at the base of nearby cliffs. The body of this species *(Batrachoseps aridus)* is slender and long, with one more vertebra in the spine than is usual and a greatly elongated tail, probably energy storage to be drawn upon in times of stress. Previous to 1969 nobody knew that a desert salamander even existed, but on discovery it went immediately into the Red Data Book of endangered animals for the United States and for the International Union for the Conservation of Nature. The State of California granted full legal protection, and any human molester is now subject to a $500 fine or six months in jail or both. The canyon-bottom home of the salamander is privately owned but efforts are under way to add it to the reserve held by the University of California as a Desert Research Center.

More clear as to ancestry are the desert pupfish, sardinelike holdovers from the ice age that somehow managed to hang on as the interconnected lakes of the past shrank to scattered pools and small salty streams. Pupfish are one type of killifish, an inch or two long, depending on species, the males silvery bright with iridescent blue sides, black bars on the fin edges, and occasional yellow on their heads; females are a mottled brown. Their whole aquatic realm is now limited to about three-dozen desert marshes and waterholes and meandering streams where individual males defend territories little more than a foot across. The sites are isolated from one another, and this has caused pupfish to evolve into distinct species and subspecies. The differentiation is enormously significant. How in the few scores of centuries — which are exceedingly brief in terms of geology and evolution — did the fish develop into divergent species? And how did they adapt to the changing temperatures and increased salinity as their original waters shrank so drastically at the close of the Pleistocene? The fish in one Death Valley marsh cannot have been separated from those in a nearby stream for more than 2000 years, yet they are a different species.

Pupfish survive temperatures from almost simmering, in shallow puddles exposed to summer sunshine, to nearly freezing in winter; some bury in the bottom ooze as shield against the extremes and there wait out the unfavorable period. Many are never subjected to cold; they live in springs with water temperatures as high as 112°F., extraordinarily hot for vertebrate life.

Others live in water with as much as six times the salinity of the ocean, salty enough to kill a mackerel or tuna. One species can live in water only an inch deep and will flip across a marsh puddled by animal footprints, feeding as it goes on algae or suitable bits of organic debris.

Predaceous diving beetles attack the tiny fish and may take a toll as high as one fish per beetle every two days at Saratoga Springs, where their behavior has been intensively studied. In other springs and streams species of fish introduced by man prey on the native pupfish. Pest-control agencies have routinely planted mosquitofish in waters throughout the West without regard for the welfare of native fish or recognition of their capacity to do the job of controlling mosquito larvae. In other instances, black bass were introduced to improve sport fishing in a waterway, an action that nearly wiped out pupfish; another waterway became infested with tropical fish escaped from a hatchery (a short-lived enterprise utilizing a hot spring); and a third pupfish habitat was lost when the flow of a small stream was channeled to better serve human convenience. Scientists have long recognized both the unique value of the little fish and their vulnerability, and in the 1950s they successfully pressed for one of the largest pupfish waterholes to be established as a detached unit of Death Valley National Monument, a few miles to the west. Their feeling was that the fish are biological "national treasures," in the sense that Japan officially recognizes unique aspects of their land and wildlife. Even so, fearing the public might not care about obscure fish, the men placed emphasis on the geological merit of the site, with the fish as an added value. The ruse was successful and forty acres were set aside at Devils Hole, Nevada, a pool situated in a deep rock crevice and connected with a labyrinthine cavern.

Other waterholes need equal protection, and may receive it under a National Wildlife Refuge proposal that would safeguard the fish *and* the groundwater their life depends on. The latter is absolutely vital: as human population expands, so does the demand for water. Mining a peat bog under one small marsh all but drained a slough where pupfish had managed to survive the centuries between the moist climate of the past and the desert climate of the present. Pumping groundwater to irrigate alfalfa fields now threatens other pupfish habitats — and indeed threatens the hydrology of the entire southern half of Death Valley. The various water sources have not connected on the surface since the ice age, but subterranean connections remain. Water from the Ash Meadows region east of Death Valley still feeds into a small river that meanders mostly underground, threading from one spring to another and eventually bending

Pupfish and
saltmarsh
habitat

northward and flowing into Death Valley. There it supplies
the ponds at Saratoga Springs and largely controls the moisture
balance of the vast salt flats, then reaches its end at Badwater
(a small pond long famed as the lowest point in the Western
Hemisphere, 279.8 feet below sea level, but with two nearby
spots now known to be 2.2 feet lower still). The irrigation has
been the work of a private company, although as recently as
1969 the Bureau of Reclamation was authorized to make a nearly
one-million-dollar feasibility study for bringing 100,000 acres of
the Amargosa headwaters region into cultivation. Pumping for
the existing irrigation seriously lowered the water at Devils Hole
in 1969, the same year that study of expanded irrigation was
authorized. This posed a dire threat for the pupfish because
they feed and spawn only on rocky ledges a foot or two beneath
the normal surface of the water, and with levels falling and
the ledges drying there was real fear that the fish would die
while scientists and governmental agencies and agriculturists
argued rights and priorities. As a stopgap, National Park Service
biologists fashioned artificial algal mats replete with electric
lights, and these seemed to succeed in drawing enough fish to
provide interim hope.

The year 1972 brought two disasters that have lowered the
odds of survival. In July an earthquake centered in Alaska either
directly caused an upwelling surge of water or else set off a
rockfall that produced a surge. Either way, a wave three feet
high beat across the little pool and scoured one of the natural
rock ledges used by the fish. All of the algae, needed for food,
were destroyed and the gravel necessary for spawning and
protection of the hatchlings also was lost. Park Service men
replaced the gravel, and before long the algae started to regrow.
Then in September a cloudburst washed debris into Devils Hole
and again destroyed the algae. A census at the end of the month
showed only half the pupfish population that would have been
expected under the conditions before the quake and the storm,
bleak as they had been.

Current outlook is dire. The margin of survival already had

been pressed for these small fish, and there may simply be no leeway left. This becomes especially true since each year brings a new low-water level owing to the pumping operations. Transplants to aquariums have not been successful, although a manmade refuge built at Boulder Dam to simulate Devils Hole seems to be succeeding so far. Its shape and dimensions replicate the pupfishes' home realm, and although the sides are lined with concrete, rocks and gravel have been brought from the Hole and the ledges have been seeded with algae from Devils Hole.

Esthetically and ethically pupfish seem entitled to life; they have survived under difficult circumstances, where so many of their fellow Pleistocene species have had to surrender to change and disappear as life forms. The pupfish also have enormous research value. Their body adjustment to high temperatures, low oxygen concentrations, and extreme salinity is eyed with wonder by physiologists concerned about how man can adjust to environments in space or under the sea radically different from what he has known in the past; and geneticists think of the rapid mutations that have separated the fish into different species in so few centuries. Might there be applications to the mutation threat man now faces because of increasing radiation levels? Extinction of course has been part of life's flow from the beginning, but it is not easily welcomed — for ourselves or for a fellow creature. Certainly at an oasis it is life that you feel, an indomitable force, remarkably adaptable, inexorably set on survival. If the desert is land that God forgot, as some men have claimed, then its oases must be promises that He has not gone far and will soon return.

8. Bites and Stings

SNAKES PROBABLY ARE the most feared of the desert's venomous creatures, followed by Gila monsters, scorpions, centipedes, and tarantula spiders. In reality, few travelers so much as see one of these creatures, let alone have any difficulty with them, and, two rules, if followed, would largely prevent what trouble does occur. Never let your foot or hand reach where your eyes can't see. And, if you do feel something crawling over you, brush it off; don't swat, or you may merely injure and anger it.

Second nature soon makes it automatic not to turn over stones or old boards where scorpions might be hiding, and not to reach onto an unseen rock ledge where a snake might be sunning. By reflex you avoid bushes where each step cannot be seen ahead, and at night you always carry a light. Once, hiking up a wash at dawn, I felt an odd softness underfoot and looked down to find a small rattlesnake. It lay coiled and half buried in the sand, its rusty color and diamond pattern such perfect camouflage that I had not seen it. The morning was cold and the rattler had been too lethargic to escape or strike. Even stepped on, it had no reaction.

Once we did have trouble. We lived at Organ Pipe Cactus at the time and followed the standard practice of keeping beds pulled away from the wall with their legs set in empty glass jars to prevent scorpions from climbing up into the blankets. Sometimes, however, they would work up the wall and fall from the ceiling. The precaution was to inspect the bed before getting in, and during the night if something was felt crawling along, the best technique was to lie still and mentally pinpoint the exact location and the direction of the movement, then reach quickly and brush the creature onto the floor. Most of the night's crawlers were not venomous, but all comers were brushed off, just in case. In spite of all this, our three-year-old son was stung by a scorpion. It was dangerous because in southern Arizona (and only there in the United States) a scorpion's sting can be deadly to a young child.

In this case one precaution had been ignored: the boy had put on a shirt without first shaking it. The scorpion must have been clinging inside as the garment hung in the closet, and when disturbed by the motions of dressing it stung, connecting squarely between the shoulder blades. We lay the boy on his bed, put on an ice pack, watched for symptoms, and clung to outward calm. With each change of the ice we tried to will the pinprick hole into puffing and reddening, for nonvenomous stings produce a local reaction, whereas toxin of the deadly variety spreads throughout the entire system without causing particular external effects. It acts on the nerves in a way similar to strychnine. It induces spasms, drooling, numbness, temporary blindness, and any number of other alarming symptoms — none of which were appearing any more than swelling or redness. After half an hour we keyed out the scorpion as one of the nonlethal species, its sting no worse than a bee's. Off came the ice, and the day picked up routine where it had been broken off.

Thinking back, I sometimes feel that we should have started for a doctor, thirty-five miles distant. Yet we knew how greatly the odds as to species lay in our favor and we did not want to frighten the child. Fear quickens the diffusion of venom through the body by speeding blood circulation, and, as adrenalin mixes in, the toxicity can double. The result often spells disaster from grave illness to death.

Venom serves two purposes (and, properly speaking, venom is distinct from poison in that its possessor can force it into the body of a victim; by comparison, a poisonous creature has no delivery system but must be swallowed). Venom and poison both serve as a defense mechanism, and venom serves even more as an aid in getting food. Prey that otherwise could not be captured, can be subdued with venom; and since digestive enzymes usually are present, the venom begins the process of breaking down the tissue of the prey even before swallowing has started. Defense is secondary. Venom is too valuable an aid in securing food to be squandered needlessly. A snake often may bite a large attacker, such as a man, without injecting venom. It is saved for creatures that are to be swallowed.

Scorpions are an unquestionable evolutionary success. Their ancestors crept from Silurian seas 400 million years ago, the same creature then as now, to judge from fossils. Throughout the millennia, 600 species have differentiated, all of them venomous, although only five genera with a dozen species threaten any real danger to man. Two of these live in southern Arizona and Sonora; both are the color of dried grass and only an inch or two long, with delicate pinchers and a slender tail. Other species, far less dangerous to man, look much more dreadful. Of the Arizona scorpions — 21 species in all — the largest are 5 or 6 inches long stretched out, with a heavy brown body and tawny pincers, legs, and tail. The stinger is at the tip of the tail, which is long and segmented, able to flick in any direction except between the scorpion's own legs. The tail has supplied the name: the Latin word *scorpio* and the Greek *skorpios* refer to a scourge tipped with sharp points.

But the stinger marks only the beginning of a scorpion's distinctive equipment. A shielding cuticle that is laminated from layers of lipids, polymers, and waxes protects against the dry desert environment. It forms an effective seal against loss of body moisture and also against suffocating when underground retreats collapse or flood after a cloudburst. How the cuticle can be quite so effective is not fully known, but scorpions have floated as long as three hours and become completely limp, then recovered instantly when lifted from the water. Others have lived for months, kept experimentally in stoppered vials with seven of their eight primitive lungs blocked. Or, buried two or three feet, scorpions have dug free. They survive as if there were an air reserve stored within, unlikely per se, although they may be able to breathe without free oxygen (anaerobically) — a possibility that preliminary work seems to demonstrate among certain creatures.

Scorpions appear well suited for noonday activity in the desert so far as physiology is concerned; some species are able to remain unaffected at environmental temperatures as high as 150°F. Yet scorpions belong basically to the night. They are dull-witted and heedless. They have no special capacity to offset the disadvantage of darkness, no large or bulging or especially sensitive eyes, no acute hearing or keen sense of smell. Instead they rely on fate to bring a meal their way, employing neither skill nor diligence in hunting one. They simply drag themselves out of their burrows shortly after sunset, take up a random stand and wait for whatever may happen along.

From four to six pairs of eyes dot the top of the head, depending on species, but these contribute nothing beyond an ability to distinguish light from dark. The only sensory capacity so far as known comes from hairs on their pincers which seem to detect changes in air currents, such as are caused by the movement of potential prey, and from special organs called *pectines,* which probably are able to sense ground vibrations. The pectines are unique structures that look like miniature combs. They are located on the underside of the thorax and swivel readily. One investigator claims the pectines are external genitalia, male and female interlocking them during copulation. Others say the teeth are useful in cleaning a scorpion's pincers, legs, and tail. Or as receptors for taste and smell. Or as respiratory organs; and this is at least incidentally true, for the musculature of the pectines does fan air across the book lung breathing structure of the scorpion. Almost certainly, and whatever their full function, the pectines also sense vibrations.

For a year we kept a scorpion as pet in Death Valley, housing it in a jar with sand in the bottom and feeding it any insects we happened to find. Sometimes we entered our scorpion in gladiator competition against other pet scorpions in the neighborhood, although I now take no pride in those small-scale orgies. Ours was not an especially large scorpion. Outstretched it measured barely four inches, but even so it was a steady victor battling to the death and devouring all challengers. Such cannibalism is usual among captive scorpions although apparently not common in the wild. For the most part, however, "Tweezers" was a lackluster pet. He (or she) lived sprawled with pincers and tail resting languidly and only when several days had passed between meals and hunger was great would an insect dropped into the jar produce real action. Usually, having fed fairly recently, Tweezers would simply wait for a prospective meal to bumble into his embrace, and only then would clamp shut his pincers and arch forward his tail to sting.

His one abrupt leap into activity was triggered by a black pinacate beetle that shared the jar toward the end of the year. The hard covering of most beetles challenges a scorpion's puncturing ability and so they are not favored as food. Furthermore, pinacate beetles may also be distasteful; "stinkbug" is one of their common nicknames because of a pungent secretion. For our scorpion the beetle was a daily trial. Tweezers would be lying at rest, only to have the insect brush against his pincers and set off the automatic capture response. The pincers would

Scorpion
stinging
a cricket

close and the tail would arch, and then the scorpion would realize what he held and would shake off the offending jar-mate and sink back into apathy. Sometimes while circling the jar the pinacate beetle would inadvertently walk up the scorpion's tail and onto his back. This would trigger a frantic charge around the jar with the beetle clinging like a cowboy to a bronco.

After perhaps six weeks the scorpion evidently had had enough of this togetherness. He went to one corner of the jar, which was square, and scraped out a pit. This was the first burrowing activity he had shown, although in the wild some scorpions dig as much as eight feet to follow receding moisture. In time, the beetle fell into the pit. The scorpion instantly mounted guard, and as soon as the insect would claw to the top of the pit he would fling it back down. In thirty-six hours the pinacate beetle lay dead, perhaps stung or perhaps simply exhausted. Next day, the scorpion died. Returning home from school, our sons had found another pinacate beetle and dropped it into the jar. Within hours Tweezers died. His days may have run their natural course; or the beetle may have been one more plague than could be borne, and he opted out. There was no way to tell.

A study of scorpions and other venomous and poisonous animals has been the lifework of Herbert L. Stahnke. At the Poisonous Animals Research Laboratory of Arizona State University he oversees work on about ten thousand scorpions a year, plus snakes, Gila monsters, and spiders. A milking herd of several hundred scorpions provides venom which is freeze-dried and used for studying toxic effects in the human body in order to work toward improved antivenin treatment. To milk a scorpion a worker grasps it by the tail, and uses long forceps wired to deliver a mild shock. The electricity causes the scorpion to exude droplets of venom, each individual producing fluid for about four successive milkings a week apart, before being rotated back into the herd. From this work Stahnke has developed a treatment for poisonous stings and bites known as the L-C method, ligature and cryotherapy — a system sharply criticized by advocates of the T-C-S method, tourniquet, cut, and suction. Neither system of treatment is new. In fact, the idea of enlarging and sucking a wound is so venerable that its origins are lost. Probably it extends back into the realm of shamanistic practices. The procedure of making small cuts and then using rubber cups for suction was developed in Texas in the 1920s, an adaptation of the ancient method. Chilling to delay the spread of venom was suggested as early as 1906.

Each system seeks to stem the spread of the toxin within the body but they differ in that Stahnke urges chilling to slow circulation, whereas the T-C-S method relies on physically sucking out the venom. Stahnke recommends immediately tying a cord such as a shoelace between the wound and the body (to be released after ten minutes), then plunging the entire afflicted area into crushed ice and water and leaving it for from two to eight hours, or sometimes more. To get the venom out of the system, the patient should be warmed until he perspires and the wound meanwhile should be kept thoroughly chilled. This holds the venom at the site of the bite or sting, and at the same time the warming steps up circulation overall. The combination permits a slow, controlled spread of the toxic effect at a rate the body can more safely absorb. Water should be swallowed in great quantities at this stage to speed excretion of the venom by the kidneys.

The T-C-S treatment recommends instead of the constriction of a ligature that a tourniquet be used, a necktie or a handkerchief tied between the bite and the heart. This should be just tight enough so that a finger can barely be forced under it, and it must be moved and retied as necessary to stay ahead of the swelling. The tourniquet's function is to stop circulation in the lymph spaces and slow it in the veins. That done, the next step is to make incisions through each fang mark by cutting an eighth of an inch deep. As the reddening and swelling of the wound spreads, additional cuts will be needed. They should ring the periphery of the affected tissue. Suction can be applied by mouth or by using the rubber cups in a snakebite kit. There is almost no danger from swallowed venom if the mouth is used;

not even an open sore on the gums is cause for concern. The idea behind sucking is to draw out as much blood, lymph fluid, and venom as possible from each incision.

Which method of treatment is better is uncertain. Each has drawbacks. The prolonged chilling of the L-C method may stress the entire body, although advocates emphasize that the patient is to be kept warm and only the afflicted area chilled. Even so, damage is likely if local chilling is too severe or if the ligature is excessively tight or left on overly long. If the chilling is discontinued too soon or the warming is too rapid or fluctuating, the venom may linger in the wound and gravely damage tissue because of the ice-induced concentration. On the other hand how much venom actually is removed by the T-C-S method is questionable; and the cutting alone can be traumatic enough to step up circulation and worsen reaction to the venom in spite of the tourniquet. Equally serious, infection introduced by the cuts can cause serious difficulty since a frequent property of venom is to weaken the blood's defense against bacteria. So pronounced is this effect that there is indication that bacteria from the fangs cause as much pain and real hazard as the venom itself.

Between the two recommendations of treatment, and the valid countering objections, perhaps the one heartening truth is that the chances of being bitten or stung are extremely low, in the desert or anywhere else. About 90 percent of the bites and stings that occur involve professional handlers, showmen or researchers who have been momentarily careless and thereby courted trouble. Nationwide, ants, bees, wasps, and hornets cause more deaths than snakes do. The records of a five-year period show 71 deaths from snakebite compared to a total of 125 for spiders and insect bites. Scorpions were not mentioned.

Rattlesnakes excite special attention. Commonly associated with the desert but actually of wide distribution, they are mentioned as early as 1630 by a New England colonist who wrote of "Snakes and Serpents of strange colours and huge greatnesse . . . [that] have Rattles in their Tayles and will not

Western diamondback rattlesnake

flye from a Man . . . but rather flye upon him and sting him so mortally that he will dye within a quarter of a houre after." A coiled western diamondback rattlesnake, or more especially one lying in a loose "S" position, can straighten and strike instantaneously. Reflexes and muscles coordinate spectacularly, providing a striking range equal to half the length of the snake's body. The entire action takes place with such speed that man's eye cannot discern the detail, but high-speed photography has captured it. Just before making contact with whatever is to be bitten, the snake's jaws open 160 degrees and a pair of fangs normally folded against the roof of the mouth swing down and forward, ready to jab. As they penetrate the victim's flesh, muscles around the poison glands in the upper jaws contract and force venom into the hollow fangs. Even infant rattlesnakes barely out of their fetal sacks carry venom, and the ability to deliver it. So does the severed head of a freshly killed snake.

Its biting is merely random and reflex action but is toxic nonetheless, and there have been cases of men bitten by such heads without bodies.

As predators, rattlesnakes feed on mice, rabbits, ground squirrels and occasional ground-nesting birds, insects, and lizards. Sometimes rattlers enter the burrows of ground squirrels or kangaroo rats in search of a meal or merely a retreat. Thus confronted, a kangaroo rat will kick sand into the snake's eyes and then turn and flee deeper into the burrow system. With luck, it can pop out one of its loosely plugged escape hatches and run off while the rattler still searches belowground. The bellies of snakes sense ground vibrations, which helps them home-in on prospective prey. They also flick their tongues in and out to pick up smells for transfer to special organs in the roof of the mouth where they are analyzed. Heat-sensitive pits just above the eyes of rattlers and other snakes in the pit-viper group detect the body warmth of nearby living flesh; and sight gives a final clue when the distance has been shortened enough. If the prey is suitable, the snake lunges and injects venom, then waits for the effect to set in.

Finally swallowing begins, a gross process. The jaws are not rigidly joined in front and this lets a snake swallow prey larger than its own body. The accomplishment involves a slow gagging engulfment during which the prey's outline is clearly evident the whole while. The jaws work from side to side instead of up and down. The upper and lower jaws on one side are thrust forward and the teeth on that side bite into the flesh and draw the meal into the mouth. Then the jaws on the other side reach for a fresh hold and repeat the process, while undulating motions of the throat inch the prey toward the stomach. Eyes bulge, unblinking because the eyes of all snakes are without lids; throat and abdomen distend, and the scales of the skin pull apart with the enormous stretching. There is a pause to rest and breathe, then the gorging continues. A two-foot rattler can swallow a one-foot lizard, and its belly can swell out three times original diameter to accommodate a cottontail rabbit or ground squirrel.

One disadvantage is that the bulge of the stomach may be so great the snake cannot move normally until digestion is completed, and during these hours — or days — it is hopelessly vulnerable. Red-tailed hawks, eagles, and roadrunners all attack rattlesnakes. Deer occasionally stomp them to death, and coyotes will often snap at them fearlessly and suffer no harm even if bitten. Kingsnakes feed on rattlers as well as on other snakes, although rattlers evidently recognize the odor of an approaching kingsnake. They try to get away, gliding off with head and neck close to the ground and trying to ward off the kingsnake with heavy blows of the body if overtaken. The kingsnake's tactic is to throw a loop or two of its body around the rattler, constrictor style, then begin swallowing at the head so that the scales won't catch in the throat and keep the meal from going down.

Rattlesnakes do not necessarily rattle before they strike. Dry shell-like nubbins form the rattle, and when vibrated they rub against each other and produce a distinctive loud buzz. According to the late Laurence Klauber, dean of rattlesnake authorities, there may be as many as one thousand contacts per second within the rattle. Each segment has three or four lobes, and six or eight rattles to a string are usual. Occasional strings of up to twenty-five rattles have been accurately reported, but these are rare; anything longer must be discounted. New buttons form with each shedding of the skin, but since the strings break easily they seldom are long.

The purpose of the rattle is not fully known. Certainly as a warning it is defensive rather than altruistic. Its message of impending danger is not addressed as a tip-off to prospective prey but as a threat against an intruder. Sometimes the system backfires. Men often would not know of a snake's presence if it weren't for the rattle; but, knowing, they find it and kill it. Presumably in response, rattleless rattlesnakes have begun to be noted in California. They probably are descended from snakes with poorly developed rattles, which provide the survival advantage of relative silence. The ability to buzz evolved long before men were dominating rattlesnake country. It may have served its purpose and switched now from advantage to detriment. If so, rattling may be on its way toward oblivion. Some observers do not agree. They believe the sound contributes to courtship, although since it is not heard seasonally this seems unlikely. Or it may be that the sound, or simply the visual blur of the moving tail, may bewitch rodents as the waving hat of a hunter will transfix an antelope.

The motion of a rattler, or of any snake, is rhythm incarnate: an effortless glide and an unending fascination for man, whose own experience is the stiltlike striding of legs. Snakes move by alternately edging forward the scales of the underbelly and pulling them back again, wave after wave. Evolution has led so far away from the legs of the lizard progenitors of snakes that few species now have even so much as a rudimentary pelvic girdle or vestigial limbs. Only boas and pythons and one or two others retain any external sign of legs — odd little bony spurs capable of vigorous but totally useless movement.

Sidewinders, and their African counterparts the sand vipers and side-running cobras, belong to a special category of locomotion, a sideways flowing that minimizes resistance and maximizes traction. Gentle looping motions apply pressure only straight down, avoiding lateral thrusts that would give very little useful force in so loose a medium as sand. One or two small portions

Sidewinder
tracks in sand

of the body serve as anchor for the snake, and the pressure is perpendicular to the surface while the rest of the body skims forward above the sand. The points bearing the weight then are shifted, the aerial looping repeats and the snake moves along at about a thirty degree angle. The track left in the sand looks like a succession of "J" marks, each entirely separate. The sidewinder is never stretched for even a moment along the whole length of any single J. The movement is fast and efficient, if oblique.

All rattlesnakes belong to the New World, ranging from the Canadian prairies to the Patagonian Desert of Argentina. Of the thirty species found in the United States seventeen are in Arizona, their range shared by only one other venomous snake. This is the Arizona coral snake, a species rarely seen, although the similar false coral snake — actually one species of kingsnake — is fairly common. Both the true coral and the false coral are gorgeously banded with cream, black, and coral red; but they are easily told apart because the bands come in a different order, red adjoined by cream for the true coral and red adjoined by black for the false coral. Also, the false coral has a light snout instead of black. There is no record of a coral snake ever having bitten a man, perhaps because they are small and shy and so gaudy as to give warning to anyone who is alert. They are venomous, but scarcely to be feared.

Of all the world's snakes, some 250,000 species, about one-twelfth are venomous and only 100 species are harmful to man. Among lizards, which total 3000 species, the record is even more innocuous. There are just two venomous species both of them in the Sonoran Desert: the Gila monster in Arizona and Sonora (not California or Baja California) and the Mexican beaded lizard found only south of the border. The two belong to the same genus, an ancient one dating back 30 million years to the Oligocene epoch. Little seems to have happened in an evolutionary sense during that vast period so far as these lizards are concerned; a fossil skeleton appears no different from a modern one.

Both species measure slightly over a foot long, with snouts that are blunt, eyes small and squinty, bodies chunky, and tail fat and dragging. Splotches of pink and tan mixed with black pattern the backs of Gila monsters, and their tails usually are alternately banded with dusty tan and black. The skin texture is beaded rather than scaled, and its mottled coloring blends against desert gravel and twigs in perfect camouflage. The Mexican beaded lizard is similarly patterned and those belonging to the damper portions of the range (which extends clear to Chiapas and the Isthmus of Tehuantepec) are darker than those in the desert. This fits the usual rule for populations within a species: heavy pigmentation in the tropics, paler at higher latitudes. The Gila monsters, found only in the desert, do not show this variation.

The manner of both lizards is consistently lugubrious. Instead of survival through the fitness of intelligence, it has been simple persistence on the part of Gila monsters and beaded lizards. No evident glimmer beyond bald reflex guides them. Even a half try at escape is enough for eluding a Gila monster or beaded lizard, which must rank with tortoises as having the slowest crawl in the desert. Perhaps as compensation, the lizards can go without eating for remarkably long periods — as much as three years if need be. They simply stay inactive, withdrawn into the coolness of underground retreats and living off fat stored in the tail. Under normal conditions bird and reptile eggs furnish staples for their diet, supplemented by hatchlings and immature rabbits and squirrels. Smell is the key to locating food. In captivity Gila monsters have dug out eggs buried in six inches of sand, and have followed the scent trail of an egg dragged experimentally in zigzags. They dart their tongues in and out, in the manner of all lizards and snakes, sampling the air and picking up the odor. In spring Gila monsters are active in the daytime; then as the heat of summer builds they shift toward nocturnalism; and when winter comes they hibernate.

A crushing bite deals death to prey, and swallowing begins immediately. Venom glands are located in the lower jaw with

Gila monster

ducts leading to the base of the grooved teeth. When the lizard
is irritated, it drools and opens and closes its mouth. This pools
venom into a special fold in the lower lip, and as the gnashing
continues the teeth are bathed in the venom, filling the grooves.
Both the upper and the lower teeth (about twenty in all) become
loaded with venom, which permits instant delivery by the initial
bite. Gila monsters hold this bite bulldog fashion, chewing the
venom in. They may even roll onto their back still holding
the bite — awkward but with the advantage of gravity-flow from
the lower-jaw glands. The amount of venom can be copious.
As much as forty drops have been milked from a Gila monster
in just four or five minutes, a far greater supply of venom than
snakes usually store. Bacteria in the saliva of Gila monsters
increases the toxicity of their bite, although through a different
chain of biochemical reactions than that triggered by the venom.

The bite hurts a man intensely and will cause dizziness,
numbness, sweating, and weakness, but it rarely is fatal. Deaths
after a bite actually have come more from psychic trauma or
from alcoholism than from the direct effects of the venom. A

survey undertaken by Charles M. Bogart and Rafael Martín del Campo disclosed 300 written mentions of Gila monsters between 1882 and 1939, and of these only 47 referred to bites and 15 to death. Among the deaths just one had been really investigated and the reports of it noted that the victim "had a weak heart and drank to excess." This case and many of the early cases involved showing off in a saloon, where Gila monsters often were kept as tormented mascots. In other instances gross misjudgment lay behind the bite. For example, one early-day Tucson resident rode with a "dead" Gila monster loosely tied behind his saddle, only to find the animal less dead than he had supposed. According to the newspaper story the next day: "Those jaws with the long, sharp, daggerlike teeth closed on Vail's finger, [and he] had to dissect head and jaws to get his finger from their grip." The bite healed but word of it spread and local folklore claimed for decades that on each anniversary of the bite Vail's hand would swell and turn black.

As recently as 1950 a somewhat similar incident took place when a hitchhiker north of Phoenix picked up a Gila monster and, not knowing what it was, carried it in his shirtfront the rest of the day and throughout the night. The next morning the lizard became irritated and bit. The hitchhiker was picked up exceedingly ill by a passing motorist and driven to the nearest town for treatment. He survived with no lasting aftereffect. The catching of Gila monsters is easy, they are so slow. Furthermore, their bright color and miniature-dragon appearance have made them vulnerable to collectors seeking pets or oddities, as well as to hunters seeking to eliminate them as dangerous. Extinction began to loom in Arizona, and consequently the state legislature in 1952 passed a law protecting Gila monsters, the first legal protection ever granted a venomous species.

Scorpions, rattlers, coral snakes, and Gila monsters are the only actually venomous creatures of the American desert. However, other species also have undeservedly bad reputations. Solpugids are an example. Tan, an inch and a half long, and scorpionlike in appearance (except without a tail), solpugids look

Right, solpugid;
below, tarantula

fearsome but are harmless to man. They move with the effortless grace of ballerinas, pouncing on insect victims and ripping and sucking and chewing them to pieces with remarkable speed; spitting out a ball of exoskeleton and pouncing onto a fresh catch to begin all over again. One investigator who kept a solpugid in a jar for months reported that it never refused to eat an insect, no matter how many it had just devoured. Probably no other creature in the world is equally rapacious; yet man, who must battle insects himself, should rejoice over such an ally, not feel revulsion.

Similarly, tarantula spiders are widely feared although they are among the desert species not harmful to man. Some are

Centipede

nearly as big as the human hand, their bodies five inches long and with four pairs of dark hairy legs to exaggerate the impression of size. Fangs are large and bacteria carried on them may cause infection that is far more troublesome than the actual tarantula venom.

Centipedes are another unjustly maligned creature, feeding on insects and spiders and in the case of Arizona's largest species (six or eight inches long) able to catch small lizards and mice if luck and exceptional appetite happen to coincide. Capturing such gigantic prey requires the centipede to wrap its body around the victim, pinioning its struggles. Then begins a wait for death and the chance to start feeding. The first pair of a centipede's legs are adapted into fangs and carry venom — but the bite seldom is more than slightly painful for man. All of the ordinary legs, two pairs to a segment, are tipped with sharp claws that often carry bacteria. They have no venom. Nonetheless, a man who has a centipede walk across his arm may find a double row of burning pinprick welts, an annoyance even though healing is sure and usually swift.

For us, horseflies probably caused more trouble in the desert than all other potentially bothersome species combined. An inch long and equipped with a vicious hinged proboscis, they inevitably zero in when your skin glistens with sweat and your hands are too full for swatting, such as when hanging sheets out to dry on a clothesline. The mere twitch of a muscle will not get rid of them; it takes annihilation or at least a close call with injury. Once, when cementing a new cover for a well in the southern end of Death Valley, my husband found the flies so frantically annoying that he ringed the carcasses of a dozen or more around where he worked. Somehow the survivors read the message and went away. But horseflies are scarcely the dangerous situation expected by those who think of the desert as a land cursed with creatures deadly to man. In reality the desert is neither hostile nor gentle. It is simply what you choose to make of it, and for species living there — men included — a variety of adaptations override factors that otherwise could be troublesome.

9. Desert Adaptation: Heat

ONE OF THE BLESSINGS OF SUMMER in the desert is time to think, to muse. It's too hot for much else. You sit sweating and drinking iced tea, complaining of the heat even while the evaporative cooler hums. Yet out there in the sunshine the antelope ground squirrels are running over the superheated ground and stuffing themselves on dry mesquite beans, and at night while you lie sleepless, longing for the temperature to drop, you hear the thumping and leaping of packrats in the attic; or if you are sleeping outside you catch the motion of kangaroo rats jumping silently, and perhaps see the shine of their bulging, lustrous black eyes.

These are the creatures sharing the desert heat with you, and seeming to fare rather better. How do they manage? No sandals to insulate their paws, or sun hats to keep their brains from baking. No iced drinks, or cold showers. No clever technology. The desert, more than gentler lands, sets the mind to thinking about other life forms, perhaps because desert land is essentially still and empty, and you can see and hear whatever stirs. Or maybe it is because the harshness prompts empathy for all who share it with you.

When it comes to heat, these "others" have three basic means of coping: they fight it, endure it, or escape it. As an illustration consider the white pelicans of California's Salton Sea, a desolate desert basin flooded by the Colorado River in 1905. The largest western waterfowl other than swans, these snowy pelicans have ten-foot wingspans. They are magnificent fliers undaunted by distances. Most of them winter in Mexico and colonize northern inland lakes in the summer, generally as far north as Yellowstone Lake and on into Canada. For nearly sixty years, however, the Salton Sea rookery dotted the desert heartland, beginning almost as soon as the river burst its banks and formed the salty lake that still measures about forty miles long. The very year after the lake formed the pelicans arrived, remarkably ready to take over new territory, even one with so little that seems ideal. Each nesting season until the early 1960s the birds returned, but by then increased drainage from irrigated fields had raised the water level and drowned their favorite site. Also, burgeoning water recreation had replaced the desert hush with the roar of outboard motors and the sound of human voices. Probably the pelicans will come no more now, but in the years that they summered at Salton Sea they displayed impressive adaptations to desert heat.

Along the former shore where the birds nested, six or eight sandbars used to build up each year as sediments were carried into the lake by storm runoff — tiny disconnected islets that were battered and nearly destroyed by waves from the time of one sediment load's arrival to the next. Yet each new rainy season with its fresh runoff would start the cycle of rebuilding, and by April and May the pelicans would arrive to add to the process. They scooped up soft silt from the lake bottom with their bills and pulled in bits of driftwood, thereby creating nest sites raised barely above water level. The late Lewis Walker, naturalist with the San Diego Museum of Natural History at the time, told of watching several hundreds of the great white birds at work.

He watched throughout the incubation period and came to know the temperature of the day by the position of the parent birds above their eggs. Developing embryos can tolerate a range of only a few degrees. Above 105°F. or below 95° they die. But Walker found that whenever the temperature fell to 80°F. the parent birds would squat close to the eggs so that their feathers formed a blanket over them and heat flowed by conduction from their warm bodies to the eggs. Then as the day warmed, the birds raised their bodies, and the process of brooding switched from incubating the eggs to shielding them from the sun. By midday with the air at 110°F. or above, the pelicans would leave the nest every twenty or thirty minutes and wade into the water to splash briefly. Returning, they would hover close to the eggs, wetting them with their breast feathers. After that they again stood tall to shade the nest and let the wind caress the wet eggshells and ruffle the birds' breasts, moistening and cooling the air.

Walker set thermometers in the ground under several clutches of eggs as a check on the efficiency of this air-conditioning system, and he found that nest temperatures held within four or five degrees of 100°F. regardless of air temperature. Somehow the birds adjusted the amount and timing of moisture and the position of their bodies to maintain this narrow range. When the eggs hatched and the featherless, fuzzless, salmon-pink young lay sprawled at the parents' feet, the adults continued to provide cool moist shade. In fact Walker, sweltering in his observation blind and unable to slosh himself with water, confessed that he roundly envied the care given the infants.

Later workers studying the rookery checked the body temperature of nestling pelicans. They found a chick about a week old, newly covered with down, prostrate and panting in direct sunlight. A cloacal thermometer gave a reading close to fatal. The men sprinkled the chick with water, as a parent bird returning from the lake would do, and in just one minute the young pelican's body temperature fell a full degree; three minutes later it dropped an additional degree and a half. Next they ceased supplying water or shading the infant, and its down quickly dried. In five minutes its temperature rose back to the starting point and it was again panting.

Almost as soon as pelican chicks peck their way out of the egg, they start to flutter the loose skin of their throat pouches as a means of cooling themselves. The motion is exceedingly rapid, four times or more per second. The skin of the pouch is thin and richly laced with blood vessels that bring heat from deep within the body to the surface, where it can be given off. Fluttering the throat accomplishes for a pelican what sweating does for a man: moisture is evaporated and the entire body is cooled. The process draws on internal reserves, and so would pose a severe problem under desert conditions if it were not for the birds' habit of waddling to the edge of the lake and lowering their bills into the salty water without drinking. This wets the outside of the pouch and doubles the square inches of body cooling surface without costing so much as a droplet of additional water. Both inner lining and outer surface evaporate water, and the odds in favor of survival are increased by just that much, an amount — however small — that can be crucial since desert margins are often exceedingly narrow. The wetting completed, the flightless young waddle back and rejoin their peers, packed into a heap with each one seeking the shade of the others.

Relieved of constant nest responsibilities as the young start to mature, adult pelicans at Salton Sea used to soar aloft and ride thermals as high as 8000 or 10,000 feet above their sun-baked rookery. In the high, cool air they would circle with scarcely a wingbeat, and by not exerting themselves they were able to give off the body heat accumulated in the desert. Even during the weeks of brooding, off-duty adults commuted to this coolness overhead. Sometimes they stroked on as far as the San Diego Mountains, fifty miles distant, there to feed and rest on lakes favored by breezes and moisture fresh from the Pacific Ocean. Work at Duke University has shown that birds flying in a special wind tunnel can operate with a fuel efficiency about ten times greater in proportion to body weight than that of a jet airplane — the equivalent of a man running for an entire day at the pace of a four-minute mile. This sort of efficiency made the pelicans' commuting possible. They spent the hottest hours in the mountains, or soaring. Then in late afternoon when the sun's fire began to ease, they returned to the desert and relieved their mates.

Pelicans are oddities in the desert. Most of the high dots riding the unseen currents of desert thermals are black instead of white. It is the circling of ravens and vultures which fully belongs. Their soaring may be the only motion at noon when ground squirrels have gone into their burrows and lizards have retreated to the shade of bushes. A raven's voice is the one sound to counterpoint the silence. Rasping and evocative, it will carry over the rock walls of a canyon to where you are climbing in search of a wild palm oasis; or it will come from far out over a shimmering plain as you reach with a pole to knock ripe saguaro fruit from the high branches. Ravens do not belong exclusively to the desert but they belong whole-heartedly, and memory of their call even at noontime lingers forever in your memory. Of course where they soar temperatures are a full ten or twenty degrees below what you are experiencing at ground level. Furthermore, a man is doubly exposed to the sun's heat as it both pours from the sky and glints back from the baked earth.

Vultures, too, paint their black silhouettes against the china blue of a desert sky, and thereby stay cool as well as watch for meals. Once I timed a turkey vulture tracing circles above the crags behind Guaymas, Mexico. It floated for four minutes and twenty-eight seconds without so much as a single flap of the wings. It glided close and low to look us over; then with wings still outstretched and unmoving it swept past sideways, caught an updraft, and circled back aloft to continue soaring. Seen thus, the sheer competence of a turkey vulture gives it magnificence. The wings arc gently up in a vee and the terminal feathers spread like fingers. The head, which is naked, wrinkled, and fire-engine red, is drawn in against the velvet-black body and becomes a pleasing accent instead of an offense. Our sons used to lie spraddle-legged on the desert floor feigning death and waiting for a vulture or two to circle overhead on the lookout for food. When this happened they would leap up, laugh, and scamper on to some other amusement.

There are ways on the ground itself to find coolness, or at

Jackrabbit

least to minimize heat. For instance, jackrabbits ramble about the desert as the red glow of a new day begins to streak the east and catch hold on the peaks. They browse away the dawn, but as soon as the mercury climbs and a summer day has arrived in earnest you see no more jackrabbits. They disappear into the shade of mesquite or beneath a tangle of lycium bushes and there crouch motionless in shallow pits called "forms." Here both the soil and the air are relatively cool. Even the slight depression of a form acts as a sump for cold night-air drainage, and since it is doubly roofed by both the bush and the jackrabbit's body its surface never gets heated by sunshine. A form is cool when a jack enters, and it stays fairly cool.

Spending the daylight hours in these shaded depressions may be the prime factor in survival for desert hares, according to Knut Schmidt-Nielsen, pre-eminent authority on how mammals adjust to desert harshness. Without resting in a form, a nonburrowing animal the size of a jackrabbit would have to drink and evaporate a prodigious quantity of water, an amount hardly feasible because of desert scarcity and also because of jackrabbits' inefficient evaporative cooling. They seem able to unload only about one-third of their excess body heat by panting and sweating compared to man's ability to rid himself of all his heatload by sweating, provided he has enough water. For hares, however, the preponderant heatload must be lost by conduction and radiation to the soil and air. Enormous ears serve well if the air temperature is below body temperature. They are nearly big enough for a donkey, as much as eight inches long for a two-foot jackrabbit. This is more than a third of body length and is the largest in proportion to overall size of any mammal in the world. Richly veined and lightly furred, the ears readily radiate heat to the surrounding atmosphere when air temperatures are low — and they would just as readily absorb heat when temperatures climb if it were not for a unique shut-off system. As the temperature of surroundings begins to equal or exceed body temperature, the blood supply to the ears is shut off, thereby minimizing the rate at which the ear surface picks up heat and transports it deep within the body.

Packrats also successfully fight the heat by behavior. They are fully at home in the hottest desert, yet in laboratory tests are decidedly unable to endure high body temperatures. Even white rats fare better when exposed to heat and given a dry diet, surviving two or three times as long as their desert cousins. This suggests that the conditions packrats actually experience are not so harsh as commonly supposed, in spite of the desert setting. By behavior they control circumstances. They depend exclusively on succulent food, without need to drink, and their young, unable to feed independently yet needing a steady supply of moisture as well as nutriment, attach themselves to their mother's teats at birth and cling there day and night. The female will feed and run and sleep with her litter clamped on until they are half grown. So marked is the tendency that a Tucson pet shop owner even reports that nursing mothers run on an exercise wheel with their young hanging to the nipples, flopping unheeded and unheeding. Above all, packrat dens protect against heat. They are more deliberately constructed than their

Packrat in den

haphazard appearance suggests. The piled debris is a deliberate mix of dead twigs and green cactus, a combination that simultaneously provides air circulation and evaporative cooling as the cactus gives off its moisture.

For many small mammals and reptiles, burrowing offers an answer to summer heat. By digging beneath the surface even a little way they enter a far more moderate environment than that aboveground. Air temperatures may stand at 110° or 120°F. within the tangle of a bush where a roundtail ground squirrel is gathering seeds, or may reach as high as 190° on the ground surface; yet within the earth, moderation reigns. A scant foot belowground, maximum temperatures reach little more than half what they are aboveground, and burrowing even a couple of inches will drop the temperature twelve or fifteen degrees. Furthermore, the maximum underground temperature comes about ten hours after the aboveground high has been reached, thereby giving the best of two worlds to nocturnal desert animals. They avoid the heat of the surface world by sleeping belowground throughout the day; and they leave their burrows to forage under cool night skies before the subterranean realm has reached its maximum.

A similar lag in temperature occurs seasonally. Heat accumulates within the earth throughout the summer, sinking increasingly deep. In winter the flow reverses and heat slowly dissipates back to the atmosphere. The situation is ideal for burrowing animals. Warmth stored from summer raises burrow temperatures during the winter, but by the time the next summer has come this stored heat has been dissipated and replaced by winter coolness. The earth acts like a reversible temperature reservoir — a condition utilized by humans as well as rodents, as witness the pit houses of primitive peoples, the "soddies" of prairie homesteaders, the "dugouts" of desert prospectors, and the buried heat pumps of modern buildings.

One of the great burrowers of the desert is the kangaroo rat. Named for the habit of leaping rather than running, some species are about the size of laboratory white rats (although unrelated); others are smaller. All burrow by whirring their short forelegs like a mechanical auger, then kicking away the accumulated sand with their long hind legs. As the tunnel deepens a kangaroo rat will push excavated dirt out of the entrance, using chest and chin as a bulldozer blade. You see a three-inch oval hole slowly fill with a moving load of earth, incongruously topped by bulging lustrous-black eyes and a set of silken whiskers sprayed

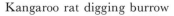

Kangaroo rat digging burrow

out like delicate threads. A brief emergence of the little animal, a tumble of its half-cup load of sand, and back it goes to scratch still deeper. In just five minutes a kangaroo rat can completely disappear within a sand dune, plugging its hole and leaving no sign to betray its presence. We once found a kangaroo rat at San Quintín, Baja California, abroad at midday and completely lacking fear. It would burrow; then we would flick open the sand plug and gently pull it out by its tail, watching and timing and photographing the process over and over again. There was a small wound and incipient tumor on top of the animal's head which perhaps had affected its mentality and accounted for its fearlessness. Nevertheless, actions and coordination seemed normal and there was no apparent panic or displeasure even at being tugged backward out of the burrow and having to start anew.

Wholesale burrowing by kangaroo rats aerates the soil beneath bushes and provides a remarkable amount of fertilizer. Soil scientists estimate an average of 10 pounds of nitrates per burrow mound. Multiply this by the market value of fertilizer and the vast number of kangaroo rats there are, and for a single range in southeastern Arizona where tests were conducted the figure comes to $31,000 worth of fertilizer. Add the droppings of pocket mice, grasshopper mice, ground squirrels, cottontails, snakes, and lizards (all known to take over abandoned kangaroo rat burrows or even to share active ones) and the nitrate value pushes still higher. A study near Tucson showed an average of from 4 to 10 kangaroo rats per acre, and about 20 to 30 antelope ground squirrels and the same number of pocket mice; various other species were uncounted.

Through years of digging by successive generations and with continual extending and altering of galleries, mounds become as large as ten or fifteen feet in diameter and two feet high. Doorways are located well above the general level of the ground as protection against flooding by summer cloudbursts; and sleeping chambers may be as deep as two feet beneath the surface, where temperatures are cool. Food storerooms vary from thimble size to generous pantries. An astonishing fourteen bushels of stored seeds and dried grass cut into short lengths were removed from the burrow of one kangaroo rat by an investigator, and amounts half that great are fairly common. Different kinds of seeds usually are stored separately, or if a chamber holds several kinds each one will be piled by itself. Various ripening times may account for this; or a kangaroo rat may concentrate on harvesting a favored species first, then turn to a lesser choice. Either way, the seed caches serve well on rainy or brightly moonlit nights when venturing forth is not prudent.

Within burrows, not only are temperatures moderate but humidity is also more favorable than in the aerial world. It holds much higher, largely because of kangaroo rats' habit of keeping burrow entries loosely plugged most of the time. Absolute humidity in the passageways and chambers of a mound remains fairly constant at seven to fifteen milligrams of moisture per liter of air, three or four times more humid than is usual for summer air aboveground. Seeds stored under these conditions actually absorb moisture and provide a slight water reserve when eaten.

Perhaps the champion burrower of the desert is the fringe-toed lizard, several species of the genus *Uma* which are superbly adapted for life on, and in, sand. Their quick nose-diving into a dune gives easy escape from the temperature extremes of the desert, both hot and cold, and also offers protection from predators: roadrunners stalk the dunes where fringe-toed lizards live, and sparrow hawks hover overhead; badgers occasionally follow a fleeing lizard onto the sand to dig it out; and a few snakes such as sidewinders prey on them. Fringe-toed lizards are about eight inches long from tip of nose to tip of tail, their backs a mottled brown patterned and shaded to match the sand they live on — dark where the dunes are dark and light where they are light.

When startled, they dash across the loose surface of sand, running as fast as fifteen miles per hour, their weight balanced on hind legs and their tail lifted; then they nose-dive and

Fringe-toed lizard

disappear beneath the surface. Two particular adaptations permit this abrupt submerging. The toes of the hind feet are long and have flaps of skin that fold out when the lizard is running or "swimming" through the sand. These flaps double the bearing surface of the foot and greatly increase its thrust. On the forward stroke the fringes fold against the toes and offer no resistance; on the downstroke, friction unfolds them. A shovel-shaped head is the other adaptation that eases the dive. Running at full speed the lizards simply dip their long flattened snouts into the sand and wriggle their necks and shoulders, which are equipped with rough scales that help them dig in. In addition, the lower jaw is countersunk, eliminating drag that might otherwise force open the mouth. The forelegs flatten against the body and streamline it. The hind legs do all the stroking. Body scales, except at neck and shoulder, are reduced to mere granules, which give a velvet texture to the skin and further lessen friction. Thus equipped, a lizard can sand-swim a distance equal to four or five times the length of its body. This permits total concealment and gives a cruising range great enough to provide temperature control by choosing depth within the sand. A bare submergence will net a temperature only slightly below that of the surface. Going deeper will permit greater cooling.

Such extensive refinement of physical characteristics suggests a long period of evolution in a sandy environment. Fringe-toes have become so specialized that they now live only where there is loose sand. This usually means sand deposited by wind. Water-deposited sand may be acceptable in texture but it seldom harbors the lizards, because its location, in a stream bed or on a floodplain, is too subject to fatal inundation. Also, sand deposited by water often has a lightly cemented quality when damp, unsuitable for diving into or moving easily through; or if it is coarse, lizards shun it because its drag against their bodies is too great. Struggling against such sand would be exhausting, and a lizard escaping noonday heat or a predator might settle for partial burial and leave itself vulnerable to disaster.

In burying, fringe-toes nearly always plunge into a dune on the lee side of its crest, an instinctive action that assures their not subsequently being unburied by wind. They breathe the air of spaces between sand grains, and even have a system to prevent choking on the loose particles pressed against their snouts. They gulp in air before submerging, then exhale it explosively as soon as they settle into the sand. This creates a small space between nostrils and sand, forcing away fine particles. Large ones remain, but, being angular, they tend to lock together into a "grille" which holds back fine particles that otherwise might cause choking. As further protection, blood rushes into a network of vessels in the lining of the inner nostrils and produces a gorging much as erectile tissue is gorged in mammals. This constricts the passages and lessens the chance of sand getting far into the nose. Furthermore, a valve closes the outer nostril to a mere crescent-shaped slit, and the inner nostril angles upward so that sand grains must move against gravity to penetrate far.

The shape of the nasal passages provides an additional preventive. They are narrow at the opening, even when not reduced to slits, then widen to form a cone with the large end toward the inside. This shape magnifies the force of the exhaled breath. The air gets rammed from the wide inner end of the tube out through the narrow opening and the pressure mounts as it goes. The compression responsible for this comes from the lizard's tongue, which is pushed against openings between the roof and the nasal passages. In the case of inhaled air the situation is reversed. The velocity of the breath falls off as air enters the narrow nostrils and passes into the expansiveness of the widening inner passages. It loses pressure instead of gaining it and whatever sand may have gotten through the outer protective system is dropped. This acts as a safeguard against choking. Still one more preventive is a U-shaped doubling back of the upper nasal passage, which functions as a last trap for any sand making it that far. Removal is accomplished by means of mucus coating the walls of the U passage, plus cilia (minute waving hairs), which push along any particles into the mouth, where they are swallowed.

Protection for the eye is even more elaborate than for the nose. Eyelids have no muscles for closing, but two distinct mechanisms substitute. When a fringe-toed lizard is in the act of submerging, the pressure of sand dragging against the lids closes them. When aboveground, there is an entirely different two-stage system. It consists of a gorging of blood and lymph similar to that which narrows the nostrils. This swells the lids shut and in the process raises a special set of scales that festoon the edges of both upper and lower lids. They interlock to form a barrier and prevent sand from scratching the eyeball when the lizard dives belowground. A double row of ridges along the edges of the lids contributes a virtual double-seal effect. But if sand gets into the eye even so, there are countermeasures for getting it out. Special muscles let lizards protrude their eyeballs and quite literally give them a shaking. If this fails, a "third eyelid," a nictitating membrane, can be unfolded across the eye, gently pushing sand particles to the outer corner. If sand still clings to the eye, the lizard reaches with its hind foot and brushes away the troublesome bits. Most remarkable of all, the shape of the toenails on the hind feet precisely matches the configuration of the eye. When the foot is brought forward into the brushing position, the nails fit exactly parallel to the cornea and thereby minimize the risk of scratching.

To test lizards' vulnerability to environmental temperatures Charles Lowe and Robert Vance once sealed tree lizards from Sabino Canyon, Arizona, into glass capsules fitted with copper tubing to permit breathing. They then put the capsules into water heated 104°F. and every half-hour raised its temperature one degree. At each step the lizards' body temperatures matched the water temperature within five minutes. Even when heated close to 112°, the fatal limit for this species (*Urosaurus ornatus*), the lizards had no physiological means to hold their internal temperature below that of the environment — no sweating or panting. Trapped within the capsules, they had no escape from death; and this was the point of the experiment. Lizards have no internal way of solving heat problems, but in nature they cope very well by behavioral adaptation. Some dive underground. Others run on tiptoe across the sun-scorched sand. They streak for the safety of a bush's shade and, once there, stand stiff-legged, holding their bodies as high as possible off the ground. Desert iguanas feed on creosote bush blossoms and then stretch out on a branch, to sway with whatever breeze stirs the desert air and enjoy temperatures much cooler than at ground level. Their tails are faintly banded with alternating light and dark and their backs are mottled, letting them blend into the patches of light and shadow within the bush. Chuckwallas, fifteen-inch miniature dragons, escape from heat or enemies by

Chuckwalla

fleeing into deep rock crevices. If pursued they gulp air and
puff themselves up to wedge in tightly. No predator except man
can pull them out; desert Indians used to puncture the ballooned
lizards with sharp sticks and add them to the stewpot or roast
them over coals.

As "cold-blooded" creatures — that is, lacking inner temperature control — lizards and snakes often are believed the helpless
victims of environment, but they really are not. Misunder-
standing on this point began early in the twentieth century when
a British physiologist noticed that mammals can keep their body
temperatures fairly constant regardless of circumstances, whereas
reptiles must depend on environment. His conclusions gained
wide credence. Too wide, especially since depending on environment is not synonymous with being the helpless victim of its
temperature extremes. There is no evidence that any desert
vertebrate can tolerate body heat beyond about 108° to 110°F.
for an extended period. Yet men watched reptiles stretch out
motionless to bask in full sunlight and, because they knew there
is no physiological means of temperature control, they assumed
that these creatures had a preference for elevated body temperatures. Investigation disproves the idea.

Rattlesnakes experimentally forced to endure direct sunlight
die in about ten minutes at air temperatures of around 100°F.
and with the soil surface at only 132° (mild for desert summer
conditions). Lizards are similarly unable to tolerate direct
sunshine, except on their own terms — and those terms permit
a surprisingly precise degree of control. For lizards, the optimum
ranges of body temperatures vary from 76° for geckos (which
are nocturnal) to 97° for chuckwallas; at body temperatures
varying from about 104° to 116°, lizards will die. The degree
to which each species can manipulate circumstances to control
its own temperature is shown by whiptails and spiny lizards,
two species that occupy the same range. They are exposed to
identical air and ground temperatures, yet whiptails stay ten
to twelve degrees warmer than spiny lizards. They have a higher
optimum temperature, and by behavior they maintain it.

Horned lizards furnish an impressive example of body temperature control through behavior. They can flatten their body, and this pancake shape together with a fringe of sawtooth scales along their sides allows them to submerge quickly into loose sand and unload heat. Or, aboveground, their flattened body lets them expose maximum surface to sunshine if the day is cold and they need to warm up. Conversely, on hot days they squeeze in their sides and become the cylindrical shape typical of most lizards. Also, they orient themselves to the direction of the sun's rays. They face into the sun and thereby minimize the rays that strike them if the day is hot, or they stand at right angles to the sun if the need is to bask and warm up. In addition, sloping ground allows them to intensify or lessen exposure according to body demand.

Cold is as much of a problem as heat. The chill of early morning leaves lizards sluggish and uncoordinated, prime prey for the sharp eyes of flesh-eaters until their bodies can warm to functioning temperature. As protection, various species start the day by lying with only their head out of the sand, soaking up warmth so as to become active as soon as possible and thereby gain added minutes to hunt food before the heat of midday forces them back into retreat. If they emerged completely and exposed their entire bodies to the dawn, they could absorb heat faster, but this would be more risky than exposing just their heads. Consequently, they preheat with merely their heads out,

Lizard
preheating

Horned
lizard

and blood there warms as much as seven degrees above the temperature of blood in the body cavity. A constriction arrangement unique to reptiles permits this. Muscles that ring the veins at the base of the skull can be tightened to greatly reduce the flow of blood returning to the heart. This causes it to pool within the head and remain long enough to be heated.

Horned lizards carry the system an additional step unknown in other species. They have a special shunting system for the blood in the head which lets them fully capitalize on the heat differential between their head and their body cavity. Normally the arteries that carry blood from the heart to the head lie close to the veins that return it to the body cavity, and this puts cold blood from within the body practically in contact with blood heated in the head. Only the walls of the two vessels separate the flows, a wasteful juxtaposition because the warmed blood loses heat as it flows past the cold blood. Horned lizards avoid the loss by squeezing off the veins that ordinarily return blood to the heart, shunting it instead into special veins well separated from the arteries carrying blood from the heart. This allows the warmed blood to reach the body cavity with its heat intact. Additional heating — and according to some studies a more important source of heat — comes directly into the body by conduction from the sand, which also warms as morning sun strikes it.

The veins in the head of horned lizards also have another function. They help with the shedding of the skin, a normal part of growth for all reptiles but difficult for these lizards since the skin of the head and protruding horns is uncommonly tight. However, engorgement of the hairlike vessels around the eyes, lips, and nostrils bursts the skin and starts the process of shedding. Blood control also lets them spurt a stream of blood from their eyes. It jets as far as six feet and startles predators into seeking something else for dinner. The blood squirts out through pores in special glands located at the outer corner of each eyelid. Possibly an irritant is picked up from the eye membranes and shot with the blood to make it distasteful as well as alarming, but researchers are not sure of this. The entire action has seldom been observed under conditions where any kind of check was possible. An estimated 2 cc of blood can be shot at a time — a considerable amount (nearly the same in volume as a penicillin injection, which typically ranges from 1 to 4 cc). The direction of the spurting is to the side and slightly backward. The eyes are closed and an audible sound accompanies the rush of blood, a mechanical sort of hissing.

Nocturnalism offers another answer to the problem of temperature control for desert creatures, birds and mammals as well as reptiles. For many it is the key factor permitting desert life. A study of snakes in California showed a marked increase in nighttime activity for those living along the margins of the desert compared to those in coast chaparral. The single adaptation to being able to forage in the coolness of the night seemed to be so crucial that various species cannot extend their range away from the coastal slopes because they cannot make this one adjustment in their behavior. They are daytime creatures, unable to switch to feeding at night and therefore unable to leave the coast. Other snakes, capable of changing their habits, are extending their range. Actually, about the only adaptation they need is to develop night vision, and this poses little problem since it need not be keen: snakes generally rely on senses other than sight for locating prey.

With lizards the situation is different. Snakes feed mostly on rodents, which are active at night, and so nocturnalism serves them well; but lizards feed mainly on leaves and flowers or on insects. They take flesh only if they happen upon nestling birds or lizards smaller than themselves. This means, generally speaking, that they are keyed to diurnal life by the dictates of their stomachs; plants are most easily located by sight and in bright light, and the daytime insect supply is ample. There is one notable desert exception to this daytime rule — the banded gecko, a member of an essentially tropical family of lizards, which thrives even in Death Valley because it is geared to nightlife.

About five inches long, these lizards move in perpetual slow motion and present an appearance of great frailty. Their skin is a blotched pink-brown and sufficiently semitransparent to show faintly their internal organs. Instead of the usual scales of a lizard's skin, theirs is softly beaded. Legs are thin, toes plump, and tails enormously fat. Snouts are long and pointed, and after each meal of a succulent moth or grub geckos lick their chops like contented puppies. In short, these particular lizards look decidedly unsuited to life in the desert — yet there they are, and well enough adapted to forage about on windy nights when so small a creature would seem likely either to sail off into the black void or be sandblasted into mincemeat.

Coupled with geckos' nocturnalism is an opportunism that allows them to gorge for three or four days, doubling their weight, then to live off stored fat for as long as six to nine months if need be. Their tail serves as a major depot for the fat, and some is also deposited throughout the body, necessary because the tail breaks off easily and acts as a decoy for predators while the lizard runs on to safety. Tail vertebrae simply split in half, aided by matching cleavage planes in the layers of fat, the muscles, and the skin. Sphincters in the arteries to the tail can all but cut off the blood supply so that the severing is quick, painless, and bloodless. Furthermore, a new tail soon grows, although with a cartilage-like rod in place of true bony vertebrae.

We had a pet gecko when we lived in Death Valley, kept in a jar next to the pet scorpion's jar. At night we let the lizard out to patrol the house for insects. He would stalk a moth drawn to our reading light, fairly oozing forward to close the final gap and almost nosing the prey before he would open his jaws and capture it. Then would come the delightful puppy-dog licking of his lips all the way up into his eyes, followed by a slow walking over to the next tidbit. When disturbed, Geck could utter a distinct, although faint, *eek* — the only lizard genus in the desert with a voice. Tropical geckos, cousins of the banded gecko, are renowned for their vocalizing. In fact the name "gecko" is said to be an onomatopoeic rendering of the call of one species. Some chirrup so steadily that they are mistaken for birds. Others, including the world's largest gecko, a two-foot New Caledonian species, can bark and even growl like dogs.

As is frequent among nocturnal creatures, the eyes of geckos are equipped with a tapetum lucidum, a "bright carpet" that lines the inner retina and functions something like a reflecting mirror in a camera. In a usual vertebrate eye adjusted for daytime, a special coating prevents internal reflections that might blur an image or produce multiple images, much as a coating for a camera serves a similar purpose. Under nighttime conditions, however, a bouncing of what dim light there is can increase perception. Cameras sometimes are specially built with a coating of mercury behind the film plane to reflect light back through the emulsion a second time, and in eyes the tapetum lucidum seems to function in about the same way. It allows rods (the cells sensitive to dim light) to receive incoming light and almost simultaneously be stimulated a second time as the rays bounce back. This may increase the apparent brightness of an object, or it may function as a brilliant screen against which shadowy objects are more clearly silhouetted. Either way, the tapetum enhances the lizard's ability to discern objects. It also produces

Gecko

the familiar "eyeshine" that gleams in the darkness as car headlights pick up the eyes of nocturnal creatures, whether bobcats and kit foxes or geckos.

Dim light is the expected light for such eyes. Bright light can be damaging. As protection many nocturnal species control the opening of their pupils with vertical slits like those of cats. These can be widened or narrowed to let in more light or less, depending on circumstances. Opening or closing the eyelids and thereby adjusting the length of the slit gives added control. Geckos' eyes have these characteristics plus one more, an improvement on the general principle which prompts Gordon Lynn in his standard reference work *The Vertebrate Eye* to credit geckos with "perhaps the most remarkable of all pupils known." Fine notches are paired along the sides of the slits to form a series of pinholes even when the slits are closed. Images thus are formed on the retina, although the pupil is essentially closed as protection from glare. No single pinhole lets in enough light to make an image that could be discerned by itself, but the series of images superimposed on one another is bright and also is considerably sharper than it would be if formed by a single opening, even one equivalent in size to the sum of the separate pinholes. The system lets geckos see well in the daytime if they need to, without risking damage to their superbly nocturnal eyes.

Our gecko died after two years with us when we stupidly

left him in the car parked in the sunshine. The temperature must have soared to 130°F. or more, and Geck had no means of saving himself.

Twice I placed a pet horned lizard in similar jeopardy, once when photographing and once when I had gone visiting. Our standard photography arrangement for small creatures was a milk bottle to form a slippery pedestal, with a flat stone set on top as stage. The combination prevented escape and gave a surface with enough space for natural action and body positions. Horny was tame and easy to work with, but we chilled other reptiles and insects in the refrigerator for a few hours before photographing. This caused them no discomfort. It simply rendered them lethargic and gave us a few minutes of slowed-down motion as they gradually regained normal temperature. My mistake came in leaving the horned lizard too long in the sunshine. She was already warm when the session began, and by the time the cumbersome positioning of a Leica in its closeup device was done, it was a sad lizard that came into focus. Her round, pink tongue was lolling from her mouth and her abdomen was heaving as she panted desperately to try to cool off. Escape was impossible, so this squandering of body moisture was the only hope of survival. As soon as I saw her plight I put her in the shade, and she quickly recovered.

The other such occasion was on a visit to the Indian Village at Furnace Creek in Death Valley, where I took regular lessons in basketmaking. My teacher, one of the elderly Panamint Indian women, always sat with me beneath a mesquite tree close by her wickiup. The flies buzzing lazily about made it easy to toss food into Horny's jar, satiating her and eliminating the need to catch additional meals for her for several days. This particular morning I grew too intent on willow withes and finger motions to notice that the shade of the mesquite had drifted off the jar and left the lizard in direct sunlight, again panting and nearly in death throes. One of the Indian boys noticed and remarked, quite offhand, "Your horned toad is dying." A move into the shade again reversed disaster. In the case of the

Young kit fox panting

gecko and both instances with the horned lizard it was unnatural
circumstances that endangered life. Escape was thwarted — no
possibility of wriggling into the sand or running to the shelter
of a bush — and so there was no alternative but to take on the
temperature of the environment, just as with the lizards sealed
in Lowe and Vance's experimental glass capsules. Panting was
the only hope, a short-term emergency measure, effective while
it lasted, and for Horny sufficient to grant ultimate survival.

In reality panting can be effective. The problem for small
animals comes because they have so little water available to
spend in body-cooling. The panting itself probably is more

efficient than sweating as a means of dissipating body heat. It may well be *the* most efficient way, drop for drop and degree for degree, especially when combined with spreading saliva onto the body surface to give additional evaporative cooling. Members of the dog family (in desert terms, coyotes and kit foxes) are physiologically well equipped to maintain a safe body temperature by panting, although limited water tends to make nocturnal behavior a more substantial part of their desert success. Birds employ panting quite regularly. The Salton Sea pelicans are an example. So are mourning doves, ravens, and any number of others. The sight of an overheated bird panting dejectedly, its wings held out, seems pitiable because of what such behavior implies for a human; yet for birds it is a normal and successful way to cope with desert heat.

The role of color in the lives of desert creatures has been studied for over a century, but even so is not fully understood. Variables, interrelationships, and exceptions to the rule seemingly have no end. Basically the question revolves around three considerations: protective camouflage, temperature control, and the screening of light rays. In general desert creatures are light gray or buffy-colored rather than saturated in hue. This is true even among English sparrows, birds that in the slightly more than a century since their introduction into North America have evolved into many separate races. Those in the desert are decidedly paler than those in regions like the Pacific Northwest, perhaps partly owing to protective coloration, since bare desert land tends to be light compared to the forest-cloaked land to the north. Or the paleness may be a direct physiological response. A cool climate means a greater need to absorb and hold heat, and this ability is related to dark pigment. In arid regions the reverse is true. The crucial consideration is to escape heat during much of the year, not to absorb it.

Seemingly the two roles of camouflage and heat regulation coexist, although at times one may outstrip the other at least temporarily. Horned lizards, chuckwallas, spiny lizards, collared lizards, and several others can change the color of their skin from light to dark and back again depending on circumstance and need of the moment. They may be dark when they emerge and start to warm up for the day, then light-colored through the hot midday, and again dark before they retreat back into the sand or rock crevices to escape the chill of night. Predators see these lizards more easily while they are dark-colored, because of the contrast with generally light surroundings, but evidently this potential danger is less pressing than the immediate need to absorb warmth. Consequently camouflage takes second place and the urgent need of warming to active temperature dominates. The skin can be darkened by the expansion of melanophores (special heavily pigmented cells) within the skin. As these cells flatten out they tint the skin dark. When they contract, the other less pigmented cells of the skin predominate and the overall color lightens.

Creatures that have no systems of warming or cooling within their own bodies need to be able to adjust quickly to environmental temperature, and studies indicate they can. In one study thermocouples attached to the bodies of brown-shouldered lizards registered changes in temperature much faster than thermometers exposed to the surrounding air at the same time. The skin was absorbing heat and warming up faster than the air. In this regard small creatures have an advantage over large ones. An animal the size of a dinosaur would need to bask a theoretical six hours to raise its body to an active temperature after a night that had chilled it even five or six degrees below acceptable range. The process would take so long that there would not be enough time left to feed before the next period of chilling arrived. During the age of the dinosaurs' ascendancy, world climate must have fluctuated little from day to night and from season to season; later, when temperatures became more varied and ranged from hot to cold, the great reptiles could not keep pace, and died.

In several cases color matches background remarkably well. At least three species of lizards living in the gypsum dunes of White Sands, New Mexico, are pale and the same species living on black lava immediately adjacent are dark. Similarly, in the Algodones Dunes near Yuma, horned lizards and sidewinders are slightly more pinkish than the same species in tan-colored dunes only sixty miles away in Coachella Valley, California. Among chuckwallas those from certain cinder craters in the Mojave Desert are a definite black and those on the adjoining desert soil are light-colored. Furthermore, lizards taken from one of these areas to another do not change to match the new surroundings. Their pigmentation evidently is genetically coded, having been initiated by environment at some early point in their ancestry and selectively bred through the generations because of survival value.

Examples of amphibian and mammal coloration that matches surroundings are equally common and documented. Nobody really questions existence of the phenomenon for a wide variety of animals, but the reasons and mechanisms underlying it have not yet been sorted out. One theory correlates color and climate. According to this explanation aridity hinders the development of dark pigment whereas humidity stimulates it. Yet where pale-colored lizards (or amphibians or mammals) are found in one area and dark ones of the same species in the immediately adjoining area, climate obviously cannot explain the matching; there can't be that much temperature difference in such short distances. Another theory argues that predators do not necessarily see the colors and patterns of animals and ground surfaces the way humans do and so coloring may not serve the protective purpose we ascribe to it. Other investigators counter with the fact that background-matching is too widespread to be easily dismissed as merely random. Skin on the back of fringe-toed lizards, for instance, precisely matches the reflectivity of the sand they live on, even when delicately measured with instruments. Furthermore, the skin is dotted and streaked with the identical combination of blacks, browns, rusts, and whites possessed by the sand grains of the individual lizard's home dunes. Certainly if predators do see color alike there is survival value in an animal's matching its background, and even a slight degree of added

Black vulture

safety can be crucial for the individual. If color blending
safeguards against a few predators on one or two occasions a
mouse may survive and breed longer than its counterpart that
does not have this advantage, however slight. Lee Dice, working
with mice in dim starlight, found that those matching their
background as his human eyes perceived the match were the
same ones that escaped from owls appreciably more often than
those appearing conspicuous to his eyes.

A third aspect of color's function in holding back the sun's
rays is of more clearly understood value. Sunshine definitely
can damage body tissue, both through the buildup of heat and
through harm from the rays themselves, especially in the ultraviolet range. Yet desert creatures live surrounded by light: excess
seems their fate. Even their underbellies receive the sun's rays,
reflected from sand and rock. Black would seem a poor color
for desert creatures exposed to such intensive sun. Its absorptive
characteristics might be expected to negate any chance of staying
cool; but just the opposite happens. Black pigment prevents
sunlight from penetrating into the body — or, more precisely it
blocks the rays and we see the result as black because all visible
wavelengths have been absorbed instead of transmitted. The

black pigment generally is in the skin or the peritoneum, an inner lining between skin and body wall. Or concentration around the central nervous system or the gonads may form a shield. This is common in diurnal species of reptiles although not in nocturnal species. Even among desert creatures with a light outer surface, dark inner membranes usually are present.

Certain characteristics of skin and hair seem also to help guard desert animals. The scales of lizards' and snakes' skins are highly reflective. Antelope and roundtail ground squirrels have a skin that is thicker than that of forest squirrels, and also is endowed with scaly folds and a greater surface concentration of both melanin and keratin, a special horny substance. Only diurnal desert rodents show these modifications, and this perhaps indicates the skin's value as protection against solar radiation and in reducing water loss. Among nocturnal animals, hair tends to be finer for desert species than for nondesert species, and the hair shafts of both kangaroo rats and pocket mice are flattened and loosely held by a peculiar fatty film, which form shingle-like plates. Presumably these characteristics of scales, skin, and hair help insulate the fragile lives encased within, although exactly how is not yet really understood.

Animal fur in general tends toward the hairy in hot regions rather than toward the woolly fur prevailing in cold regions. Hair can withstand extreme heat with little effect, and at the same time will act as a barrier and break the flow of heat from environment into the body. Schmidt-Nielsen reports temperatures on a camel's back of almost 160°F. and on Merino sheep he recorded 185° while the body temperatures of the animals were holding around 104°. Hartebeests and zebras on the African plains have been found able to rid themselves of 20 percent of their heatload by panting and sweating. The insulation value of their coats does the major job. Both species have thick shiny coats that immediately reflect more than one-quarter of the sunlight striking their backs and sides. Of the heat that does impinge on them, 80 percent reradiates directly back to the environment without ever penetrating their coats. Thus, only a small portion of the total heat they are exposed to is actually available for conduction to the animals' bodies.

Hair also serves well in the desert because it permits air movement, which in turn allows convective cooling. For animals that depend on sweating to dissipate body heat, the exact site at which evaporation takes place is important. There are two possible locations: at the outer surface of thoroughly wet fur or at the skin surface with vapor diffused through the fur to the air. The latter results in significantly more cooling. This is because it takes heat to change water from liquid to vapor, and if the water is evaporated at the skin this heat will be drawn from the body instead of from the air. The result is more body heat dissipated per drop of sweat than if evaporation took place at the outer surface of the coat. A hairy or furry animal consequently can cool more efficiently than a man does, although proper clothing restores to man the body insulation he lost through evolution when his skin became bare.

Part of the problem of heat is the loss of body moisture usually entailed in staving off a temperature rise. For small animals this can be disastrous, because of their large moisture-losing surface in proportion to moisture-providing body volume. Even with the protection of skin and pelage developed to its fullest degree many cannot afford to risk the desert sun; hence the behavioral adaptation of escape belowground or into the shade. Checking the problem with various desert birds, George Bartholomew and William Dawson found a moisture loss equivalent to 17 percent of body weight in just twenty-four hours for small species such as house finches. This was at temperatures of only 77°F., with no exercise and no direct sunshine. The birds were placed one at a time in cylinders filled with absolutely dry air. Wire mesh allowed feces to fall through into mineral oil so that no moisture would be present except what was exhaled from the bird's lungs. If fecal matter caught on the mesh above the oil or on the sides of the cylinder, data for that particular test were ignored. The finches' loss was the highest recorded for any species. For larger birds such as mourning doves the moisture loss was equivalent to 2½ percent of body weight in twenty-four hours.

Small mammals have a comparable problem, and some of them solve it by opting out, dropping into torpor. When vegetation is at its most lush in spring and early summer ground squirrels are everywhere — more readily noticeable than any other desert rodent because they are daytime-active. They search out seeds and shoots, standing upright stretched to their full seven- or eight-inch heights to survey their domain. If alarmed they chirp with a birdlike note, mouth open and chest heaving in mighty spasms. Near Guaymas, Mexico, one April afternoon we heard repeated chirps overhead and turned our binoculars to a flowering mesquite tree expecting to see a bird. Instead we found a roundtail ground squirrel perched high above us. For twenty minutes it alternately scolded and feasted on the yellow flower tassels of the mesquite. It would reach with its forepaws to pull a fresh blossom to its mouth, then nibble it like an ear of corn, holding and turning it, while golden pollen coated its face and chest almost like the dripping of melted butter. Such feeding would continue until summer was half spent and seeds had gradually replaced flowers as an item of diet; then this roundtail and all of its kind would forswear active life until the following spring and drop into dormancy within the earth.

In a few areas prolonged dormancy termed "estivation" when it occurs in the hot season and "hibernation" during winter's cold makes it possible for species with highly similar food demands and daily rhythms to coexist. In parts of California, Mojave ground squirrels, antelope ground squirrels, and round-tail ground squirrels overlap their ranges. Theoretically this is not possible because of excessive competition, but adaptations of the Mojave and roundtail ground squirrels bring the problem within manageable bounds. The two stay dormant half the year. From August to March they are in their burrows and so the actual competition between species occurs only during the months when vegetation is at its maximum and able to support them all; throughout the unfavorable months the antelope ground squirrels have the field to themselves. During spring and early summer the Mojave and roundtail ground squirrels eat enough to double their weight and to reproduce; then they withdraw and "sleep out" the late summer heat. When winter arrives they slip from estivation to hibernation without stirring, and in point of fact the two are the same physiologically. Under laboratory conditions the squirrels go from one state to the other with nothing but the calendar to mark the dividing line, and presumably the same is true in nature. Fifty grams of fat could supply enough energy for half a year of dormancy, and ground squirrels easily put on twice this amount during their months of activity.

Pocket mice and kangaroo mice similarly rely on dormancy as a means of survival, although their exceptionally small size constitutes a formidable theoretical disadvantage. With a great surface-to-mass ratio, they are in danger of absorbing heat too readily and suffering a deadly temperature rise on every summer day. The importance of surface in proportion to mass can easily be envisioned by thinking in terms of two stones brought from a cold room into direct sunlight. If one is a mere pebble and the other is the size of a baseball, it is obvious that the smaller one will become hot while the larger one has hardly changed temperature. This is because of large surface in relation to mass. Or, suggests Knut Schmidt-Nielsen, think of the matter by imagining a block of ice smashed into pieces. Its mass will be unchanged by breaking it, but the total surface area will greatly increase. This alone will speed absorption of heat and ultimate melting. In the same way, a small body with its proportionately large surface is readily subject to overheating. The physics of heat is the same between inanimate and animate objects, and for small animals the problem is intensified because the production of metabolic heat happens to also be more directly proportionate to body surface than to mass. On both counts small size worsens the problem.

A pocket mouse has about ten times the surface of a man in proportion to mass, and seventeen times that of a camel.

Relying on evaporative cooling alone would bring death on the first day of summer. The mouse would have to evaporate water equivalent to 20 percent of body weight each hour in order to survive. Perhaps because of the impracticability of swallowing this much water fast enough, even if it happened to be available, pocket mice (and also kangaroo rats and ground squirrels and many small rodents) lack sweat glands except for an insignificant few on their paws and around their noses. Panting and drooling saliva onto their chests suffices as an emergency measure, but the real means of combating heat lies elsewhere. For kangaroo rats, nocturnalism is the answer with the daylight hours spent in the coolness of their burrows. Roundtail ground squirrels estivate to solve the problem. Pocket mice also rely on dormancy, but in their case it comes in short periods. Rather than commit themselves to long seasons of true estivation or hibernation, they drop in and out of torpor according to immediate need. They idle back physiological processes as if in deep dormancy, but they accomplish it quite abruptly. No particular preparation is needed, and the state lasts only a few hours at a time. It is as if a man could drop his body temperature to 40°F., his heart beat to just six or eight throbs per minute, and his respiration rate to one breath about every four minutes.

Perhaps because this system is effective metabolically, or perhaps because it provides removal from the world's dangers a fair percentage of the time, pocket mice tend to live longer than kangaroo rats, antelope ground squirrels, or grasshopper mice, according to a study of longevity made at Joshua Tree National Monument, California, by Robert Chew and Bernard Butterworth. The men studied the same plots for two successive years, livetrapping rodents, marking them, and releasing them. They found that pocket mice captured the first year were recaptured during the second year about twice as often as any other rodent species. Corroboration of exceptional lifespan came from a different study, which found pocket mice as old as three to five years, a remarkable age for so small an animal and doubtless of survival value for the species. Without this longevity the mice might fall into widespread die-off during prolonged drought, or a series of generally dry years. Their metabolic demands are so high while active that they are hard pressed to find enough food even during favorable times, and small size further worsens their lot. If it were not for being able to periodically escape desert reality by plunging into torpor, they would be competitively weak in relation to other rodent species. Any environmental temperature up to around 80° will do for dropping into dormancy; this means any time of year, since burrow temperatures stay low even on hot summer days. The mice in effect take intermittent time out, and thereby lengthen their lifespan.

Antelope ground squirrels act as if they had no problem with desert heat. The human spirit wavers and fails long before theirs, and other mammals, reptiles, and birds will seek retreat while the squirrels are still running around flicking and arching their saucy white tails. They act like windup toys with unlimited spring tension. They may dash belowground briefly at noon, but their one usual concession to desert harshness is to flatten against the soil of a shaded area from time to time and unload body heat by conduction. They sprawl their legs, with chin, chest, and belly pressed tight to the earth; then after a few minutes of this they are off and running again. An antelope ground squirrel timed in the laboratory at the University of California at Los Angeles dropped its body temperature by seven degrees this way in just three minutes. Succulent leaves and occasional insects provide the basic moisture the squirrels need, and they drink whenever they find water. If exposed to protracted extreme heat they pant and drool, but under usual circumstances they simply live an asbestos life.

For a time it was thought that antelope ground squirrels were able to elevate their body temperature without harm, but subsequent evidence is counter to this. For certain other mammals, though, and for lizards and birds, labile temperature does hold true, and is the major means of adapting to heat. This capacity is perhaps especially valuable for birds in the desert.

Antelope ground squirrel cooling against soil

They evidently have no particular metabolic adaptations for meeting the problems of heat and aridity. Thus, house finches flitting about desert Mexico seem to have the same water metabolism as those among the rain-soaked willows at the very edge of an Alaskan glacier. The only difference is that to maintain moisture balance the southern finches have to consume about four times as much water as the northern races need. For desert living, the built-in capacity of all birds to let their body temperature fluctuate seems to be adaptation enough. An internal temperature range of several degrees is perfectly normal. If the day is hot, birds simply become hotter. Their body temperature not only rises to meet desert heat but to a point exceeds it. In this way they unload heat stress onto the environment and maintain temperature balance on days when most mammals are forced either to retreat into their burrows or to squander water as sweat.

As an illustration, at air temperatures of 104°F. Abert's towhees can let their body temperature rise enough to lose about two-thirds of their excess body heat by radiation and conduction, which leaves only one-third to be taken care of by panting. The insulation of feathers is something of a drawback in this cooling, although birds reduce the disadvantage by compressing plumage, and they also sit with wings held out to expose lightly feathered undersurfaces, from which heat dissipates fairly efficiently. In some species the flow of blood increases to featherless sites, where heat loss is relatively direct. Legs and feet are examples; also combs, wattles, and gular pouches.

Among mammals two African arid-land antelopes have received the most study with regard to elevated body temperature in relation to desert survival — the eland and the oryx. Both are large. The eland weighs up to half a ton and stands six feet at the shoulder, and the oryx is only slightly smaller. Both get along well in hot, dry country, but the oryx ranges farther into true desert than the eland. The two have been proposed for introduction into the American Southwest as range animals better suited there than Herefords to the production of meat. Oryx tested near Phoenix have done extremely well, although more gentleness must be bred into them before they are a good gamble economically. On their natural range they require a vast area for survival and they pugnaciously resist capture, which augurs against easy roundup and shipment. Yet if the oryx were fenced and fed, its unique capacity for desert living would be negated, and beef, with a proven market value, might better continue to be raised. Eland, on the other hand, with meat reported as veal-like in flavor, are beginning to be ranch-raised in Africa and cropped from game herds running wild. In the Ukraine they are undergoing tests as a dairy animal. Their milk is rich in butterfat, has a high protein content, and even is said to remain fresh for days in a hot climate.

To check into the remarkably successful adaptation of these two animals, C. Richard Taylor and Charles P. Lyman of Harvard University worked under controlled conditions at a veterinary research laboratory in Kenya. They found that as daytime heat builds, both eland and oryx are able to let their body temperature climb as high as 108°F., which is twelve or fourteen degrees above their dawn temperature. They hold this high as long as twelve hours — in effect storing heat throughout the day for unloading at night. If the animals gave off heat as it mounted within them, they would be spending body moisture. Evaporation from skin or respiratory tract would be the only possible means of cooling physiologically (and they are far too large to reduce heat load by behavioral retreat into burrows or by wriggling against cool soil). Instead, they hold body heat until after sundown and then disperse it directly into the night-cooled air through convection and radiation. No water is required.

One hazard in the system might be damage to the brain caused by such sustained heat, but Taylor and Lyman found this not the case. Blood precooled in the sinuses circulates to the brain and protects it against overheating without any added cost in body moisture or in behavioral adaptation. The carotid arteries carrying blood from heart to brain branch into an enormous network of fine vessels within the sinus passages, where each incoming breath provides automatic evaporative cooling. By these means the eland and the oryx readily endure desert heat. They don't fight it or escape it, they simply live through it as if temperature extremes were the norm for all the world, as indeed they are for the desert world.

10. Desert Adaptation: Water

AMONG BIRDS that most truly belong to the desert, succulent food may supply more water than drinking does. Waterholes and rain storms often are far between, but every grasshopper and scorpion and juicy leaf is a minute reservoir. Perhaps no bird better demonstrates the point than the roadrunner — *el paisano,* or "countryman" to the northern Mexican people. Fully at ease throughout the desert's fiery worst, these birds may slow their pace at noon in midsummer, but they do not really alter their habits even then or lose their cocky joie de vivre. They drink water if available, and are not in trouble if it isn't.

Roadrunners are cuckoos, literally, and as members of that family they uphold the word's figurative slang connotation. They are large, nearly two feet from the tip of their long stout beak to the end of their tail. Plumage is dark and streaked, an indeterminate steely hue misted with velvet green when seen close and in certain lights. A crest of two-inch feathers rises jauntily from the head in times of excitement or curiosity. Toes point two forward and two backward and are long, to provide the needed bearing surface to run over loose sand — and run the birds do. They seem never to walk and only occasionally to leap into the air and volplane across rough ground. While running they hold their lanky bodies horizontal and their legs pump at a rate of about twelve steps per second, carrying the birds across sand, gravel, and rock at speeds of fifteen to twenty miles an hour. Their stride is nearly as long as their body,

including beak and tail. For a man the pace would be comparable to a broadjump of five or six feet.

"A digestive tract encased in feathers," someone has called
the roadrunner, and rightly, for anything goes so far as their
palate is concerned. Furthermore, so powerful are their stomach
juices that every shred is digested — chitin, bone, scale, it makes
no difference. No pellet is expelled in the manner of an owl.
J. Frank Dobie, revered chronicler of the desert Southwest, once
reported the stomach contents of a roadrunner he had collected
as a museum specimen on a cool spring day. Included were:
21 snails, 1 cutworm, 1 bee, 1 spider, 3 daddy-long-legs, 2 pods
of stinging nettle, 2 crickets, 7 unidentifiable small beetles, and
2 Junebugs. Scorpions, centipedes, and tarantulas are common
items of diet. Occasionally small birds are eaten. Cactus wrens,
sparrows, and meadowlarks all have been reported as eaten by
roadrunners, sometimes taken as nestlings, sometimes as mature
adults. Mice and rats are also acceptable; so much so that
householders in desert Mexico are said to steal young roadrunners
from the nest and raise them as mousers.

So far as availability and opportunity permit, roadrunners
feed more on insects and animal flesh than on plant material.
Testing the effectiveness of this as a source of water, Robert
D. Ohmart and colleagues in the Zoology Laboratory of the
University of California at Davis simulated desert conditions
by feeding roadrunners only white mice and denying them
drinking water. No problem. The birds simply cut their daily
water requirement by about one-third. More than half of what
they needed under the new circumstances came from moisture
in the tissue of the mice they were eating, and the process of
digesting it formed enough water as a by-product to supply the
rest of the daily requirement.

In nature the luxury of a dependable mouse supply probably
does not occur, but roadrunners are masters at hunting all
manner of prey. One observer tells of watching a roadrunner
follow a family of quail. He assumed the chicks were being
stalked, then noticed instead that the roadrunner was feasting

on grasshoppers stirred up by the scratching and feeding of the quail. More often roadrunners flush their own insects by flicking out their wings and flashing their white markings. When raised in captivity they instinctively follow this wing-flicking habit. There also is a story of a pair of pet roadrunners that used the principle of a tool as an aid in hunting. George Sutton tells of them in *Birds of the Wilderness,* speaking of boyhood strolls across the hot Texas prairie accompanied by the two. For the birds' benefit he often teased tarantulas out of their burrows by twirling a blade of grass barely within the opening, and in time the roadrunners learned the essence of the trick for themselves. Spying a likely hole they would drop in pebbles and then wait for one of the great hairy spiders to emerge. When it did, one of the birds would pounce upon the tarantula and slam it against the ground until all fight had more than disappeared; then quickly swallow it, legs and all.

Pounce-and-slam is the basic feeding technique of roadrun-

Roadrunner

ners. If a victim is large, say a lizard or a snake, there may
be thirty or forty whomps against a stone to reduce the meal
to hamburger. Swallowing is an indelicate choking and gulping
of a time duration commensurate with the physical length of
the prey. A two-foot snake simply cannot slip easily into a
ten-inch gullet, and the excess dangles from the side of the bird's
beak until space becomes available for additional swallowing.
Often the protruding tail seems an annoyance. A roadrunner
will shift it nervously from side to side, uncomfortable with its
beak forced agape, until the final morsel is engulfed.

Appetite is voracious, as might be expected for so large and
active a bird, especially where food supplies both nutrition and
water. Perhaps for this reason laying continues even after
incubation of the first egg has begun. The system spaces hatching
out over a period of several days and the body heat of the first
dark-skinned, white-haired infant birds thus becomes available
to warm embryo siblings. The parent birds are given the
advantage of a graduated demand for food, instead of a whole
nestful of even-aged hungry hatchlings. This is no small consideration in view of an adolescent roadrunner's capacity. A chick
raised by its parents in the laboratory, where it could be carefully
observed, ate four newborn rats on the tenth day of its life, six
on its eleventh day, and nine on its twelfth day — amounts about
equal to half the bird's own body weight. Such a demand from
an entire family at once might be impossible to meet. However,
since accelerating food intake tapers off after the twelfth day,
the parents are free to focus their efforts on satisfying the peaking
demands of the next nestling.

Young roadrunners are fed directly by regurgitation and the
adults seem to add a squirt of a digestive enzyme as they poke
spiders and lizards and rats endlessly into the maws of their
progeny. At least ornithologist William Calder reports once
seeing a quick gleam of fluid as a parent bird fed its young,
and he surmised this might be an enzyme. In an experiment
he had been unable to raise chicks in an incubator, and it seemed
plausible that a previously unknown enzyme might be the

explanation. His chicks had failed to digest the minced beef kidney and moth larvae he fed them, although the diet was identical with that being supplied by parent birds to the healthy young in an adjoining cage.

In one way roadrunner nestlings reward their parents, with a sort of recycling of water. The chicks void urine and feces in membranous sacs, body moisture that the adult birds reuse. The basic system is fairly common among woodpeckers and other cavity-nesters as a means of sanitary control: the voided sacs are regularly removed from the nest by parents for cleanliness and probably also to lessen the threat of predators drawn by scent. Roadrunners, on the contrary, swallow the fecal sacs instead of simply removing them. This is a help in maintaining moisture balance, because the fluid waste of chicks has only half the salt concentration of adult urine and therefore can serve as a valuable source of liquid. There usually are from 3 to 5 or 6 young in a roadrunner family, and sometimes as many as 12. Using an average of 5 chicks, Calder calculated the daily "water potential" of a nest of young. Each individual voiding by a half-grown bird would provide about 5 milliliters of wastes (nearly a teaspoonful). Allowing 3 occurrences per day and 5 chicks to a nest, this would total to 75 milliliters. About one-third would be usable water, which would result in a 10-milliliter supply per parent per day. Time and again Calder would watch an adult roadrunner put food into the gaping pink-blotched throat of a nestling, then turn attention to the opposite end and wait for expulsion of the sac containing the waste from the preceding feeding.

Desert quail also depend on food as their source of moisture, although mostly on vegetation rather than the insect-and-flesh diet of roadrunners. Quail tested in the laboratory were kept for six days on a diet of dry grain with no water available, then cabbage leaves were supplied along with the grain. The birds still were allowed no free water, but moisture in the leaves was enough for them to regain the weight they had lost by dehydration. Identical results were found by using mealworms instead

Gambel's quail

of cabbage. The experiment supported field surmise that food
alone can easily supply all the water quail need. Furthermore,
even when succulent food is not available these birds stay in
normal health. They tolerate dehydration sufficient to shrink
their bodies to only half of normal weight, a much higher
percentage of loss than is reported for any other bird, or indeed
for any other vertebrate. Quail are not strong fliers and cannot
commute to and from watering places. Nonetheless, by choosing
territories with the right kind of plants and then waiting out
dry spells, they claim the desert as their own — so much so that
the sound of quail calling at dawn and dusk comes easily to
mind as one of the main harmonies of dry washes and hillsides.
This applies especially to Gambel's quail, which seem to range
farther into true desert country than California quail (except
for Baja California, where California quail are common and
Gambel's quail are all but nonexistent).

Quail get along on as little as a half-teaspoon of water per
day, an amount easily obtained in food. Lycium, pursley,
greasewood, hackberry, and a score of other common bushes
offer the needed combination of cover, nutrition, and this amount
of water. Sometimes the fruit of prickly pear cactus is added
to the diet, an excellent moisture source throughout the hot
summer months — and one that stains the quails' beaks and faces
a deep red. Mesquite thickets, a point of concentration for many

forms of desert life, are not suitable for quail unless other plants
are present too; mesquite beans are too hard to crack open and
the leaves are not fleshy enough. But wherever there are plants
with fruits or with fleshy leaves, coveys will gather. They may
number hundreds of birds, although the usual range is from
twenty to fifty. On Tiburón Island off the Sonoran coast,
Gambel's quail live as far as six miles from freestanding water,
a distance that is at least three times their possible daily range
if they depended on drinking. Yet heat seems to pose no
particular problem, even at nesting time. Patterns of plant
growth are responsible. Thundershowers pound the island during the hot summer weeks, assuring ephemeral puddles for
drinking. More important, they initiate plant growth, and soon
tender new sprouts let coveys that missed the direct wetness of
a shower reap its benefits nonetheless.

Owls, which are nighttime-active and therefore ready-
equipped to beat the heat, evidently solve their moisture problem
through succulent diet just as quail and roadrunners do. Joe
Marshall reports watching flammulated owls feed almost like
goatsuckers, flying after insects at dusk and dawn. They would
swoop out from one perch and land on a new one. At the same
time, whiskered owls were hunting by fluttering nonstop through
the treetops to pick caterpillars, crickets, beetles, and moths from
the foliage. And screech owls were pouncing onto lizards and
mice which they tore apart with talons and beak. They also
made easy catches such as insects, and in the case of large moths
simply folded them double and gulped them whole.

The most ingenious of the desert owls in hunting prey must
surely be elf owls, as watched by Lewis Walker from a photography blind several years ago. He found that the adults
specialized in scorpions as food for their young and always
delivered them with the stinger removed or at least crushed.
Insects and spiders also were brought to the nestlings, but no
flesh. Unlike most owls, elf owls fly with wings swishing, so
noisily that Walker could hear them coming from twenty feet
away. Probably this alerts small vertebrates and sends them

scurrying, whereas invertebrates, less sensitive to sound, can be caught. Noisy or not, elf owls are adept hunters. They catch prey on the ground, swoop after it on the wing, and also have a third approach, which Walker discovered when he rigged photographic lights close to a flowering agave that the birds were visiting regularly. He had noticed that adults with nestlings would head directly for the agave as soon as they emerged from their hole in a saguaro, and with the help of the lights he saw why. The birds would veer up on approaching the agave, then grasp the underside of one of its sprays of blossoms and hang there upside down, clinging with talons and beating their wings. A cloud of insects would rain out, whereupon the birds simply circled and took their pick to supply the hungry progeny in the nest. As for the intrusion of lights, the owls not only got used to the illumination but quickly capitalized on it. They learned to perch on the reflectors and pick off insects attracted to the beams.

Carnivorous desert mammals, including kit foxes, badgers, bobcats, and coyotes also draw body moisture from the juices of the animals they feed on. They drink if they can but often must survive without daily access to freestanding water. Kit foxes make the nocturnal rounds of their territories by trotting systematically back and forth like trained hunting dogs, seeking likely spots for prey, stalking and chasing and killing. When there are pups to feed, the adults face an enormous task. Based on laboratory tests where meat was freely available in unlimited quantity, a family of five pups can eat an average of nearly a pound every twenty-four hours throughout their two months of infancy. This means that each growing ball of tawny fluff can gulp down fully half as much food as is needed by an adult. Supplying the family must require a total catch of 500 or 600 kangaroo rats and ground squirrels and other rodents, allowing for bone and hair and including the parents' own requirements. For kit foxes, which themselves weigh scarcely more than four pounds when mature (the smallest of the North American foxes), this is a considerable feat. Evidently they rely more on hearing

Kit fox

augmented by smell than on vision. Their ears are notably large, like sound scoops raised and swiveled to catch clues for transmittal to the brain for evaluation. Lew Walker reports testing their hearing while camped at San Felipe, Baja California, in the quiet days before its invasion by American sports fishermen. He found that he could toss bits of food past their eyes without their seeming to notice, yet as soon as they heard a piece land they would leap in its general direction, then locate the exact spot by sniffing. Even the tiny plop of pieces of a pancake, inaudible to the human ear, was enough to coax the bravest among the kit foxes into coming quite close.

Desert carnivores often show an opportunistic ability to devour any sort of moist food they happen across. Talking about coyotes, J. Frank Dobie points out that their favorite food is anything they can chew. Among items found in scat he lists skunk bones, peccary bones, rabbits, mice, kangaroo rats, paper, grapes, rubber from a tire, horned lizards, centipedes, a harness buckle, grass, mesquite beans, bird feathers, bird eggs, rattlesnakes, honey, fish, ants, peanuts, and cactus fruit that sometimes had been rolled on the ground to remove thorns and other times had been swallowed spines and all. Such omnivorous tastes are perhaps more frequent in the desert than in gentler lands where being selective is more practical. Peccaries basically are plant-eaters, feeding heavily on cactus pads and fruits but also supplementing their diet by rooting out and devouring all the lizards and insects they happen to find. Hognose skunks, ringtails and coatis follow a similar pattern: they snuffle along the relatively favored courses of dry washes at night or crisscross the pine-oak forests of the desert upland, scratching and digging and pouncing in accord with whatever opportunity presents itself.

Antelope ground squirrels feed mostly on green leaves, which, dry as they seem much of the year, nonetheless average more than half water. This proportion can be increased by feeding at dawn, while dew covers leaf surfaces and the leaves are transpiring freely and in their own most moist state. How some animals manage to maintain water balance is something of a mystery even so — antelope ground squirrels perhaps more than other American desert species because they remain undaunted no matter how intense the heat. George Bartholomew and Jack Hudson measured daily evaporative water losses from these squirrels' skin and lungs equal to 15 percent of the total water in their bodies. The amount seems a high daily turnover, but apparently green food augmented by insects, lizards, and carrion sustains the animals well. Certainly drinking water is totally unavailable for them much of the time.

In their study of the eland and the oryx Taylor and Lyman found that even such large animals could get along on the water found in desert vegetation, acacia leaves for the eland and grasses and shrubs for the oryx. The acacia proved a surprising 58 percent water, measured during drought. By calculating the volume an eland normally eats and multiplying by the moisture thus supplied, the professors found that the theoretical moisture need of the animal and its actual intake were in flawless balance. For the oryx the question was more

Ringtail

Hognose
skunk

puzzling. The grasses and shrubs they browse are dry enough to fall apart at the touch. Their moisture content measured only 1 percent, far too low to sustain the animal; yet thriving they were, and drinking they were not. The answer lies in the oryx's feeding at night. Leaves of desert plants can collect water from the air even when no dew forms. This is because as the night temperatures drop, the relative humidity of the air goes up but that of the leaves and twigs remains unaffected. The vegetation is therefore proportionately dry compared to the air and can absorb moisture; the same leaf that registers only 1 percent water at noon may have a water content as high as 42 percent by midnight. This allows the oryx to greatly increase the water content of its food simply by waiting till after sundown to graze.

Handy as it sounds, this dependence solely on the moisture in food has the disadvantage of added salts to dispose of at the same time there is a vital body need for water conservation. This is true whether food comes from insects and animal flesh or from vegetation. The researchers working with roadrunners at Davis noticed salty crusts around the birds' nares during the simulated hot desert conditions when no drinking water was being supplied. They found that sodium was secreted through a nasal gland capable of producing a concentration six times what the kidneys could handle. Under moderate conditions with water freely available this system was not used; salts were handled by the kidneys. But when water was not readily available the nasal glands took over.

Chuckwalla lizards also handle salts through their noses and seem able to cope with potassium as easily as chloride, the only terrestrial species known so far to have this capacity. They need it. Their feeding territories often are in alkaline soil where every leaf is high in salts. Chuckwallas on some of the Gulf of California islands illustrate this. They feed heavily on pickleweed, a plant that grows in soil which may be crusted white with salt. Bean-shaped glands acting as auxiliary kidneys are located in the nasal passages. Their discharge flows through ducts and collects just inside the nostrils; whereupon the lizards simply sneeze it out. Various marine birds have similar salt glands.

Somehow Savannah sparrows carry the process further. They have no nasal glands yet can safely drink salt water and thereby greatly increase acceptable living sites, since desert marshes and springs often are brackish. These birds can actually drink ocean water if need be, as is the case on many of the islands in the Gulf where no fresh water is available. According to one investigator the Savannah sparrows excrete an amount of salt per day equivalent to 2 percent of their body weight, an enormous amount since the full load has to be handled by the kidneys.

For kangaroo rats, too, an efficient kidney is a big part of the desert success story. They never drink, do not utilize dew, or even feed on succulent vegetation. Their diet is dry seeds and nothing more; yet they thrive, "both fireproof and waterproof," as the early-day naturalist William Hornaday put it. Studies show a population density of from one to seven or eight Merriam kangaroo rats (one of the smaller species) per acre, each ranging over one or two thousand square yards as home territory. Translating this into terms of seeds typically obtainable as food is not thoroughly possible because data are not available, but Lloyd P. Tevis, of the University of California desert research station at Deep Creek found a total production of one and one-half billion seeds per acre in the California desert, including all plant species present. The potential yield for a few individual plant species has also been calculated, assuming a "usual" rainfall, flowering, and setting of seed. For bunchgrass the yield per acre per season approaches thirteen pounds of seeds. Yucca comes next among the plants inventoried, with ten pounds of seeds, and creosote bush has a production of eight pounds per acre.

Given an average territory this would mean seed for a Merriam kangaroo rat equivalent to sixty times its own body weight from creosote bush alone, the most widespread single plant species of the North American desert. Food clearly would not be a problem. The question of water is another matter, one that has been well detailed by the classic work of Knut Schmidt-Nielsen and Charles Vorhies and others. Seeds alone have been proved adequate as the source of all the water kangaroo rats need — an "all" that actually is astonishingly little, so small that it must be hoarded in every possible way. Staying underground during the day is one readily noticeable means of conserving body water, although obviously not effective enough to be the whole answer. Through a long series of separate experiments Schmidt-Nielsen and Vorhies sought understanding. In one study several kangaroo rats were kept in the laboratory for seven weeks, fed only dry oats and barley and given no water. If they endured the desert by tolerating unusual body dehydration, this should establish the fact; yet at the end of the seven weeks their tissues measured 67 percent water, which is usual for mammals. The next question was whether kangaroo rats might somehow store body water for later use during deprivation. To test this, separate groups were fed diets ranging from moist to dry; no differences in body moisture could be detected. Another possibility was that they might hold body wastes for later excretion when water was again reasonably available. African lungfish do this, burying in the mud of a dried marsh and letting urea build up in their blood to be eliminated when rain fills the pond and reactivates the normal metabolism of the fish. However, the kangaroo rats' waste concentrations after two months showed no variation regardless of diet.

The pieces of the puzzle now included the facts that kangaroo rats do not endure unusual drying out, or store water within their body, or concentrate waste for later excretion. Yet they neither drink nor need moist food. Their only possible source of water had to be what forms as a by-product from the digestion of seeds. Such water is part of digestion for all animals as food is chemically separated into constituents and atoms of hydrogen and oxygen are recombined into molecules of water. However for most species the volume of this metabolic water is of negligible value in relation to the total amount needed. What distinguishes kangaroo rats is not the production of metabolic water but the ability to subsist on it without any additional source of moisture.

Seeds are the ideal food for such a regimen because they are starchy, and starch takes less oxygen to metabolize than fat does and also uses less water in the elimination of nitrogenous waste than protein does. Regardless, the net amount of water from the digestion of seeds is so minute that kangaroo rats have to be exceedingly miserly in how they spend it, else they could not survive. Staying underground throughout the day avoids the need for evaporative cooling, a vital savings of body water. In addition, nasal passages are about 45°F., which is considerably lower than the overall body temperature. This provides a reclamation system. Air exhaled from the lungs cools as it passes through the nose; and having cooled it no longer can hold all the water vapor that it picked up on leaving the lungs. Droplets condense on the inside of the nose and are absorbed back into the body. The water thus regained is infinitesimal, but it is important in the tight economy of the kangaroo rat.

Savings in the elimination of body wastes are even more important. The kangaroo rat kidney is about the most efficient in the world, producing urine with more than 20 percent urea, four or five times greater than the concentration of human urine. Solid waste also is handled efficiently. Feces are exceptionally dry and small in amount, and after expelling them a kangaroo rat often picks up the pellets and swallows them, gaining a second chance at digestion and also profiting from vitamins produced by bacteria as the fecal matter passed through the lower intestine the first time. Furthermore, the habit recirculates a tiny amount of water.

Curiously, fat serves as a reservoir of water as well as of energy. Camels and Brahma cattle, a successful desert breed, have fatty humps, and the tails of fat-tailed sheep and several species of lizards are heavy with adipose tissue. Perhaps comparable among humans is the steatopygia of African Bushmen, the enormously (and stylishly) fat buttocks of the women. Such deposits serve as a store of potential water because when fat is oxidized within the body each gram produces slightly more than its own weighT in water, a greater amount than is produced by the oxidation of either starch or protein. Fat tissue also has value as a reservoir because of its capacity at least in some cases for the direct storage of water. Experimenting with the desert lizard *Varanus grislus,* Robert Chew injected distilled water into the skin in amounts equivalent to 5 to 15 percent of body weight — enormous quantities, which if translated into human terms are as if a 170-pound man were given injections of from one to three gallons at a time. Even so, the lizards formed no extra urine. Instead, tissues throughout their bodies held the water (except for spinal cord, brain, bone, and skin tissue). Fat held by far the most; it registered a dramatic 20 percent gain in weight. Seemingly this indicates a means of maintaining water balance during drought, and it may prove the basis for fat's fame as an internal canteen. More work needs to be done before anybody can say.

Internal reservoirs have been suspected for at least two thousand years, especially in the case of camels. If it isn't the hump of a camel reported as a virtual water tank it is some other part of its anatomy. Pliny knew of sacs lining the walls of a camel's rumen, which is the first of three stomachs, and he wrote that the function must be to store water. The idea prevails, and reports still suggest the sacs as a means of salvation for thirst-crazed Saharan men. Yet anatomy alone makes this impossible. The musculature of the pouches consists of straight bands instead of sphincters, the only type of muscles that could close them off into watertight compartments. Schmidt-Nielsen once investigated the rumens of thirteen butchered camels and found only watery, greenish, well-chewed food both in the main chambers and in the wall sacs. He did find the sac tissue dotted with literally millions of glands that produce a copious salivalike flow, a discovery that led to speculation that the function of the sacs might be to provide additional gland surface. This would increase production of the fluid believed to be indispensable for digestion. The liquid is foul-smelling, but could be swallowed by a man who was thirsty enough; and it might save his life.

Natives in the waterless Empty Quarter of Arabia drink the rumen liquid of addax antelope as an emergency source of water. They place the pulpy rumen contents on a lattice of sticks supported by the horns of the beast's severed head, and then let the fluid drip down onto the hide spread beneath.

Even without a built-in canteen, camels are remarkably adapted to the desert — so famously so that under orders of Jefferson Davis, at the time Secretary of War, two shiploads were brought to the United States in 1856 and 1857. Price: $30,000 for 60 animals. When water is scarce camels adapt in several ways. They pass even drier feces than kangaroo rats do, and can let their body temperature rise as high as 108.6°F., which narrows the gap between body temperature and air temperature and thereby lessens the demand for sweat. They go as long as a week without water if need be, and their size lets them carry heavy loads. The usefulness of camels in surveying the desert West, developing wagon roads, and hauling freight seemed worth testing, and both single-hump Arabian camels and two-humped dromedaries were imported by the government. Private operators also brought in the great beasts, using them to pack mine machinery in the High Sierra of California as well as in the desert south as far as Sonora. There also was a brief, abortive use of camels to carry freight from Laredo, Texas, to Mexico City. During the heyday of the experiment, camel trains vied with mule trains in hauling. The strange gawky animals appeared as a new basketry motif among desert Indian women, and were outlined in stones on a barren hillside, a giant effigy six or eight times life size.

The experiments were successful. A desert newspaper account published in 1861 comments that "where the trail was so rough that the mules were bothered, the camels went forward without hesitation, browsing from side to side as though they were at home." Another early report mentions that the camels "feed happily on cactus and sagebrush and can travel 100 miles a day or even 150." Despite this success, the end came in the 1880s. Camels were practical in America but not popular. They spooked horses, mules, and oxen; and few Americans were trained in handling them correctly, or were willing to learn. It was easier to resent camels as intruders than to bother to work with them. They were turned loose or sold. Several ended up packing ore and freight in British Columbia during gold strikes in the Cariboo country, and one is said to have roamed free in Beacon Hill Park, Victoria. As late as the 1950s, when we moved to Organ Pipe Cactus National Monument, professors at the University of California asked us to keep an eye out for feral camels. Not that they really expected any, but there just might have been some in the remote reaches of the Arizona-Sonora borderlands, a region little visited in those days before the advent of dune buggies and all-terrain vehicles. We saw none.

The last wild camel known with certainty dates to 1894, when one was lassoed north of Yuma by a Mexican vaquero carrying mail from a mine. About the only physical evidence remaining of the camels is a gleaming skeleton housed at the Smithsonian and a bronze camel bell of beautifully clear tone at the Southwest Museum in Los Angeles. The bell had been given to the desert poet and novelist Mary Austin by General Edward F. Beale, who as an Army lieutenant commanded one of the first surveys to utilize the camels. Only these two tokens remain, plus the fossil footprints of the ancient ancestors of the camels, for the fact is that the nineteenth-century "imports" actually had American origins. Camels roamed the Southwest for millennia before the last ice age and the imprint of their broad, flat, hoofless feet remains in desert stone today.

The idea of internal water reservoirs does have basis in fact, but the reptile family is where to look, not mammals. For example, chuckwalla lizards captured toward the end of the plant-growing season may have a pair of sacs filled with fluid lying along the sides of their abdomen. Those that live under the most severely arid conditions, such as Isla Angel de la Guarda or San Esteban off the Baja California coast, have large sacs extending all the way from lower jaw to groin. Evidently such sacs belong to the lymph system, since their fluid is a clear amber color and clots on standing. Specimens captured after long drought invariably have empty sacs, which suggests that the fluid had been used up in supplying body moisture. To check this, laboratory chuckwallas were given lettuce and other moist food to simulate the favorable conditions of the field growing season. Their sacs slowly filled to capacity. The animals then were switched to fasting, all food and water withheld, and the sacs gradually emptied.

Desert tortoises and various toads also store water in their bodies. Australian Aborigines who live in waterless parts of the Outback, will dig out toads and carry them on crosscountry treks as readymade canteens. Desert tortoises are similarly endowed as living reservoirs. Vernon Bailey writing in 1928 about the Galápagos Islands, commented that by squeezing a tortoise "a good drink that might save human life could invariably be obtained." The amount ran as high as half a pint at a time. In these cases the liquid is urine of a special dual-purpose type unknown among mammals. It holds wastes in chemical suspension instead of in solution, and thereby leaves the liquid portion of the urine available as a moisture reserve for body needs.

Desert tortoise

The ultimate dependence of life upon water belongs in that large category of body needs so basic they seldom are consciously considered; but in the desert the problem of supply accentuates awareness that only a frail shield of moisture divides life from death. Water is requisite, whether or not readily at hand, and any means of getting it is valuable. A few species can nose moisture out and dig to it. In the Serengeti, elephants somehow sense underground wetness in times of drought, and stomp out shallow wells in dried stream beds. In the sandy mesquite hummocks of northern Death Valley we once found a similar well, dug by a coyote. We were driving and walking, enjoying a slow sampling of a small area much richer and more varied in life than a first glance can suggest. In three days our zigzags probably had scarcely totaled fifty miles. We had found a Shoshone Indian wickiup of mesquite branches, probably abandoned about fifty years before, and also two or three chipping sites where much earlier Indian toolmakers had sat and whacked obsidian and chert into points and drills and knives. We had watched kangaroo rats leaping in the starlight as we lay in our sleeping bags. And we had kept running count to see how many species of newly sprouting seedlings we could find, for this was New Year's and faint green was beginning to herald the yellows and reds and purples to come in another few weeks when petals would unfold. On one of these seedling strolls we chanced on the coyote hole. It was hollowed at the base of a head-high dune that had a scraggly mesquite growing from its top, and it reached nearly three feet into the sand, like a slightly off-vertical funnel about fifteen inches across at the top and tapering to three or four inches. Animal tracks of several kinds converged into worn paths as they neared the lip of the well, and fresh claw marks gouged the moist sides. In the bottom of the hole was water about an inch deep.

This ability to dig to water is so well recognized that the place name Coyote Wells appears on many desert maps. Locations may be where the water table lies fairly close to the surface, as was probably true of the coyote hole we found; or the excavations may be into special "sand tanks," which are one of the desert's hidden sources of water. These form when flood runoff carries a heavy load of sand, filling a cavity and producing an ephemeral reservoir. The presence of sand in the runoff is essential to the formation of the tanks. If floodwater is clear or with only a small sand load, they cannot form. The water may pool, of course, but it soon evaporates. Yet if sand and water combined are swept into a cavity, the moisture usually lasts a considerable time. The upper sand quickly dries, and the interstitial spaces between grains prevent the water from rising by capillarity and evaporating from the surface. Consequently, the lower sand holds its water, sealed against contamination and protected from the bloom of algae that often fouls an open-air pond. Coyotes readily reach such water sources, kicking aside sand and gaining access to the saturated subsurface layers. In summer these drinking holes are often vital for coyotes and for other creatures that come upon them, including man.

Among birds, those incapable of long daily flights to water or of tolerating great moisture loss within their bodies must restrict their summer range to the immediate reach of water or else leave the desert. The bird lists of desert locations from Death Valley to Tucson to Guaymas may total 200 or 300 species; but of these only about 10 percent will be year-round residents. The others pass through, using the favorable seasons and moving on: hummingbirds, flycatchers, thrushes, vireos, warblers, tanagers, grosbeaks, buntings, sparrows. Wave after wave and species after species the majority come and go. A few, such as mourning doves and white-winged doves, come for the summer rather than the winter, relying on their wings to see them through. They must drink daily but can travel as far as twenty or thirty miles to commute between their brooding, feeding, and watering grounds. They arrive at a waterhole by the score, and produce a soft brown cloud as they flutter for position. In just five minutes they may drink an amount equivalent to 18 percent of body weight — the same as if a 160-pound man were to swallow three and a half gallons of water.

White-winged
dove

The anatomy of doves' throats, unlike that of most birds, lets them suck up water through the bill and swallow it without raising their heads. They will drink more than they actually need to replace daily water loss, up to twice their actual physiological requirement, as if preparing in advance for the coming bout with the day's heat. This surplus feeds their young, and since doves are avid breeders (raising from three to six nestfuls of offspring per year) this is a need that often lasts all summer. Both male and female doves produce a milky secretion in their crops chemically similar to mammals' milk and equally ideal as a source of food and water for the young. They pump this fluid from their bodies into the gaping mouths of their hatchlings, a liquid diet with about 15 percent protein and 6 to 12 percent butterfat. It is so nutritious that the young birds develop fast enough to fly only about ten days after hatching. The whole process from when the egg is laid until the bird leaves the nest takes less than a month. Then the adults start all over again.

Bighorn sheep are another of the desert's creatures with ability to survive by commuting to water, and drinking every few days is adequate in their case. Nevertheless, they face a threat more formidable than the desert itself, and one to which there seemingly is no adaptation: their ancestral watering holes have become man's watering holes to such an extent that experts worry about the future of bighorn sheep. Formerly they grazed all of the western continent from Alaska to Mexico and inland as far as the Rockies and the badlands of the Little Missouri and Platte Rivers. They were as common as deer. Juan Mateo Manje, writing in 1607 about an Indian village near the present town of Florence, Arizona, mentioned a pile of 100,000 sheep horns stacked as some form of communication with the gods, probably a trap to filter the influence of evil spirits from the area and assure good weather. Far earlier, Pedro de Castañeda de Naçera, chronicling Coronado's march of 1540, made the first written mention of the species other than Indian petroglyphs chipped into rock. He told of finding a sheep horn on the bank of the Gila River, and proceeded to exaggerate about it excitedly: "It was a fathom [six feet] long," he wrote, "and as thick as the base of a man's thigh. From its shape it looked more like the horn of a he-goat than any other animal. It was worth seeing!"

Bighorn sheep are oldtimers on the continent. They probably came from Asia via the Bering land bridge along with woolly mammoths and bison and man himself. There are two distinct species: thinhorn sheep and bighorn sheep. The former include the northern White (or Dall) sheep and Stone sheep. The latter are spread throughout terrain so diverse that they have developed into distinct races: Rocky Mountain sheep, Nelson bighorn, California bighorn, Mexican bighorn, peninsular bighorn (belonging only to Baja California), and the now-extinct Audubon bighorn of the Dakotas. Vast as the desert is, the strongholds of sheep there, as elsewhere, have been threatened, first by turn-of-the-century mining booms and now by off-the-road recreation vehicles from Jeeps to dune buggies to all-terrain vehicles. The hunting of bighorn sheep posed a threat until recent years, but is now illegal in California and Mexico and allowed only by limited permit in Arizona. However, water still holds a final key to survival or extermination, and versatile as desert bighorn are this problem looms large. They can feed on the stiff twigs of bushes such as Mormon tea and wire lettuce, although they prefer grass. They relish the dry tops of brittlebush and the slight saltiness of desert holly. Thistle is acceptable. They even eat cottontop and barrel cactus, so armored by thorns that a man needs a strong machete to cut them open. Food is no problem for bighorn, but water is.

For eight years Ralph and Florence Welles studied sheep in Death Valley, totaling 1700 hours with the animals actually in sight through binoculars and cameras, plus uncounted hours of searching and of bedding down virtually with the bands to wait for dawn and a chance to watch some more. They came to know their subjects well enough to name them — Full Curl, Old Mama, Mischief, The Stranger. Certain peculiarities gave the clues. The ram Full Curl was "potbellied, but still sleek and intimidated by no one." Old Mama was "old [and] runny-nosed but tough and worldly wise in bighorn ways." Another ewe, Peel, "got her name because of the peculiar quality of the gray of her coat. She and her lamb lived somewhere on Pyramid Peak and came down across Paleo Mesa now and then on their way to water at Navel Spring." And so on, through forty-eight others, as recorded in the official account, *The Bighorn of Death Valley.*

The study's approach was to watch and note every possible action of the sheep; which ram courted what ewe; how many times a day a sheep urinated; how long one stood motionless (over an hour, staring intently but never moving); how often two rams in rut butted heads (forty-eight times in one day, with a great *clonk* reverberating into the quiet desert air each time). Anything and everything became the researchers' business, and as a result they began to formulate for the first time a real understanding of how the desert's most elusive creature was faring. Often they followed feeding bands. Other times they set up at known waterholes and waited.

It is distance to freestanding water that determines the roaming of bighorn. So long as they can drink every three to five days sheep get along well even under drought conditions. In fact, they sometimes fare better than other desert creatures. Through one particularly dry summer the Welleses reported "no food in the canyon washes or on the mountain wall above them . . . In Wildrose Canyon we found no flowers, no insects or birds, no lizards, rodents, cottontails or jackrabbits. One dead coyote, reported to us 5 days earlier, had already been picked clean when we found it. As we approached the carcass, a live coyote in very poor condition got to its wobbly legs and made off. Miners throughout the area reported the least wildlife they had seen in many years. Yet on November 25 with the two-year drought still unbroken, we observed 18 bighorn at Navel Spring in optimum condition."

The way bighorn feed contributes to this success during drought. They nip a few bites in passing rather than eating a plant to the ground. Bushes recover quickly from such browsing and groundcover annuals receive only light trampling. During a dry cycle when the trip from waterhole to forage has length-ened, sheep tend to travel single file through areas where the food is exhausted, but on reaching the feeding grounds they spread out and nibble at random. As the days of summer grow hotter and drier and water supplies dwindle, the need for water increases. If possible, sheep will drink every day. The rigors of the environment are at a peak and so, ironically, are the demands of the animals' own systems. Rut is on. For the males, especially, this involves an enormous additional outpouring of energy, for they must both chase ewes and challenge other rams. They may be literally on the run across rough ground at temperatures in the 120's. The Welleses watched one ram chase a ewe for three days, often at thirty miles per hour but with no apparent lessening of energy or interest and with no time out to drink.

One noon they watched a ram approach a spring and, checking the records, realized he had not come to drink there during the last two days. Either he had been without water for that time or he was now trekking in from another waterhole, at least eight very rough miles distant. The new arrival, Tabby, was met by a ram already at the spring which had finished watering and was resting in the shade. For two hours, with the temperature at 113°F., the rams blasted each other, rearing, aiming, and hitting horns forty times. Then, their hormones satisfied, they separated. Tabby drank for twelve minutes; ate a little grass; rested until the day had cooled to 102°, and set out briskly up the wash.

Bighorn survive partly through this ability to "take it": to extend themselves regardless of circumstance and to recover quickly. When they finally are able to drink they swell out the way dried prunes do; their flesh rehydrates and their vigor is restored. The Welleses first realized this as they watched an emaciated ewe and lamb drink. The legs of the pair as they approached the waterhole were spindly, with knobby joints and stringy muscles. Their coats were rough and their hipbones, ribs, and skulls lay under drawn and shriveled skin. As the sheep drank their sides filled out and their bellies distended. The lamb

Bighorn ram and ewes

seemed almost too full to walk when the two finally moved off to the shade of a mesquite to rest. Half an hour later the siesta was finished and mama and the lamb began to climb the peak that stands behind this particular spring. "I was watching [them] climb, briskly, easily, despite the grueling slope and the gathering heat," Ralph Welles writes in his report, "and I was marveling at how two animals in such poor condition could do this when I suddenly realized that they were no longer in poor condition! The potbellies were gone, the legs were no longer spindly, and the muscles were smooth and rounded beneath the glistening hides of animals in perfect health. Now I suddenly realized that the apparent emaciation of their bodies when they had first appeared at the spring half an hour before was a symptom not of bad health, but of acute dehydration."

If water is available, even every few days, bighorn will fare well. This is true no matter how hot the summer. But water pockets evaporate and springs get choked. Earthquakes probably cause some of the loss, although evidence is difficult to assess, and floods roaring downslope after a cloudburst often block seeps and small springs by burying them under yards of gravel and rock. In the Death Valley mountains this happened to three springs during the course of the Welleses' study — 3 out of a total of 289 water sources where small pools form at least sometimes. At this rate several springs must be lost each year in the Southwest desert as a whole, when one considers the frequency of cloudbursts. Of course many will be uncovered again some day later when floodwaters strip off detritus instead of depositing a new load of it; but that "some day" may not come for centuries, and unfortunately bighorn sheep are not flexible about dispersing into new range. They are traditionalists, making the same rounds of foraging and watering that their forebears made, and passing on the same routes and ranges to their offspring. Ewes do not even drive off their yearlings as a new lambing season approaches, and the young therefore do not explore and claim new range. Rather than shift territory, bighorn make do with whatever is left; and if it is inadequate, they die.

Consequently, each waterhole increases greatly in value under present-day pressures. Man and sheep do not mix, and since bighorn can spy a motionless man a mile and a half away, they frequently drift off with their thirst unslaked rather than risk going to a waterhole to drink. Throughout the late 1800s and early 1900s mining boomed as riches and supposed-riches were discovered in desert mountains. By the depression of the 1930s desperate men headed into the hinterlands to mine as a livelihood, not so much because it was promising but because alternatives were so few. Camps and mills sprouted wherever there was water, and this included the wildest, most forbidding reaches of the desert. Laws permitted staking a claim at a spring, and that meant a place in which to live with water to drink and perhaps enough to also grow vegetables or fruit. A show of ore was almost beside the point. Men claimed the desert, and bighorn sheep became so hard pressed that extinction loomed in many parts of their range. Following World War II mining fell off, but jeeping and camping replaced it from the bighorns' standpoint.

Further competition has come from a burgeoning population of wild burros. These are imports. Their distant progenitors were the wild Nubian asses of the African desert, domesticated by the Moors before the time of Christ. Their immediate ancestors are the donkeys brought to the New World by the Spanish. Once arrived on this continent burros helped to carry the flag and the cross into the northern frontier, and when history rolled back the Spanish tide, the Mexican successors continued to use burros as pack animals. Many escaped or were abandoned, disappearing into remote desert washes and canyons. American prospectors and miners next used burros, and more animals escaped and were abandoned. Today nobody needs burros, but their herds have built to an estimated total of 8000 roaming ten western states. They run wild, cropping shrubs and grasses to the roots, churning and trampling the soil. They are easily in evidence, their hoofmarks plain, their droppings large, their voices loud. Bighorn sheep, on the other hand, are seldom seen and their sign is not widespread. Burros have been increasing and bighorn decreasing, and for a time it looked as if the shaggy little asses were going to take the final blame for the bighorns' troubles. Management programs were launched against burros to eliminate them or at least to reduce their numbers radically.

Even in the roughest and hottest desert, burros can thrive impressively well. In studies they have proved capable of walking fifteen miles without water, the thermometer at 104°F., yet their body temperature was low and they showed no stress. They can lose body moisture equal to 30 percent of their weight, then drink all the water they need to completely rehydrate in just a few minutes, sucking and swallowing so fast they scarcely take time to draw breath. In one study a burro was clocked gulping down more than five gallons of water in two and one-half minutes. So far as known, only a camel can better this sort of a record. They can go twice as long without drinking as a burro can, and lose twice as much proportionate body weight without damage.

As might be expected of so successful an introduced species, burros compete with bighorn for food, water, and space. This creates a severe problem in an environment where balances are already inherently delicate. Expert opinion concluded that the conflict focused especially at oases. Burros generally come to drink at night and bighorn during the day, so it was not so much of a matter of competing presence as that burros supposedly fouled springs to the point that bighorn are forced away. Ralph and Florence Welles jeeped and hiked to check actual field evidence on the issue instead of inferring it — and they found the assumptions wrong. To be sure, burro droppings lay near springs where there were no bighorn droppings, and square yards nearby might be churned to mud by the drinking, fighting, and mating of the burros. Nevertheless, seeing "evidence" is not the same as reading it right. The burro droppings rarely were *in* the water, but close by it. Contamination could not be the singularly determining factor it was held to be. The brownish color and stench of many springs thought to come from burro

Wild burros

urine was found equally strong at springs in the Funeral Mountains east of Death Valley, where there are no burros. Chemicals within the earth were responsible. As for bighorn sign, it was scarce both at springs and away from them. The Welleses' notes began to lengthen: "The Nelson bighorn leaves remarkably few droppings, apparently using up a great percentage of their food material . . . The dark-brown to black exterior lubricant [on the droppings] will dry in 10 minutes, and the entire pellet can be pulverized to dust, leaving no moisture or discoloration and very little, if any, odor on the fingers."

Observations began to turn to how sunshine, wind, ground salts, and burro trampling affect sheep pellets, and the trouble at the waterholes started to change appearance. The answer to the specific conflict over springs proved as simple as the fact that bighorn sign is inconspicuous to begin with and tends to vanish quickly, whereas burro droppings and tracks are more plentiful and more persistent. The two animals share water while

the supply lasts. Forage comes closer to being a crucial problem: burros have adapted so well to the American desert that in places they could eat themselves as well as sheep out of a future and at the same time threaten the well-being of quail, certain lizards, and small mammals, and also eliminate a few plant species. Their pressure is especially keen close to waterholes, where wholesale feeding, trampling, and contending for females may destroy the cover needed for protection and nesting by birds and small mammals. Cottonwood trees, the green sentinels of the desert traditionally marking a spring, are so tasty that they become endangered where burros are rampant. The new shoots of seedlings and saplings stand no chance of living long enough to replace mature trees. And in small garden areas such as Arcane Meadows, high on Telescope Peak overlooking Death Valley, burros' food choices are changing the vegetation. The continuation of bush lupine is threatened and phlox already is essentially eliminated except where it grows in the tangled centers of large shrubs, safely beyond reach.

The burros are too successful. The idea that they drive off bighorn sheep by fouling waterholes may not have proved true but there is no doubt about the range problems they create or their competition in dry years, when even a small band may gulp down all the water of a particular tinaja or the flow of a small spring and leave only death for other creatures unable to wait until the depleted source recovers or unable to range as far as the next drinking hole. As an introduced species, the burros inevitably fit disruptively into the balances of the American desert — much as does modern man, who also is too successful a competitor, too populous, and too dominant. Yet solutions are emerging. For a while warfare was directed against burros. They were hunted for meat and were rounded up wholesale for slaughter as pet food. Today they are protected against these activities in several states, including California and Arizona, and have been given special sanctuary in Saline Valley, on the northwestern edge of Death Valley, decreed by the state legislature as a burro refuge in 1957. Interlopers they are, but their appeal is immense and their tenure has been long. The burros are here to stay, although they need watching and controlling for the sake of all.

As for the water problem, another manipulation of the ancestral springs of bighorn sheep has begun, this one beneficial. "Guzzlers" (aprons of sheet metal) are being installed on certain key hillsides to catch rainwater and snowmelt and channel it into underground storage tanks. Pipes lead from the tanks to drinking containers. The romance of a primeval oasis suffers from such a contrivance, but bighorns, burros, birds, and all forms of wildlife are guzzling and surviving.

11. Man and Thirst

A MAN STRANDED IN THE DESERT will die in one day at 120°F. if he has no water. If he has one gallon, his life will be lengthened to two days. At least this is the rule of thumb. What actually happens will depend on several factors: Is he exerting himself or resting? Shirtless and in the sun, or clothed and in the shade? Panicky or calm?

The factor of attitude alone can override practically all else. Men have died of thirst in one day with the temperature scarcely above 110°F. although they have walked only a few miles and may even have canteens of water or jugs of lemonade left in their stalled car. They have expected death, and have found it; but in these cases death comes partly from the desert and even more from having crossed into the shadowland where physiological problems merge with psychological. By different attitude other men shape their destiny in the opposite way. Consider as an example the time that Lewis Walker was stranded in Mexico with a Russian colleague named Vladimir Solotov. Walker had offered to take Solotov to Isla de Guadalupe, one of the desert islands in the Gulf of California. Even the desert-wise can get caught without water, and, since prolonged bad weather isolated the two men, this is exactly what happened.

They decided to walk the twenty miles to the Mexican Government barracks at the north end of the island carrying fifty pounds of cameras and scientific gear. After twenty-two hours of walking, which included a 4000-foot climb, Solotov gave out. Walker pushed on. He reached the barracks, got help, and returned. By then the Russian had been two days and into the third without water at temperatures that fortunately had peaked at only a little above 100°F. He was painfully thirsty but calm and in reasonably good condition. His first question after drinking enough to regain speech was whether the gear and collections were safe — a question that marks Solotov as a scientist and also points to a force that can sustain life when physical factors alone mount against it: namely, a concern beyond oneself.

In the same vein, the botanist Robert Humphrey (in his late sixties at the time) tells of a car breakdown while he and his wife were studying boojums in Baja California. "The situation at this point begins to look a little serious," his diary records, "because it can be days or even weeks before anyone comes by on this road . . . " The next day he wrote: "I shall try a few more tests to see if I can locate the trouble, but am not particularly optimistic. Failing in that, I plan to collect some insects in a good stand of cirios about a mile up the road. We can then run some line transects while we wait." Instead of panicking, here was acceptance of the situation and of the opportunity for leisurely study that it unexpectedly made possible. The Humphreys had some water, and were careful about using it. They dealt rationally with the immediate physical plight, and then got on with matters of significance beyond themselves. After a day and a half, Humphrey decided to walk to help. The next morning a carload of campers happened by and of course offered help to Mrs. Humphrey. Together they found Dr. Humphrey, who had succeeded in reaching a small village.

This kind of a strong tie to an interest or a person has frequently proved decisive in desert survival. Saint-Exupéry, writing in *Wind, Sand and Stars,* speaks of seeing his wife's face float before him in the days following a plane crash in the Arabian Desert. His whole being cried out to surrender to the agony of thirst and die; but thinking of her he couldn't.

The opposite emotion of hate works equally well, or at least it was credited by a Mexican gold prospector for sustaining his life under what must surely be the most remarkable tale of survival in all the literature of the desert. He had done nothing right to save himself, and had no knowledge of survival techniques. He simply and stubbornly wanted to live in order to take revenge. And he did.

The case was described by W. F. McGee in a lengthy article titled "Desert Thirst As a Disease," published in 1906 in the *Interstate Medical Journal.* By surviving, the man had confounded all medical odds, although perhaps it should be added that present-day physiologists, while not discounting McGee's account, do comment that some of the descriptions are essentially anecdotal rather that scientific. The report concerns a man who wandered about in the harsh borderlands where Arizona and Sonora meet, surviving for nine days with essentially no water at temperatures in the nineties and low one-hundreds.

McGee, director of the St. Louis museum at the time and vice president of the National Geographic Society, was camped southwest of Yuma, Arizona, at a waterhole known to all early-day travelers through the region, Tinajas Altas. This was the only sure water between the spring at Quitobaquito, in what is now Organ Pipe Cactus National Monument, and the Colorado River, about 125 miles, distant. The route had been pioneered by the Jesuit priest Father Eusebio Kino to link the roads of Sinaloa and Sonora with California's El Camino Real, a road still leading from mission to mission between San Diego and San Francisco. However, this portion had become known as "El Camino del Diablo" because death claimed an appalling toll throughout the days of the padres and on into the era of prospectors stampeding for the 1849 goldfields in the Mother Lode. The worst stretch of all lay between Tule Well and Tinajas Altas, a distance of sixty miles. Graves here lined the way two or three to a mile, and there were forty clustered within the last half mile of Tinajas Altas. Most of these pathetically concentrated graves were — and are — on a knoll within sight of the pools of Tinajas Altas, for again and again men crept close to the salvation of water, then lacked the strength to climb to the first tinaja even though the slope is gentle. Or, succeeding in the climb but finding the pool dry, they failed in the struggle up the steepening slope to the next higher pool A later, stronger traveler would bury the pitiful remains.

McGee camped at Tinajas Altas from May through August 1905, devoting himself to meteorological observations and a study

Tinaja

of the effects of radiation on desert life. One noon two vaqueros reined in: Pablo Valencia, aged forty, and Jesús Ríos, sixty-five. They were en route to lost mines that Valencia had recently rediscovered, and were two days out from Yuma equipped with food for a week and four gallons of water. The pair stayed overnight at McGee's camp and rode out with the morning star.

The following night, Ríos returned. He had both horses, and reported that he had come for more water while Valencia continued on foot toward the mine carrying a partly full canteen. The two were to rendezvous the next day, but the meeting never took place and no amount of searching picked up any trace of Valencia. All believed him dead. Then at dawn on August 23, eight days after he had set out, Valencia reappeared. McGee and the Papago Indian who was camped with him awakened to a wild bellowing which in a half-dream McGee first mistook for the thirst-crazed cry of cattle.

"We ran down the trail . . .," McGee writes, "and on the arroyo sands, under an ironwood tree at the foot of the Mesita de los Muertos with its two-score cross-marked graves, came on the wreck of Pablo. He was stark naked. His formerly full-muscled legs and arms were shrunken and scrawny; his ribs ridged out like those of a starveling horse; his habitually plethoric abdomen was drawn in almost against his vertebral column; his lips had disappeared as if amputated, leaving low edges of blackened tissue . . . His eyes were set in a winkless stare . . . Even the freshest cuts [on arms and legs] were as so many scratches in dry leather, without a trace of blood or serum . . . Skin clung in a way suggesting shrunken rawhide used in repairing a broken wheel . . .

"We soon found him deaf to all but loud sounds, and so blind as to distinguish nothing save light and dark. The mucous membrane lining mouth and throat was shriveled, cracked and blackened, and his tongue shrunken to a mere bunch of black integument. His respiration was slow, spasmodic, and accompanied by a deep guttural moaning or roaring — the sound that had awakened us a quarter of a mile away . . . His extremities were cold as the surrounding air; no pulsation could be detected at wrists, and there was apparently little if any circulation beyond the knees and elbows . . ."

McGee and Papago Jose treated the pitiful husk of a man by sloshing water over his whole body and rubbing it into his limbs, which "absorbed it as greedily as a dry sponge, — or more exactly, as this season's rawhide." Within an hour Valencia could drink a little, and after two hours he could eat. In three, he could walk to camp with help. "By this time," McGee continues, "he had ingested and retained about 1½ ounces of whiskey, with 5 ounces of water, and 2 or 3 ounces of food. His external tissues were saturated and softened, circulation was restored sluggishly in his extremities, and his numerous wounds began to inflame or exude blood and serum. Articulation slowly returned, and in a cracked voice, breaking involuntarily from bass to falsetto, he began to beg pathetically for '*agua, agua,*' water . . ."

When Pablo Valencia could think and speak, he told his story. He had stretched his one-day supply of water to last for three days by gargling it without swallowing. He also had added his urine to the dwindling liquid within the canteen, and he had eaten insects and scorpions and chewed the leaves of agave plants, as the only sources of water he could find. Coyotes trailed him, and by the seventh day buzzards grew bold enough to come almost within hand reach whenever he lay gasping. He felt convinced that Jesús Ríos had deliberately abandoned him and gone on alone to claim the mine, and sheer mad wrath spurred him on with the one aim of living and knifing his betrayer.

Finally, on the afternoon of the eighth day, Valencia gave up. He uttered the prayer for the dying, made the sign of the cross, and felt that he died. But exceptionally cool night temperatures breathed awareness back into him; consciousness returned, and on the ninth morning he somehow sensed that McGee's camp was near. It was then that he bellowed.

Valencia was in what McGee defines as the third stage of thirst by this time. The first stage, common dryness, is the familiar cottony feeling in mouth and throat which accompanies great thirst. It builds a deep craving for liquid but can be satisfied simply by drinking. The second stage in McGee's terms — functional derangement — brings the onset of pathological disturbance. The tongue clings to the teeth; the ears drum annoyingly; the eyes smart; and hallucinations may begin. At this stage companions often quarrel and separate. Delirium comes, "wild and paralyzing in tenderfeet," as McGee describes it, "and in the desert habitué, concentrated on the central instinct of the trail and the way to water . . . [There is] talk, talk, talk, without pre-vision of the next sentence or memory of the last — and all the talk is of water in some of its inexpressibly captivating aspects."

Ranchmen had told McGee of being cut off without water when an earthquake had drained a spring, and through the entire ordeal they had murmured with longing and agony of water; of rivers they had forded, and the verdant bluegrass where one had been born, and a creek in flood which had drowned a friend; of watermelons growing and ripening, and a long discussion of what would be the ideal form for a canteen. In this stage thirst can be relieved by water — water swallowed by the quart, snuffled into the nostrils, dashed over face, head, neck, chest, arms. But if there is no water, saliva soon stops flowing and mucus dries. Lips retract, gums shrivel, eyelids stiffen, and articulate speech ends. Only moanings and bellowings continue. "Numbness creeps over the face, then over the hands and under the clothes, imparting a dry, rattling, husklike sensation so nerve-trying that few [can] longer resist the impulse to cast off clothing in an automatic outreaching for relief."

C. Hart Merriam, the renowned biologist who was a contemporary of McGee, had once experienced this grave second phase of thirst with its onset of mental disorientation. As McGee tells it, Merriam reported being impressed by the beating of his own heart and he had a conscious sense of the slow thickening of his blood. He felt its liquid portion being evaporated. He reached the point of blindness, yet kept mental discipline and enough sense of objectivity to observe and report the intensifying sensations within his body.

McGee himself had been without water once and had held on to himself only by constant effort, aided by a broken bit of mirror which he used to keep his tortured mind linked with the reflection of his "distorted face in which motionless eyes were set." The whole while his chief emotion was regret: "Keen quivering, crazy remorse at the memory of wantonly wasting — actually throwing away on the ground — certain cups of water in boyhood."

Water by the gallon can relieve this phase of thirst, but in the third stage — structural derangement — the tenderfoot quickly passes on to death, whereas a man hardened to the desert may go through "progressive mummification, beginning with the extremities and slowly approaching the vital organs." At this point the more mild symptoms recounted by McGee include the fingers mechanically wandering over the tumid tongue and lips, producing no sensation, the throat feeling plugged, and "lightning in the eyes and thunder in the ears." Thoughts become mere vague flashes of intelligence, although "a threadlike clue may be kept in sight by constant attention — the trail, the trail, the elusive, writhing, twisting trail that ever seeks to escape and needs the closest watching . . . The forbidding cholla, spiniest of the cruelly spined cacti is vaguely seen as a huge carafe surrounded by crystal goblets, and the flesh-piercing joints are greedily grasped and pressed against the face . . . The shadow of shrub or rock is [seen as] a pool in which the senseless wanderer digs desperately amid the gravel until nails and even fingers are torn off . . . In this final phase there is no alleviation, no relief save the end, in which senses cease and men die from without inward, as dies the desert shrub whose twigs and branches wither and blow away long before bole and root yield vitality."

So writes McGee. Desert thirst for him was more than an academic concern, as it inevitably is for anyone who lives or works in the desert for long without the modern shield of air-conditioning. You come to know the land as home and to see its beauties; but you never forget its awesome character. Without water, the silences of the desert, its vastness and emptiness and total indifference to the plight of any individual — man, animal, bird, plant — reach an intensity and dimension unparalleled in gentler lands. Yet, for all the hostility, both real and exaggerated, the desert evidently has been man's home for as long as the forest or the tundra. Every major racial division has been represented in the desert for millennia: Negroid peoples in Africa, Caucasoids in the Middle East and Africa, Australoids in Australia, and Mongoloids in Asia and America. (Indians are a mongolian people who crossed to America from Asia during various periods when glaciers held so much of the earth's water locked into ice that the level of the ocean stood lower, and land bridged the continents in the Bering Strait region.)

No particular blood type or body build seems better suited

Cholla

for desert life than any other, except possibly for the tendency toward low body weight and long arms and legs among native desert peoples. Not all investigators agree on this point, but if it ultimately proves true it will bear out accepted zoological principles. Bergson's rule states that similar or related animals are smaller-sized in warm regions than in cold, and Allen's rule is that long spindly legs and necks and tails, instead of short heavy ones, tend to characterize the animals of hot regions.

When it comes to skin color, no overall principle has yet been found to tie together all observable aspects. Dark-skinned peoples obviously belong to the desert, yet their pigmentation could be a disadvantage, since a dark surface will absorb the sun's heat more readily than a light one. On the other hand, pigment's capacity for screening ultraviolet rays may be of even greater importance; it may more than offset the apparent liability of absorbing heat. A study of Hawaiians was made to check on this point because they live and work together under the same conditions, yet offer widely varying skin hues. White-skinned peoples fared by far the worst. Their sweat glands showed much more damage from sunshine than was true for native Hawaiians or Orientals, or any mixture of races, and the rate of skin cancer was forty times greater for Caucasians than for darker-skinned people.

Any person who moves into the desert — regardless of his race — or who goes to work in a situation of intense heat such as a steel mill will make certain rapid adjustments to the stress of the new surroundings. Additional skin capillaries will develop, easing the circulation of blood at the surface of the body and thereby contributing to more efficient cooling. The kidneys will excrete slightly less salt, and the proportionate amount of salt lost in sweat will drop even more significantly. The rate of sweating will increase by as much as 20 percent, but no new sweat glands will develop. Somewhere between two and eight million of these tiny glands dot the skin of an average-sized adult, a greater number per unit of surface than for most other mammals. A curious aspect is a correlation between the number of functioning sweat glands and the climate of the area where the person was raised during the first two years of life. It is only during these early months that sweat glands become activated, and consequently how many are readied for life will depend on the environment experienced by the infant. Persons raised in a hot climate, no matter of what race, may have as many as four times the rate of active sweat glands of those born into a cold climate or living there as a baby or toddler. Nothing changes this basic physiological equipment; moving to a hot situation later in life does not increase the number of glands (nor does the opposite of moving to a cold climate reduce the number).

Primarily it is sweating that fits man for life in the desert. The human body temperature normally holds within a degree

Death Valley
basketmaker

or two of 98.6°F., yet desert surroundings may easily fluctuate thirty or forty degrees between noon and night. The human steady temperature is true even though the body itself produces enough internal heat to raise its temperature two degrees Fahrenheit in just one hour while resting; and the heatload from the desert environment on a moderately hot day may be ten times as great as this metabolic heat. Fortunately, only vital organs need constant temperature, not the entire body. A muscle at rest can be fifteen or twenty degrees cooler than the same muscle during exercise without any harm; and mountain climbers or polar explorers who suffer frostbite of fingers and toes and noses usually experience no real problem other than pain. In making one circulation through the body, blood may vary almost forty degrees without any particular consequence.

Two centuries ago studies began on how man succeeds in keeping his temperature normal while exposed to heat. In 1775 the *Philosophical Transactions of the Royal Society of London* published Charles Blagden's "Experiments and Observations in a Heated Room." Blagden told of going with colleagues into a room heated to 260°F. and staying for nearly an hour. As a means of comparison they took a dog with them, kept in a basket to protect its feet from the scorching floor of the chamber; and they also took in a piece of raw steak. At the end of the experiment the men and the dog emerged uncomfortable but unharmed. The steak was cooked. This, Blagden pointed out, demonstrates that living tissue is capable of cooling itself, while nonliving tissue lacks the capacity.

In a second experiment, Blagden placed two pots of water in the room, one with oil floating on its surface and the other without it. The water in the first pot began to boil while that in the second pot was still far below boiling, just as had been expected. The film of oil made the difference. It prevented evaporation from the surface of the water and thereby forced the heat to build up within the water. To apply this to human physiology, Blagden next flooded the floor of the test chamber and returned a third time. However, he could not stay. Humid-

ity caused the same temperature that previously had been
bearable to be totally impossible this time. Sweat clung without
evaporating, which of course proved the intended point — that
human adaptation to heat depends overwhelmingly on cooling
the body by the evaporation of water from the skin.

The rate of evaporation needed under desert conditions can
be far more prodigious than is commonly realized. Sweat
evaporates the moment it oozes from the pores, and the skin
stays dry. Yet on a day that is only in the 110° to 115° range,
three gallons of water may be evaporated as sweat. The exact
amount will of course depend on variables such as how much
one is exercising, what the humidity is, whether the wind is
blowing, and so on. Sweat rates as high as one gallon per hour
have been recorded, a volume nearly equal to the total water
in the human bloodstream. A normal man can manage this
much sweating and keep his body temperature steady, providing
he drinks enough. When we lived in Death Valley and my
husband was patrolling the valley floor in summer, I would fix
three one-quart vacuum bottles of iced tea for him to drink
with his lunch, which he ate in the relative coolness of a mine
tunnel whenever possible, a midday retreat commonly shared
with packrats and occasionally with a snake. In addition he
carried several one-gallon waterbags hanging on the front
bumper of his pickup truck — tightly woven canvas bags that
keep their contents cool by slow evaporation — and he had a
fifty-gallon drum of water in case of emergency. He drove in
his stockings, which were absorbent terrycloth sweat socks, and
he kept a bucket of water on the floor of the truck convenient
for plunging his feet in and out of, to keep them wet and thereby
provide additional evaporative cooling He also kept a wet cloth
on his head, and he rigged the windshield washers so they
squirted on the inside, spraying a cool mist onto his face, much
to the amazement of occasional passengers. Temperatures inside
the cab reached 140°F.: no air-conditioner was available.

Until World War II and the sudden need to send American
troops to the Sahara, virtually no detailed studies of man's

physiology in desert heat had been made. Commanders readying troops for battle in North Africa looked at the fact that water would be scarce and they sought to conserve it stringently during training. General George Patton, working with troops in the California desert, tried to toughen his men to get along on a quart of water per day, or even a pint. This included all purposes, bathing and cooking as well as drinking. The result was a saving of the camp's water supply and an expenditure of men. Maneuvers were conducted in the blazing sun at temperatures of 110° to 120°F. Sweat glistened on the men's faces and stuck their shirts to their backs in spite of the General's orders, and no amount of will power held this loss of water in check or kept body temperatures from climbing as dehydration set in. Through sweating alone, men were losing a quart or two of water per hour. The toughened campaigners the Army wanted failed to develop, but medics gained enormous experience in treating heat cramps, heat prostration, heat stroke, and all manner of desert malaise.

Physiologists were also gaining experience. By observing and testing they worked out the amounts of water needed per man under various desert conditions and degrees of exertion. For the first time it was established scientifically that every ounce of water a man loses in sweat must be made up if he is to continue to function. Formulas for water supplies were worked out to include factors such as the anticipated air temperature, humidity, and wind speed, and the exercise planned for the men. The result of these considerations was then multiplied by the number of men to be involved, and this was how much water would be needed. It was that simple, and very nearly that universal. For in spite of tales about desert men being able to get by on mere mouthfuls of water, no actual investigation over a prolonged period has ever borne this out (although there are fantastic short-term examples such as McGee's account). Obviously individuals differ, but within a rather restricted range. The only way the body can cool itself is by sweating; and thirst is a signal of deep body need, not merely a matter of discomfort or a dry mouth. Water used as sweat must be made up. If it isn't, the extent of damage done will correlate precisely with the size of the debt.

Each two-degree rise in Fahrenheit air temperature calls for forty more grams of sweat per hour; and if direct exposure to sunshine is added, the sweat rate will jump by five times. As the various factors compound each other, a man's thirst increases proportionately — thirst scarcely understood by people in pastoral lands. The English language, for example, has no word to distinguish the sort of discomfort that prompts a child to call out from his crib for a drink from that which kills a man stranded beneath a desert sun. "Thirst" expresses both sensations. Not so in Arabic. Three separate words describe common thirst to an Arab, and additional terms distinguish between the thirst that makes a man giddy, the burning thirst that drives him to madness (which happens to be the same word as for passionate love), the thirst that kills, and every other possible shade and feeling of thirst.

Not long ago, a soft-drink company sought to capitalize on the drama of desert thirst by arranging through an advertising agency for a young stalwart to walk across Death Valley in July. The sponsorship of the feat was kept quiet, and consequently the press started covering the event as a human-interest feature. Interviews were given at the end of each day's march, with the young man available for photographs. The hope was that he would be drinking the sponsor's beverage, but by the time the stunt was a few days old, knowledge of its backing had leaked out, Death Valley was living up to its summer reputation, and thirst had become painfully real for the youth. His "preferred drink" became water — plain, pure, cool water. The soda pop supposed to profit from testimonials was outspokenly rejected. Body need was crying out and economic incentive had vanished.

A similar choice among beverages was shown under more academic circumstances by 19 young Israeli men who hiked a 370-mile course. Their sweat rates averaged from 6 to 11 quarts per day, a loss they were allowed to make up with a free choice of water, cold tea, milk, soft drinks, citrus juice, or beer. Each man was allowed to choose but was required to stick with that one beverage for twenty-four hours at a time. The overwhelming choices were water and citrus juice, selected by 17 out of the 19 men. Milk gave diarrhea. Soft drinks produced a sensation of fullness before enough had been consumed to satisfy the body's craving for liquid, and beer gulped a quart at a time made the men drunk and therefore that had to be eliminated from the options after the first few days. (Nevertheless, if it weren't for the drunkenness, beer would have an advantage over soft drinks. Alcohol affects the pituitary gland and increases the rate of urination, which relieves the fullness and simplifies continued drinking.)

Not much is known about the sweat differences between men and women. Some work has been done but not enough to be statistically valid. Tentative evidence suggests that since women are better insulated with fat than men are, their skin is less effective as a conductor of heat. In a warm environment this means that a women's skin will average about three degrees warmer than a man's and the heat from the environment will not pass as readily from her skin into her body. At the same time, a woman's metabolism will stay as much as 20 percent lower than a man's under the same conditions. For this reason, women are slower to begin sweating than men; they incur less of a heatload from the desert environment, and their internal production of heat is less. Men's sweat glands become active at air temperatures of about 85°F., but women seldom sweat much until about 90° has been reached.

Both sexes and all races and body types steadily lose salt in sweat, as well as water, although the loss is not consciously noticeable. The body has a mentally recognized urge to drink whenever internal moisture decreases, but no comparable sensation warns of the loss of salt, even though the effects of its imbalance are also serious. During a single hot day as much as ten to thirty grams of sodium chloride may be sweated out, plus lesser amounts of potassium and other salts needed in blood and plasma. In one exceptional documented case, a man working at 100°F. with 80 percent relative humidity lost more than one-seventh of his body's total supply of salt in two and one-half hours. Unless such losses, even when less spectular than that in the example, are compensated, muscle spasms set in. Today these spasms are called heat cramps. Earlier they were known as miner's cramps or stoker's disease (for stokers in the steamships, whose work was extremely hot and therefore sweaty). Incapacitating cramps kept occurring in these occupations, although until the 1930s no one fully understood why; miscellaneous observations had been recorded, but no real study had been made. It was recognized, for example, that Scandanavian seamen were not much bothered by heat cramps compared with British seamen working under comparable circumstances. This was puzzling until food differences were noticed. Diet on Scandinavian ships was high in salt fish, but the British used fresh fish and meats. In a similar way, men began to realize that folk sayings in Norway had been stating physiological principles for centuries. One advises the addition of salt to beer in haying season, empirical wisdom based on the fact that the long sweaty hours of haymaking brought on a loss of body salt. Somehow farmers discovered that they felt better and worked better if they salted their beer, although they did not know this was compensation for a heat-induced deficiency. A second saying cautions against drinking heavily from a brook in summer without also eating. This too is based on experience. The salt in food can supply the body's need, whereas stream water in rural Norway cannot, since the land is laced by glacial melt-streams that are conspicuously lacking in minerals. Drinking any real quantity of such water on a day of heavy sweating supplies water needs but worsens salt balances; hence the advice to eat as well as drink. This need for salt is an urgent body requirement. Wars have been started over salt, and trade has been based upon it. Salt has even been weighed up against gold, so highly is it valued. Considerations of flavor are of superficial importance compared with the physiological role of salt.

About the time of World War II, as scientific investigation began to determine actual salt needs and rates of loss, salt tablets came into popular use. They seemed to be the easiest way to be sure the body had enough salt, since a man sweating heavily must make up the salt expenditure as well as the water expenditure. However, imbalance in one direction swung to the opposite extreme: too much salt instead of too little. There wasn't always enough water to drink along with the tablet, or nobody cautioned about this point, or there wasn't time to drink adequately. Nausea and dizziness were the price paid, and salt tablets fell into slightly less favor. They have value, but the best answer under most circumstances is also the simplest and oldest: add a little extra salt to food during periods of unusual heat.

Thirst as a sensation seems to stem from the concentration of salt in the blood. In experiments with goats, salt solutions were injected close to the hypothalmus, which controls thirst. This sent the animals into an insatiable round of drinking. Ordinarily goats stop drinking when the stomach becomes distended to a certain point, behavior already known from previous experiments conducted by gently inflating balloons placed in the stomachs of the goats. In the new experiment salt triggered the hypothalmus and the signal for thirst was sent out, overriding the normal sensation of "enough." The animals drank on and on until they had swallowed an amount of water equivalent to half their body weight, a volume that would correspond to a 160-pound man drinking nearly ten gallons of water. Evidently the mechanism that produces thirst in mammals depends on the osmotic concentration of blood reaching receptor cells of the hypothalmus, and so the injection of salt close to those cells in the goats stimulated unquenchable thirst, completely unrelated to actual body need.

Under hot conditions, men tend to dehydrate themselves even when water is available. Thirst prompts drinking enough to compensate partly for sweat losses, but the resupplying lags and the deficit grows. By natural inclination, a man may dehydrate himself by an amount equivalent to 3 or 4 percent of his body weight and then make up for it at meals. Seemingly this is the body's way of recognizing the danger of salt imbalance, since a slight tissue dehydration is less damaging than flooding the body with water and risking drastic dilution of salt concentrations. Therefore the tendency is to delay balancing sweat losses by drinking until there is also food to make up the lost salt. Furthermore, man is a slow drinker. During an experiment salt losses were replaced hourly, but even so men allowed themselves to partially dehydrate between meals if allowed to decide for themselves when to drink and how much. It is uncomfortable, or even impossible, to drink enough to keep pace with the sweat losses of extreme conditions. Man is less of a desert animal in this regard than a camel is, or a host of other species. Man needs time to consume all the water he requires for proper regulation of body temperature and dehydration.

The physiologist Knut Schmidt-Nielsen tells of becoming deeply impressed in this regard once as he watched a donkey drink. It could suck up a vast amount of water in a short time, and Schmidt-Nielsen decided to test his own capacity against the animal's. He went for several hot miserable hours without drinking, until he desperately wanted water and yearned to drink a huge amount. The donkey's rate of gulping water was nearly two gallons a minute, and although Schmidt-Nielsen had no expectation of even approaching that level, he measured out about a quart of water, and when feeling thirsty enough, reached for it. "It proved hard to drink the full liter," he reports, "and I could barely down it . . . All desire to continue with another liter was gone, and I could only drink additional mouthfuls by forcing them down."

About two-thirds of the human body by weight is water, which is distributed in the blood and tissues. Nobody knows exactly what proportion of this can be lost without fatal result, since experiments obviously cannot be carried to that point. The probable tolerable loss is somewhere around 15 to 25 percent, influenced by differences between individuals and variable external factors such as environmental temperature and the rate at which the body is being forced to dehydrate. McGee estimated that Pablo Valencia had lost thirty-five or forty pounds, mostly water, during his ordeal. This would be roughly a 22 percent loss of body weight, and a defiance of all the known odds of survival. Actual observations have never been allowed to go beyond an 8 to 11 percent body dehydration, which is the point of extreme discomfort and beginning derangement — nothing that drinking and resting won't correct. The victim of this degree of dehydration may safely be allowed to gulp as much water as he wants, as fast as he wants, although ice water should be avoided because it chills the stomach abruptly and may cause cramping.

Beyond that degree of dehydration, voluntary drinking alone is not enough. Water must also be given intravenously, through the rectum, or by stomach tube. If it is not forthcoming in sufficient quantity at this stage, the cells are drained of fluid, the blood thickens, and the heart beats faster in an effort to maintain the flow of increasingly viscous blood. Heat exhaustion may result, an automatic safety valve for the body much like a faint. The dehydrated person collapses and breaks out with clammy sweat. This has the effect of stopping all exercise, which reduces the load on the heart, and at the same time the automatic sweating cools the body. Heat stroke is more severe. The temperature-control center within the brain breaks down, sweating slows or stops, and body heat builds explosively. The blood cannot carry deep-body heat to the skin fast enough, and with the sweat system malfunctioning, cooling is no longer efficient in any case. Unless help is at hand, death quickly follows.

The need to rid the body of excess heat dictates the need for water, and so it obviously follows that the only way to reduce the amount of water required is to reduce the heatload. This can be done either by less exertion, thereby cutting the production of heat within the body, or by insulation from hot environment. The first method is limited, for humans have no way to drop internal heat production below the metabolic normal while at rest. We can't hibernate, at least not until the techniques of cryogenics are perfected. That leaves protection from environment as the prime means of reducing heatload. Modern air-conditioning accomplishes this indoors; and outdoors, clothing is remarkably effective.

On a hot day the impulse often is to take off clothing — and this does successfully increase comfort if unlimited water is available for sweating. If it is not, swaddling oneself in layer on layer of clothes can be wise. Schmidt-Nielsen tells of watching a Bedouin arrive at an oasis on a scorching June day and immediately shed two woollen burnooses and a jacket, then sit about relaxing in a long-sleeved woollen shirt. His shoes were also of wool and extended over the ankle somewhat like American Indian moccasins. Open sandals would not be practical, for they would let the superheated sand of the desert trickle against the foot. Wool actually is an ideal fabric for desert clothing, no matter how uncomfortable this may sound. If unlimited water is available, cooling by sweating is no problem; but if water is in short supply, wool offers protection against the added heatload of solar radiation and prevents excessive evaporation from the skin by wind. It does this without completely cutting off the circulation of air, an important consideration that can easily be realized by imagining the discomfort of desert clothes made of a plastic-coated fabric or a tight-weave nylon unable to "breathe." Sweat has to evaporate if it is to do any good, but the rate of evaporation needs to be slowed if drinking water is limited. This is what Arabs' loose woollen clothing accomplishes. Even a face cloth of wool covering the nose and mouth is an advantage under extreme conditions, although uncomfortable. Such a cloth feels stifling, but it helps to reduce water loss from the lungs.

Close to a one-third savings in body moisture can be made by dressing properly. The ideal is to find a balance between insulating the body against the sun's heat and ridding it of internal heat by sweating. Loose fitting garments of permeable material are the best answer. Color is less important. Theoretically white should be best, since it would reflect the sun's rays and thereby lessen the amount of heat gained from radiation. However, only about half of the sunlight reaching the earth is in the visible spectrum; the other half falls in the infrared range, which even pure white absorbs instead of reflects.

Somehow desert peoples arrived empirically at answers to survival that are now being derived scientifically. Arabs' clothing is an example. So are the precautions of Bushmen in the Kalahari Desert, who instinctively follow the first rule of staying alive through periods of great heat and little water. They avoid the sun as much as possible, resting from midmorning to late afternoon and concentrating their hunting and gathering into the early and late hours of the day. Temperatures are relatively cool at these times and sunshine reaches the earth obliquely; the rays travel a greater distance through the atmosphere and arrive more fully filtered than when the sun stands directly overhead. Consequently dawn and dusk are the times for work, and among the items gathered is a supply of *bi*, a tuberous root. This is scraped and squeezed to produce juice for drinking. Next — a pathetic mark of their desperate battle against dehydration — Bushmen pour urine from jugs onto the dry root scrapings and use this moistened pulp to line gravelike pits dug beneath whatever sparse bushes may be available as shade. There the people lie during the day, conserving energy and supplementing their frail supply of internal body moisture with what they have applied to their skin. At dusk, they rise and go again into the veldt to gather food and dig more roots.

The physiological reason underlying the Bushman custom is that heat drastically saps energy. A sweat loss of only one and a half to two quarts, which can occur within a single hour, will reduce work efficiency by 25 percent. Because of this, working under conditions of great heat, or walking for help in an emergency, should be held strictly to dawn and dusk, or night. In addition, water should be swallowed as available rather than trying to stretch a little out over a long period. This allows one to maintain full strength for a longer time, sometimes a crucial factor in handling a stressful situation. Urine, blood, alcohol, gasoline, and other liquids that frantic men have been known to drink can be applied outside the body, but they should not be swallowed. Drinking them only worsens the net water available for sweating because the body must rid itself of the solids dissolved in such liquids. The slightly brackish water frequent at desert springs may be drunk with a net gain in body moisture, but swallowing strongly saline liquids is foolish. Sucking pebbles or chewing gum contributes nothing to a serious problem of moisture, but in the early stages of dehydration it may stimulate saliva and give the mouth a feeling of comfort, which helps psychologically.

Direct sunshine must be avoided. Even a small patch of artificial shade produced by a tarpaulin can be thirty or forty degrees cooler than the same spot unshaded. Similarly, contact with the ground should be prevented. Soil surface temperatures commonly stand twenty or thirty degrees above air temperatures even on moderately hot days, and they may be as much as sixty degrees hotter. Rigging some sort of a platform to permit resting at least a foot above the ground therefore greatly reduces the heatload on the body. A thin layer of air in contact with the ground will take on very nearly the scorching temperature of the ground, but the heating effect decreases exponentially with height above the ground up to a foot or two. The slight elevation of a platform is therefore important.

Certain signs of water can be watched for in the desert: stains on the rock walls of canyons, or flies hovering above a damp place in the sand, or birds twittering at sunrise and sunset near a seep or flying toward it to drink. The contact zones between two lava flows or two sandstone strata may have water. Certain plant species mean water — mesquite, arrowweed, seepwillow — and even when moisture lies too far beneath the surface to reach by digging, such places will be cooler than the surrounding desert. The moist soil and the plants themselves act as a gigantic evaporative cooler. Some plants, such as pickleweed and salicornia, are sure indicators of water lying close to the surface, but since these species are far more tolerant of salts than the human

Arrowweed: water indicator

body is, the water they grow in should not be swallowed.
Nonetheless, it can be used externally to advantage. Pure water
is not necessary even for drinking. A waterhole scummed over
with the floating bodies of scorpions and bird feathers can taste
like nectar; its wetness is all that registers under dire circumstances.

Better yet is a solar still for emergency desert use developed
at the United States Water Conservation Laboratory in Phoenix.
The design is so simple that the needed parts can be carried
in almost any desert kit. A piece of plastic sheeting about a
yard and a half square, a hole dug into the ground, some small
rocks, and — ideally — a container for holding water and a length
of tubing to suck it up through are all it takes. If need be,
the container can be jury-rigged of additional plastic or metal
foil. The hole should be about three feet across and a foot or
two deep. In its center, scoop out a hollow to hold the container.
If tubing is available, tape one end into the container and bring

the other end to the edge of the pit, convenient for sucking the water through. Next, cover the excavation with the plastic sheet, setting it at a height of about three or four inches above the bottom of the pit and banking soil around the upper edges to hold it in place. Let the plastic sag to form a gentle cone in the center of the pit, and add a small rock or other weight directly over the water container to help the cone keep its shape and to reduce wind flutter. The plastic should touch the ground only around the edge of the pit where the soil holds it in place.

The still operates as energy from the sun passes through the plastic and evaporates water from the soil. Moisture condenses on the inside surface of the sheet and the droplets run down the cone and into the water container. From there, water can be sucked up through the tube without disturbing the still or disrupting its action; or if no tubing is available the container can be emptied and the still reassembled. In clay or slightly damp sand a yield of about three pints of water per day can be expected, and several small stills will net even more water than a single large one. Seawater or brackish or polluted water can safely be poured into the pit to wet the soil, because, distilled by the sun's heat, it will be purified and thoroughly fit to drink. Or plants can be cut and put in, assuring a good yield of moisture even when the soil is dry. Chunks of cactus become virtual reservoirs used this way. On cloudy days the still won't produce as much water as on sunny days, but there will be some. Even throughout the night, water will be produced — about a pint from dusk to dawn, according to tests made near Phoenix.

Rain of course will doubly bless a victim of thirst. The cone of plastic will fill with water from the sky; and with moisture restored to the earth, a renewed yield from the still is certain. Survival is assured, or at least greatly helped.

12. Desert Yesterdays and Tomorrows

DRIVE THROUGH PHOENIX today to sense an intermixture of how man has lived in this desert in the past together with his modern presence and intimations of what will come. Start on Van Buren heading east past motels and restaurants and signs that announce and cajole. *Earthworm Farm. Eat Here. Have Vacation Fun. Retire Now.*

Angle out Bee Line Road to where a gravel company scoops and screens the dry riverbed of the Salt River, putting it to commercial use. Stop and look for two earthen ridges about five feet high which run between the road and the river. These are the banks of an irrigation canal dating back centuries before the Spaniards arrived in America to the time when the New World was not "new" because its culture was still simply and wholly its own rather than an import from beyond the seas.

The greatest prehistoric irrigation system in North America and perhaps in all the world centered here on the lower Salt River and on the Gila, which is the next river to the south. A network of canals at least 125 miles long could still be discerned in the early twentieth century, and during the classic period of building a total of close to 300 miles of canals must have laced the desert. Their makers were the Hohokam, a people whose irrigation watered sufficient crops for a population of 50,000, yet until the 1920s a people whose culture was little known. To the north, evidence of the Anasazi, or Cliff Dweller Indians, was more obvious, more showy, and more in danger of irreparable loss from indiscriminate amateur collecting. Also, frankly, the pueblo ruins were more comfortable to investigate. The higher elevations of the mesas and canyons offered pleasant summer working conditions compared to a sweaty, dusty field camp in the low desert of the Salt and Gila river valleys where archeology had to be an ordeal. Nonetheless, excavation ultimately has shown the early Indian irrigation society of the Phoenix region as comparable to that of the Tigris and Euphrates valleys. Beginnings date to about 300 B.C. Culmination and decline came about A.D. 1400.

The name Hohokam is a modern Pima Indian word literally meaning "used up" or "no longer useful." It usually is translated more gently and romantically as "Those who have vanished," which is an apt description. To archeologists first assessing the evidence, all but the merest fragments of this once great people seemed to have shifted and gone like the blowing of sand in a desert wind. Emil W. Haury, who has patiently traced the story of the Hohokam at many Arizona sites, comments: "It sometimes seems to me that they must have planned it that way. I have probed Hohokam ruins for more than 30 years of my professional life — and the search quickly taught me to live with frustration and disappointment."

Unlike other early peoples in the Southwest, these ancients cremated their dead. Consequently their physical appearance can only be assumed. Furthermore, much of their most beautiful wares, such as clay figurines and stone incense burners, seem almost deliberately smashed, and their canals of course long ago filled with sand and grew over with creosote bush. Time and the elements have taken a toll, and so has man. By 1870 Anglo-American farmers newly come to the desert were planting the fields deserted by the Hohokam scarcely five centuries earlier. These settlers often adapted the canals of the Indians to bring water to the new crops. They leveled and reshaped the ancient fields, and erased old watercourses that they did not need. In the process they plowed under the remnants of houses belonging to the vanished Indians. Even a ball court 150 feet long by

60 feet wide and 5 feet deep was knowingly destroyed, a great loss because such courts are now known to link the Hohokam to Mexico. They make it possible to follow the thread of the culture's expansion northward. In another instance a farmer told an archeologist that he had used a mule team and scraper to clear two feet of dirt from a collapsed house. He noticed broken pottery and stone axes and seashells by the score, but he scraped on. There had been stone pestles too. Some still were flecked with soft tints of copper greens and rusty earth-reds, pigments that had been pounded and used to color jewelry and faces.

For the most part Hohokam architecture was less than monumental. Houses of poles covered with brush and plastered with mud seem to have been the style almost until the end of the fourteenth century, although perhaps as early as 1200, families had begun to draw together into consolidated villages. They started to build with adobe and caliche, and condominium living had one of its early tests. Pueblo Grande, an archeological ruin in today's downtown Phoenix, dates from this time. So does Casa Grande, southeast of Phoenix near Coolidge. Walls at Casa Grande are four feet thick and a central tower rises thirty-five feet above the surrounding desert. The engineering and labor involved tantalize the mind: think of taking mud as a material and sticks as implements, and building a structure to be inhabited for a century, then left empty and untended yet strong enough to remain standing for the next several hundred years. In 1697 Captain Cristóbal Martín Bernal, traveling with Father Kino, the pioneering Jesuit priest, wrote of Casa Grande: "We saw the whole building which is very large . . . One sees four stories with good rooms, apartments, and windows curiously plastered inside and out . . . It is also clear that there was a very numerous population and they lived in a community, and over a large area is seen much painted and broken pottery; likewise a main canal is visible of ten yards in width and four in depth, with very thick earthen banks, which extend up to the house through the plain." Bernal wrote three centuries after Casa Grande had

Casa Grande

been abandoned to the sun and the rain and the wind. Today
the old house still stands, preserved as part of the National Park
System. It is a venerable touch of the past again approached
through green fields, although the crops now are tilled by
machines and nourished by chemical sprays.

The Hohokam successfully farmed land as much as fifty-five
feet above river level, an accomplishment that required irrigation
canals heading far upriver. Contours were tested by running
a stream of water across the land, then setting to work with
stone hoes and digging sticks of mesquite and ironwood. Dirt
from the deepening canals was mounded to form banks and
also used to fill low places so that aqueducts would be possible.
Sometimes a thick coating of clay was patted against the canal
banks to reduce water loss by seepage. Intakes were built of
rock and brush, and headgates directed water from main ditches
into laterals. Canals more than forty feet wide can still be traced,
although for the most part they were ten or twelve feet wide
at the bottom and six to seven feet deep.

It may well have been this very irrigation success that eventually drove the Hohokam from their citadels, much as the realists of today — or the Cassandras, depending on point of view — predict that modern agriculturists will be driven from the land. Decade after decade the Hohokam brought water to the desert soil, and beans and corn and pumpkins and cotton turned the brown earth into gardens. The system worked. Then hardpan layers started to form a foot or two beneath the surface of the ground and the fields became waterlogged. Moisture no longer could drain away. The hardpan held it, and capillarity caused a movement upward instead of downward. Salts rose with the moisture. Crops no longer could grow.

The disaster was not regionwide, but in places ecological mismanagement rang down the curtain and forced abandonment of established centers and styles of living. The people of Casa Grande and Pueblo Grande and similar adobe cities left their irrigation networks and moved closer to the rivers to start over. Their descendants are the Pimas, noted in the earliest journals of the Spanish conquistadors and missionaries and still living along the river near Phoenix.

Today about ten or fifteen miles of remnant Hohokam canals can be traced in the Salt River valley if you know where to look. The system is to watch for potsherds as sign that an old canal is Indian rather than associated with the days of white settlement. All we kept finding at first was broken glass and smashed crockery and rusting cans. Finally, lying on the bank of the canal we walked along was a two-inch broken piece of baked clay, buff-colored with a geometric pattern of red-brown. Presumably it had been part of a pot fashioned by a Hohokam woman decades or centuries before Columbus had headed west. Presumably the canal we walked was the one we sought. And if not, no matter, for this particular day we felt more of an emotional need than a factual one. The afternoon was stormy, with clouds trailing curtains of rain to earth, and wind gusts kicked up gravel that peppered our legs. Twigs and tumbleweeds kept scudding past. It was winter and we zipped our parkas and walked with hands in pockets to keep warm. Jet planes shrieked overhead; the machinery of the gravel operation roared; cars and pickup trucks whizzed past. Yet thoughts turned easily to the time when Hohokam minds and muscles had shaped this canal and commanded the desert to yield crops, including cotton and lima beans, still grown on this soil. Creosote bushes as high as ten feet grow on one bank of the canal today, as they probably did in the days of the ancients. A mesquite tree close to us momentarily was host to a shrike, as other mesquites must have been in the past. A thrasher flew into a lycium bush; and when we lifted binoculars to scrutinize it we found two cactus wrens already in there, sitting utterly silent, also three white-crowned sparrows. They all were taking shelter from the wind. The tumbleweeds rolling in the broad bottom of the old canal would be a sight the Hohokam farmers could never have seen, for tumbleweed is an introduced species; and we found a feral domestic cat, which would also have been unknown in their day. It was crouched at the base of a brittlebush and as I ambled obliquely toward it, it held its position, taut and vigilant. Then I looked at it squarely, and it shot off across the road like a frightened rabbit, jet black, big, immensely strong and quick.

Walking the old canal gives a feeling of immediacy with Those Who Have Vanished, for you must ferret out your own directions and puzzle over whether or not you have followed them success- fully. It is not completely easy, or completely certain. You give of yourself as a person of today, and receive whispers from the persons of the past. Not that the Hohokam were the first arrivals in the Southwest. The firstcomers pursued mammoths and other large mammals through the tall grass, killing them as they grazed. These people arrived eight or ten thousand years before the Hohokam. They were rovers who moved with the herds, their population density perhaps roughly comparable to that of the Eskimos of northern Canada today, who live by following the herds of caribou. In the North this sort of relationship between land and man supports about one person per one hundred square miles; in the more gentle grasslands of the Sonoran Desert those long years ago, the human density may have been as great as two or three or maybe even five persons per hundred square miles. Contact between bands must have been infrequent and random; few ideas could be exchanged, and there was little incentive for the development of culture beyond the technology and ritual of the hunt.

Then about eight thousand years ago, the climate warmed, the glasslands dried, the great herds dwindled and disappeared — for whatever reason — and man profoundly altered his relationship with the environment. Hunting shifted from large animals to small and required new ways of stalking and killing. A new set of life habits developed. Plants, which formerly had been supplements to diet, became mainstays. Techniques of harvesting and storing and preparing became important. Small seeds encased in hard coats formerly were useless because they passed through the digestive system untouched, but now women learned to grind them into flour or to parch them, and a new food source opened. Curiosity and hunger led to the sampling of additional plants and to trying out ways of preparing and cooking. The land was growing increasingly dry, the old water sources shrinking. Families wandered smaller territories, and certain dependable springs and seeps and tinajas began to stir feelings of proprietary rights. Human population concentrated close to water, and rose to twenty or twenty-five persons per square mile where conditions were favorable, with vast empty stretches in between. Experiences started to differ from group to group and area to area. Ideas and insights and techniques worthy of exchange began to develop.

Gradually the gathering of wild food-plants gave way to raising crops. Wild, ancestral corn had first been domesticated in Mexico or Guatemala perhaps as long ago as 6000 B.C. — by coincidence about the same time the merit of wheat was being discovered on the other side of the world. The idea of deliberately planting corn to be harvested later worked slowly northward through Mexico and into Arizona and New Mexico. Pollen grains and one single partial kernel of corn found at Bat Cave,

Papago woman harvesting saguaro fruit

New Mexico, date by radiocarbon methods to about 4500 years ago. They belong to a cultivated form of corn, a popcorn type with each kernel separately enclosed by a husk. An entire cob was about as long as three good kernels from an ear of modern corn placed side by side. No matter how physically small this new arrival, however, its implication changed the lives of men and the face of the land itself. With fields to prepare, plant, cultivate, and harvest, and crops to store, men no longer had either time or need to wander far, not even seasonally. Wherever water permitted an assured food supply, population could expand and energy and thought could be focused on what would benefit the whole community. Warriors developed to protect communal property and interests, priests to intercede with the gods, farmers, hunters, masons, artisans, and artists to serve other needs. Casual farming — pressing seeds into the ground with a dibble and letting summer rains do the rest — set the stage for exploiting environment. Man gained mastery. His marks changed the earth in a way never before known.

Of course the wild desert also continued to be utilized. Rivers like the Salt and the Gila are few in the Southwest, and large-scale irrigation was in no way possible for most of the early tribes. However, food resources existed even in the bleakest hinterlands, such as the shifting dunes and waterless lava fields at the head of the Gulf of California. This region was home for the Sand Papagos, a people supremely adapted to the paucity of the land and able to wrest a living. The beans of mesquite and ironwood trees and the fruits of various cactus were fairly dependable in season, and when the tides permitted, fish and crabs could be taken in the sloughs of the Gulf. Jackrabbits could be run down in the loose sand of washes, antelope and mule deer hunted on the desert plains, and bighorn sheep pursued on the high slopes of nearby mountains. An outwash plain below the volcanic cones of the Pinacate region (just south of the present international boundary) could be profitably scratched and coaxed into yielding corn and beans and squash. Mexican rancheros today still plant these same ephemeral fields.

Even at times when heat and drought oppressed the land and all life seemed to draw back into itself, there were desert tortoises and lizards and toads to catch and eat. And there was "sand food," a little-known succulent plant *(Ammobroma sonorae)* that grows parasitically on the roots of creosote bush, arrowweed, coldenia, and several other shrubs. It is found only in the wastelands from Imperial Valley southward to the dunes of the upper Gulf; nowhere else in the world. Botanists have considered it a genus with a single species, although a probable second species has now been discovered. Very little of the plant shows aboveground, no more than a four-inch saucerlike receptacle studded with minute purple flowerlets. No stems show and no leaves, and the flowering disc lies flat against the sand. But stalks buried within the sand are as much as an inch thick and three to five feet long, and they usually form clusters. A single plant with more than one hundred stalks, weighing a total of forty-six pounds, has been reported parasitizing the roots of an arrowweed bush. Sand Papagos could locate the plant at any time of year, although to the eyes of modern men no hint is apparent except during the brief flowering period in May. Some inexplicable clue evidently guided the Indians, much as Bushmen in the Kalahari Desert are able to rely on *bi* and *ga* tubers totally indiscernible to outsiders; and, as in the Bushman's case, the fleshy stalks of sand food substituted for water, carrying men through days when death would otherwise have been certain. The plant was eaten both raw and roasted, its texture reported as tender and juicy with a flavor something like a sweet potato.

The gods send only two to five inches of rainfall yearly to the land of the Sand Papagos. Their life was totally geared to finding food and water, a nomad's life in which the people worked a vast territory for subsistence as other mammals also work territories for survival. Records even of the much more favored Papagos north and east of the Sand Papagos, where rainfall is double that of the upper Gulf, tell of a stern, disciplined life, and of ready acceptance of it. "I am telling about the month of Pleasant Cold when the [summer] rains were long over," anthropologist Ruth Underhill, writing in a 1936 issue of the *American Anthropologist,* quotes a Papago woman as saying. "Our pond had dried up. If we wanted to stay in our houses, the girls had to run far, far up the hills and across the flat land to a place called Where-the-Water-Whirls-Around . . . [When they got back] every family had two little jars of water to last for the day. But we did not mind. We knew how to use water. We have a word that means thirst-enduring, and that is what we were taught to be."

The same sort of endurance is reported for the Mojave Indians living along the Colorado River north of the Gulf. They were recognized as phenomenal runners, but their basic adaptation to the rigors of the desert probably was not exceptional however much it seems to defy modern knowledge of human potential. Small groups of men would cover nearly one hundred miles a day, trotting at a steady pace to visit and trade, carrying neither food nor weapons but blending with the desert as smoothly as any of its other creatures. "We can withstand hunger and thirst for as long as four days," the Spanish priest Father Garcés reports one of the men telling him in 1776. (The Tarahumara Indians of northern Mexico indulge in similar feats today, purely as sport. Boys of grade-school age hold informal 6-mile races on Sunday afternoons by way of an hour's diversion, and men compete seriously over 90- to 180-mile courses, kicking a small ball as they go. The terrain is precipitous in the extreme and reaches elevations of nearly 8000 feet; yet men cover the ground in 24 to 48 hours.)

Papagos made long expeditions for salt, to gain a trade item that could be bartered for wheat among the farming villages and also as a way to toughen their bodies and minds to the hardships of life and attune their spirits to the supernatural. They traveled two hundred miles across the barren land of their Sand Papago cousins to the Gulf — specifically to Salina Grande, a slough surrounded by low sand dunes and white with salt. A mining surveyor who visited there has estimated deposits of at least seven million tons of salt. Thirty or forty Papago men would go at a time ("As many as go to fight the Apaches," according to one early account). Nobody was permitted to turn back once started, and only old men who had gone before were allowed to speak as the party traveled. Eating and drinking were minimal and strictly at the leader's direction.

On arrival at the salina, men on their first trek would run the length of the salt beds four times — a total of sixteen miles of running — while those who had made the trip before ran over the beds only twice. When the rituals and the harvesting of the salt were done, the men shouldered hundred-pound sacks and started home. Practically the only water along the way was, and still is, what happens to catch and last in rock tinajas. Trails worn by the men's feet from one possible waterhole to the next still show. They were used for at least three thousand years, to judge from evidence at campsites, and abandoned only when the culture of the newcomer Caucasians finally swallowed the old ways of the desert peoples. You can follow the trails without quite knowing what it is that guides you. Partly you walk where there is a slight depression in the earth, and partly you pick the way where stones are small and easy for your feet to step among. In places the faint line of a path angles crosswise to a drainage channel, proof of having been superimposed on the natural lay of the land. You lose the trail repeatedly but follow by instinct what seems the most likely route — and come back upon it.

South of the Sand Papagos lived the Seri Indians, the people we met at Puerto Libertad while on our search for boojum trees. The desert cursed the Seris with its little water, and forced the women to make daily trips to springs five miles distant, originally carrying water in thin strong clay ollas with narrow openings to minimize sloshing and evaporation, then later shifting to open five-gallon cans. The desert tempered muscles and will and spirit; and the sea blessed with its bounty, for it was the Sea Turtle god who created this world, raising the Seris' land from the water with his great back. Poetry poured from the minds and hands of these seagoing desert people who lived closely and

Seri women

fondly with their dual environment. Women painted their faces using a clam shell of water as mirror and the chewed tip of a mesquite twig as brush. One of their motifs formed a series of wavy lines in blue: the legs of an octopus. Another, painted in red, symbolized the roots, pods, and seeds of ironwood trees, a thoroughly desert species. Sandals made of sea lion hide protected men's feet from the thorns of the desert while they hunted for jackrabbits and peccaries and mountain sheep. And conversely, when they put to sea in canoes lashed from bundles of carrizo reed, they carried cactus fruit as provisions. The Seris speared porpoises and sea lions and sea turtles from jutting rock ledges. Their lances were carved from the hard taproot of ironwood trees, and the ropes they used to haul in the prey were twisted from mesquite roots. They danced to the beat of a drum fashioned by placing the shell of a sea turtle over a hole in the ground, and they augmented its thunder by shaking rattles made from desert-tortoise shells filled with pebbles. They sang to the music of a harp made from the flower stalk of an agave and strung with gut from seals. They called their children in from desert play by blowing on a conch shell off the beach.

Along the rivers life was easier. The Pimas, relatives of the Papagos, were one of the river peoples. For them, crops held prime importance. Fields were located along the lower river terraces watered by irrigation canals in much the manner of the Hohokam. Each year the melting snows of the mountains would swell the rivers, beginning in late April or May, and by June as the floods drew back and mud no longer clung to the men's feet it was time to plant. A stick opened the ground a few inches and from four to seven seeds were dropped into the hole. "If the mice were eating seeds at the time, we put in seven," a river Indian reported; if not, four seeds were enough. The work often continued until early August: "We would watch for the Seven Sisters star every morning. When it came out we would stop planting. If we planted later than that the frost might catch the crop." Planting was very nearly all the effort demanded until time for harvesting. Scarecrows shaped from arrowweeds to resemble humans and decked out with pottery sherds and stones might be set up in the fields, and children might be stationed to throw mud clods and clap their hands to frighten birds away from the corn after ears had begun to ripen. Sometimes men would build a fire and sleep in the fields to keep coyotes away from the watermelons. A little weeding was done. But mostly it was a matter of waiting. Harvesting came in the fall, and lasted from late September to early November.

Corn could be roasted and eaten with the kernels still green, and surplus ears were sun-dried and stored in basket granaries of remarkable size. Some stood as high as five feet and were six feet across. They were coarsely woven of arrowweed and raised off the ground on low platforms, or placed on top of ramadas. Beans were stored in gourds or ollas. Squashes were cut into strips and dried. Watermelons were stored in deep pits dug in cool, sandy soil. Details of course varied between tribes but the same general pattern prevailed along the river bottoms.

Wild foods were stored along with harvested foods. In the book *A Pima Remembers,* George Webb speaks of the storeroom of his childhood home as filled with "baskets and ollas of mesquite bean cakes, balls of cactus fruit, cactus seeds, dried meat in sacks, cheese and salt. In one corner, stacked in straw would be muskmelons, watermelons, and pumpkins. Hanging from the ceiling would be bundles of foxtail weed, split willow branches, and devil claws for basket making." There also was "cactus syrup put up in little ollas" by the Papagos and traded to the Pimas along with salt in exchange for beans and corn.

Just before sunrise each morning a village leader would climb to the top of a ramada, or sun shelter, and call out an exhortation, George Webb further recalls. He would speak for about five minutes in a ringing clear voice that could be heard for a mile. When he finished, the village came alive. His words: "Now another day is coming. Awake from slumber. Look toward the east . . . See the rising of the sun which means another day to toil, another day to hunt for meat, to put seed in the ground. Arise and make use of the day, and do not get in the way of the women as they go about fixing up the camp and the needed task of preparing meals for you. Many moons, many suns, have come and gone since our forefathers here on this same ground toiled and struggled so that we might enjoy life today. So let us not waste this day. But get your tools, go out to the fields, or take down your bow and arrows and go after the game, so that your family will not be in need of meat. So now I hope you will strive to make this day the best in your life."

Into this organized, surprisingly homogeneous land came the Spanish, Mexicans, and Yankees — successive waves, each stamping its imprint on the culture of the region and the land itself. First it was the Coronado Expedition. An army of three hundred soldiers and seven hundred Indian attendants assembled on February 23, 1540, at Compostela, beyond the southern extreme of the Sonoran Desert, and they marched northward through the length of the desert and on to the panhandle of Texas and into Kansas. A side expedition commanded by

Melchior Díaz pushed west to the Colorado River. The men sought wealth, and the closest they came to finding it was the full granaries of the Indian villages. But what a sight to the unbelieving eyes of Indians along the way! No pomp was spared. The soldiers were cased in leather armor and the horses were fitted with silver-decorated harnesses. Cattle, swine, sheep, and goats stirred the dust of the advancing expedition along with the hoofs of the soldiers' horses and the sandaled feet of the Indian retinue. Such was the pattern of all Spanish *entradas*. One conquistador a few decades after Coronado is reported as carrying with him a suit of blue Italian velvet trimmed with elaborate gold braid, plus suits of rose-colored satin, purple Castilian cloth, Chinese flowered silk, three hats trimmed with ostrich feathers, and forty pairs of boots. Only the padres came modestly, first the Jesuits, black-robed; and after their expulsion in 1767, the brown-robed Franciscans. Life in the desert would never be the same. Spanish rule and Spanish religion spread across the land, lightly, to be sure, and with something of a sporadic nature, but pregnant with meaning for the years to come.

The harshness of North American desert conditions and the lack of obvious riches slowed impetus for conquering the frontier and creating a proper "New Spain." So did the reluctance of some Indians to give in to the newcomers, although the majority heartily welcomed introduction of new farming methods and even the new patterns of religion. Most of the Indians already were agriculturists like the Pima. Some were settled in river-valley villages and others at isolated rancherias. Either way, the new form of life at missions was simply a more affluent version of their old life, and tribal autonomy and lands were still intact. Difficulty arose only when respect for tribal authority was violated, when force was used instead of explanation and choice.

In 1812 Mexico wrested independent control of her destiny from Spain, and the new government continued the broad policy of "civilizing" the native peoples as begun under Spanish rule, although with changes. Schooling was now to be available without religious instruction automatically included, citizenship was to be equal for all, and individuals were to be encouraged to own land apart from tribal ownership and apart from the feudal Spanish hacienda system. However, the desert portion of the new nation continued low in priority. Reforms constituted goals, and if events shaped themselves along those particular lines, fine, if not, there were other ways. Missions continued in operation, and — tragically — so did the old policies of extermination and exploitation. As late as 1907 Yaqui Indians of northern Sonora were shot as they worked in the fields, or rounded up by the thousands and sold for sixty pesos each as slave laborers for the henequen plantations of Yucatán and the cane plantations of Oaxaca. These measures settled insurrections, and also sent refugees fleeing across the international line to found the Yaqui community still present in Tucson.

Anglo-Americans had been intermixing with Mexicans for some time, particularly in the land that now forms the border states. As early as 1827 a party of trappers, including the famous mountain men James Ohio Pattie and his father Sylvester Pattie, had floated the Colorado, planning to trade furs at the Spanish settlements they assumed to be at the mouth of so mighty a river. "We floated about thirty miles per hour," James Pattie recounted later, "and in the evening camped in the midst of beavers. We set 40 traps, and in the morning [had] caught 36 beaver, an excellent night's hunt." Furs kept increasing so rapidly that "present crafts in a few days were insufficient to carry them, and we were compelled to stop and make another canoe." Eventually the party reached the river estuary, and there found it impossible to contend with the rush of the incoming tide, which was surging and churning in conflict with the current of the river. Also, there were no Spanish settlements — only red mud and wintering waterfowl. The men abandoned canoes and pelts and struck out on foot across the desert to San Diego, where they were thrown in jail by the Mexicans. Anglos wandering unexpectedly in from nowhere were not welcome at that time.

Mounting tensions between Mexico and the United States reached their climax in the mid-1800s, and a third "civilized" government claimed jurisdiction over the northern desert. The years 1846 to 1848 brought war, which ended with Mexico ceding California, Arizona, New Mexico, Texas, Nevada, Utah, and western Colorado to the United States for a payment of fifteen million dollars. The border set by the treaty lay north of its present location, and left level land within Mexico coveted by Americans for a railroad route and for farming. Consequently the Gadsen Purchase was negotiated: ten million dollars were paid to Mexico, the signatures were affixed to the papers, and 26,640 square miles of saguaro desert and river valleys became American. Precisely where the new international border lay nobody much knew or cared, any more than they had known or cared about the technicalities of the previous ones. Surveys had been underway by the American government for years, often knowingly conducted on Mexican land but with no great concern on either side.

Prospectors streamed into the desert as early as 1849, lured to the Mother Lode goldfields of California. Many of them found ore en route and came back later to stake claims and open mines. Forts were built as headquarters for surveys and peace-keeping. Anglo farmers added new crops to the green that had clothed the river terraces of the Hohokam and their descendants. Stern-wheeler ships churned up the Colorado River through Mexican waters to supply the inland desert region, carrying cargo and passengers brought from San Diego around the tip of Baja California and up the Gulf. There was even a small shipyard at the head of the Gulf to repair hulls battered by snags and shifting sandbars on the difficult upriver passage. It was an American operation on Mexican soil; but Americans resented the final drawing of the boundary which left all of the Gulf within Mexico and cut the desert off without a port. At times they chose simply to ignore the existence of the line, and it lay too far north in too desolate a land for the officials in Mexico City to feel much concern one way or the other.

Among the Indians there was initially little reaction to still
one more alien government claiming a right to rule. The Indian
feeling toward the land was a sense of belonging rather than
dominating; they accepted land and life "as is" without trying
for radical change in either. To be sure, the previous newcomers
had brought new seeds and animals and ideas; they had caused
some disruption and some innovation, but the sun still rode the
heavens and baked the earth, the deer still came to the rivers
to drink, floods watered the fields, and cacti set their fruits.
Patterns were essentially unbroken especially in "Pimería Alta,"
the northern frontier that had been pioneered by Father Kino
as far back as 1687. His were relatively gentle, assimilable
changes, but to the south, in Pimería Baja, changes had been
overwhelming as Spaniards impressed Indians into hard labor
at mines and on ranches. Then came the Gadsen Purchase,
and within five years the Anglo-Americans began to drastically
change the land and peoples newly under their jurisdiction.

By 1858 overland stagecoaches were crossing the desert — a
wondrous sight to the Indians — and new ditches were bringing
water long distances to irrigate alfalfa for the coach horses and
to grow produce for the communities springing up around the
stage stations. The railroad came, bringing puffing monsters
that both enchanted and terrified the Indians; and wagon-trains
started to arrive, especially in the Pima villages, where kindly
treatment was assured. George Webb described the wagons as
"long boxes on wheels, drawn by oxen and with little children
peeping from under the canvas tops." Settlers usually arrived
wanting to trade metal and trinkets for wheat, but if trade could
not be worked out the Pimas gave them food anyway. "That
is how Pimas are. For centuries the rich soil and water from
the Gila had always given them all they needed. It was easy
to be generous." These latest newcomers were regarded as a
needy people, and courtesy demanded they be well treated.

Factors that had been building since Coronado's *entrada* now
converged abruptly, each reinforcing the other, and the relation
between desert and man entered a new era. American policy

was to establish reservations for the Indians, at first intending
to isolate the native peoples rather than to incorporate them
into society either by intermarriage or by wanton exploitation,
as had been the Spanish custom. The lands "agreed" upon were
seldom as large as the Indians felt were theirs rightfully by
aboriginal occupancy, and in the case of the main Papago
Reservation (not established until 1918) mineral rights were
withheld from the Indians even though the land was said to
be theirs. There was considerable unhappiness and growing
apprehension, but one decided advantage for the Pimas, Papagos,
and Opatas (who lived in Mexico at the mountain edge of the
desert) was the final containment of the Apaches — a goal the
Spanish and Mexicans had sought but never achieved. The
Apaches were a loosely affiliated tribe of twelve or more bands
who lived by hunting and gathering rather than by farming,
and for whom raiding the villages of neighboring Indian tribes
and the settlements of Spanish, Mexicans, and Anglos became
simply a logical, updated, efficient means of gleaning a livelihood
from the land. Horses were as tasty as deer, and were useful
as well. Wheat was as acceptable as wild seeds, and through
raiding it was available in large and ready-gathered quantities.
Why send women out with baskets and beaters to harvest the
seeds of wild bushes when men of the tribe could ride their
new horses and raid?

The Spanish government had tried warfare against the
Apaches but on too sporadic a basis to be effective. They then
switched to enticing some of the more peaceable bands into the
settlements and there teaching them a desire for material things
and to crave liquor and accept the convenience of rations. This
deliberate impoverishment of the human spirit was effective
enough that "tame" Apaches came to be differentiated from
"wild" Apaches; but the money gave out and rations were
discontinued, and all Apaches were again "wild." When the
new Mexican government took over they began an even more
horrendous policy: extermination. A bounty of $100 was paid
for each dead Apache, until, mercifully, money again ran out,

in 1836. Twelve years after that the Apaches felt understandable satisfaction when the United States emerged as victor in the Mexican-American War. But the welcome turned to worry as the Indians tried to deal with the Anglo-Americans, who insisted that all raiding must be stopped, even against ranches and villages south of the new border — an odd viewpoint since the Anglos themselves had just spent two years warring against the Mexicans, killing them at every chance. In the Apache view killing should be held to a minimum. It was pointless. The purpose of a raid was to make off with horses, wheat, women, and children, and it was basic good sense to leave a nucleus of ranchers or villagers in good health so that they could raise more horses, wheat, women, and children. This was wise husbandry of the resource of raiding.

Further disillusionment came as the Apaches slowly realized that the Anglos believed victory in their Mexican war had given them jurisdiction over Apache territory as well as Mexican territory gained by the treaty. Clashes were inevitable, and so was the shameful ultimate outcome of Apaches' accepting reservations and submitting to daily head counts and lessons in farming.

Other tribes, who also felt they had lived well by following the paths of their fathers, similarly found themselves under the administrative care of agents determined to "civilize" them. For the Pimas a first step was to bribe the men into haircuts, for which the reward of a hat was offered. Next, adobe houses were deemed "progress" and wagons were held out as bribes for each man who would build one. No instruction in how to build the houses was given, and no help, but the promise of a wagon was so alluring that several men built as best they could. Each followed his own ideas and often ended up with a boxy hut set with tiny doors and no windows. These were roughly styled after traditional Pima brush houses, the only pattern available. Built of the alien materials, they were unbearably stuffy to live in. Nonetheless, families could seek refuge in the odd little boxes on freakishly cold winter nights and they made acceptable storage

Papago village
(right)
and wagon

sheds. Furthermore, the "houses" had accomplished their one real objective, so far as the Indians were concerned — getting the wagons.

The wheel came in the same way to the Papagos, at least to those living in the better-watered, eastern portion of the reservation. The western portion was such harsh desert that it stayed beyond reach of an agent. But by the 1860s eastern Papagos were finding wagons remarkable resources to plan around, with whole villages newly drawn together in cooperative activity. Councils discussed trading expeditions, the hauling of wood and water, the building and maintaining of roads, undertakings that affected everyone. Men could bring in loads of firewood big enough for village needs and to sell in Tucson, thereby using one new resource — the wagon — to provide still another new resource — cash. The wagon also meant a way to get sacks of corn and wheat into town for sale. This provided incentive for larger-scale farming, which in turn called for irrigation. And with the wagon to bring household water to the villages in metal drums, family consumption sharply in-

creased; the manufacture of clay ollas fell off; and women and girls found their time free from two time-honored chores, making containers for water and endlessly walking the desert to fill them and carry them home. Men who formerly had hunted together and farmed and fought and gone to the Gulf for salt together now formed groups to clear land and grade wagon routes across washes and rough hillsides. Practically for the first time work parties from widely scattered villages coordinated their efforts to serve a common purpose, and individuals learned to specialize in new skills, some working with iron to shoe horses, others with leather to repair harnesses, or with hammers and sawn wood to keep the precious wagons patched together. As late as the 1950s, when we moved to Organ Pipe, the Papagos were still driving their wagons, occasionally coming past National Monument headquarters en route to Mexico to visit relatives who lived only a few straight-line miles from them. It was a long, tedious trip, and dangerous with automobiles dominating the roads; but there was no other legal way to get to Papago villages separated by the boundary fence that cut the Indians' traditional territory in two and divided it between Mexicans and Americans. The Papagos had to drive around the fence, and check in and out with Customs and Immigration.

For villages along the rivers, water became the inevitable point of issue. The whites tended to dig irrigation ditches upriver from Indian settlements and divert water, leaving none for Indians in dry years. The newcomers' fields would lie green beneath the sun, while the Indians' ancient fields turned to dust. George Webb told about how it was in his village. The year was 1887:

> Now the river is an empty bed full of sand. Now you can stand . . . and see the wind tearing pieces of bark off the cottonwood trees along the dry ditches. The dead trees stand like white bones. The redwing blackbirds have gone somewhere else . . . [It used to be that] some Pima boy would come along and dive into the big ditch and swim for awhile. Then he would get out and open the headgate and the water would come splashing in the laterals and flow out along the ditches. By this time all the Pimas were out in the fields with their shovels. They would fan out and lead the water to the alfalfa, along the corn rows, and over to the melons. The redwing

Papago horses

blackbirds would sing in the trees and fly down to look for bugs along the ditches. Their song always means that there is water close by ... Now you can look out across the valley and see the green alfalfa and cotton spreading for miles on the farms of white people ... Some of those farmers take their water from big ditches dug hundreds of years ago by Pimas, or the ancestors of Pimas [the Hohokam]. Over there, across the valley, is where the redwing blackbirds are singing today.

Man no longer lived in the desert simply, as one species among many. He dominated, shaping the land and the life to suit his convenience, or what he thought to be his convenience. But change was dawning even for the new Anglo overlords, change beyond their control.

In the Tucson region the change can be said to have begun in 1889. That year rain was heavy and water flooded normally across the grassy bottomlands of the Santa Cruz River. It wet fields and enriched the soil and pleased the farmers. Ducks found ample water runways for their landings and takeoffs. Fish darted to escape from otters and rose to the bait dangled in their midst by men and boys. And what few beavers were left used the high water to float new branches of cottonwood and willow to

their food caches. In short, all was normal — but for the last time, at least under what had been normalcy for the past scores of centuries. Destiny had shaped a new era, and the summer of 1890 brought the opening event. The *Arizona Daily Star* chronicled the curtain-raiser on August 5: "The flood yesterday washed a deep cut across the hospital road . . . The cut is perpendicular and the water [is] deep."

Two days later the channel had grown two hundred yards wide and nearly two miles long, and before the floodwater dried a week later the channel had doubled and tripled and quadrupled its size. Where there had been fields there was now a yawning arroyo cut deep into the valley bottom, and furthermore, the occurrence was not limited to the Tucson area. Rivers throughout southeastern Arizona and much of Sonora stopped their gentle meandering that year and began instead to sluice themselves into trenches twenty to seventy feet deep. The Santa Cruz, San Pedro, Sonoyta, Altar, and Magdalena riverbeds turned from ribbons of green to wide dry bands of sand and gravel. The year-round flow of water stopped and intermittent flow began. Once these valleys had been cursed for their mosquito-plagued marshes, but no more. The joke had even been that the citizens of Tucson would die of malaria faster than the new railroad could bring in replacements. In many of the desert valleys wild turkeys had nested in waist-high grass and muskrats had endlessly gathered sedges. Fish had been so plentiful that they were a mainstay in the diet of the Indians, boys often simply diving into the river and searching in beaver holes dug into the bank, favorite refuges of fish. The boys easily caught the fish in their hands. All this changed. No more turkeys or muskrats or beavers or fish. And no more farms. The rivers had cut too low to flow into irrigation ditches and bring water to the fields.

Why did it happen? James Hastings and Raymond Turner have analyzed causes in their book *The Changing Mile,* and with paired photographs have shown how extensive and widespread the changes are. Fire has been held by some observers to underlie the arroyo-cutting: specifically, the loss of wild range fires that once swept the river bottoms and the bajadas, killing woody seedlings but not really harming grass (which would quickly grow back from the roots). Without fire, brush and trees invaded the grasslands, rain no longer soaked in well, and runoff increased. The theory is plausible, although there is question as to how widespread fires actually were. Father Ignaz Pfefferkorn, an early-day priest in Sonora, speaks of Opata Indians burning brush to drive out rabbits, and of Pimas firing the dry stalks left in the fields after harvest, and Apaches and Seris building campfires to roast meat, then not bothering to put them out. "The fires spread easily and without resistance in the high grass ... " he writes. "[Flames] seize on trees which stand in the way, and often cause a frightful conflagration. One thing and another fills the air with fiery vapors and increases the heat, which is great enough without all of this."

Regardless of this account, there is no real indication of extensive or frequent burning by Indians; nor is it probable that lightning-caused fires happened with any regularity. The journals of early settlers make little mention of fire, and since for the most part they were ranchers they surely would have noticed. Overgrazing probably comes closer to having influenced the change. Every conquistador and missionary from Coronado on, had herded sheep and cattle through the desert. By the mid-nineteenth century thousands of head ran totally wild in Sonora and individual ranches claimed herds of 40,000 or more. Settlement by Mexicans and soon by Anglos increased steadily as Apache raids diminished. The Civil War disrupted the population growth; then the return of peace and the joining of the continent by the Southern Pacific Railroad, set the desert portion of American "manifest destiny" on its way.

Concern as to the prudence of agriculture barely existed. John Wesley Powell, pioneering surveyor, geologist, and ethnologist, had strongly stated in his *Report on the Lands of the Arid Region of the United States* that the territory west of the Missouri River differed radically from the forest and farmlands of the

East. At the same time there was a blindly naïve countervailing theory which held that rain followed the plow. The West was arid because man had not yet graced it with his agriculture, but as soon as green fields and grazing animals spread across the land the heavens would open and rain would fall. By 1880, two years after Powell's report was published, there were perhaps 60,000 cattle in southern Arizona. By 1885 there were ten times that many, and by 1890 and the onset of the arroyo-cutting the number had swelled to a million or more. "The malady of overcrowding is with us in aggravated form," commented the *Southwestern Stockmen* for January 3, 1891.

Grass cover was weakened by excessive grazing and the cattle themselves were directly disseminating the seeds of the invading scrub species that were destroying the range. The animals fed on mesquite, drawing nutrients from the green pods and depositing the beans unharmed in a moist medium ideal for germination. Nearly two thousand undigested mesquite seeds have been counted in a single cow chip, many of them still capable of germination. In fact, exposure to the acids of a cow's alimentary canal probably fosters mesquite germination since the hard seed coat needs scarification as a preliminary to sprouting. Mesquite, juniper, creosote bush, and other species invaded land that for centuries had been dominated by grass, and at the same time desert rivers changed their ancient character. A good case can be made for cause and effect. Grazing left the soil vulnerable to erosion. Wind caught sand and drifted it, smothering what grass cover remained. Runoff churned and rushed like torrents of liquid sandpaper, and cloudburst after cloudburst intensified the process. Probably this latter is a key factor, according to Turner and Hastings. The climate had changed, setting the stage for the deepening of the river channels and the loss of the fertile valley bottoms. Cattle were merely the final activating force for a change long in the making and beyond human responsibility.

More years with downpours in proportion to gentle rains came in the years from 1850 to 1890 than in the decades since, a change in pattern presumably applicable also to the preceding decades, for which no records are available. The unusually torrential and repeated floodwaters began the gullying and arroyo-cutting, and once the process had started it steadily bit farther and deeper into slopes and valley bottoms. The climate change in itself was not so drastic as the results it triggered. The totals of yearly precipitation had scarcely varied, but, owing to overgrazing and possibly also to a reduction in fire, the vegetation was in a stage of transition from grassland to brushland and even a simple shift in the nature of the rainfall was enough to set off wholesale erosion. It wasn't *more* rain, it was the new, periodic, superabundance of runoff that changed the land. Desert equilibrium seesaws on a particularly delicate fulcrum. Let one factor change and drastic effects may be set in motion more quickly than in milder lands with wider margins of moisture and fertility.

These changes of the 1890s formed only a prelude, the first threads in a whole tapestry of change. Ensuing decades brought people by the hundreds of thousands, to farm, to ranch, to mine, to work in industry, to vacation, to retire. Phoenix and Tucson have been the fastest-growing cities in the nation, with suburbs building like annular rings around urban centers. In Mexico, Hermosillo is only one step behind. Dams hold back the waters of the Salt, the Gila, the Verde, the Colorado, the Altar — every river worth the price of concrete. Lakes sparkle blue against the somber browns of the desert, and evaporate water back into the air at tremendous rates (around 750,000 acre-feet per year for Lake Mead, each acre-foot being equal to 325,851 gallons). Seven states and two nations abide by, and argue over, a compact that apportions the flow of the lower Colorado River; and the Imperial-Coachella-Mexicali valley irrigation system of southern California, northern Sonora, and Baja California is one of the greatest the world has ever known. Salt accumulations and roots drowned by waterlogging threaten disaster, as happened to the fields of the Hohokam; but plowing five feet deep solves the percolation problem, and drain tiles underlying the fields flush away excess water used to leach salts from the soil. In the Imperial Valley alone the gridwork of these tiles totals over 12,000 miles. Without it, each acre-foot of irrigation water would add a ton of salt to the soil. As it is — or has been — the salt-laden water finishes its wet work in the fields of the California desert and flows on to become part of Mexico's quota of Colorado River water. A few years ago its salts were turning Mexican fields as glistening white as if they were blanketed with snow. Protests and improved methods have rectified the matter, at least for the time being.

All manner of problems compound and add to the pattern of change spreading across the desert. Much of their trouble is based in the fact that the men who now husband desert land and determine desert tomorrows have come to this hot, dry corner of the West with humid-land attitudes and laws. They behave according to what worked elsewhere, and they persist in expecting the desert to keep pace with their economic convenience. They are unwilling to tailor dreams to fit realities. Men collect water that fell hundreds of miles off and impound it behind dams, then send it crosscountry in open canals. They pump water that fell thousands of years ago and know that water tables have dropped as much as 300 feet, yet they act as if aquifers were tanks to empty at will. Men flagrantly surround their desert homes with lawns. And they lure vacationers and additional residents by boasting of artificial lakes that undulate artificial waves suitable for water-skiing, and with gimmickry such as disassembling London Bridge stone by stone and shipping it from the Thames to the Colorado, there rebuilding it to span slack, reservoir water at Havasu City. All of this, while the United States Geological Survey estimates that by 1980 the nation's annual water consumption will exceed precipitation by a ratio of 150 to 1. This is for the land as a whole. Imagine what the figure will be for the desert!

Meanwhile the Army Corps of Engineers suggests backing water into the Grand Canyon; military gunnery ranges and atomic test sites and ammunition depots sprawl across desert

Tucson

mountains and valleys (including a bighorn sheep refuge in Arizona); weekend shanties dot five-acre "jackrabbit home-steads" in the California desert and a similar resort shoddiness spills over the international line and spreads cancerlike along the pristine desert coast of Sonora and Baja California. Dune buggies with wide soft tires race wherever the eons have piled hills of sand. Their tracks replace the pattern of wind-ripples and their wheels crash into kangaroo rat burrows and flip fringe-toed lizards from their hiding places. A documented 2600 motorcyclists and trail bikers churned the desert on a single Thanksgiving Day, racing from Barstow, California, to Las Vegas, Nevada; and increasingly throughout the desert you can't hear the song of birds for the roar of engines. Power plants supplying electricity for Los Angeles blacken Arizona skies with coal smoke, and San Francisco has asked Nevada for permission to start a garbage landfill in the desert rather than continue to fill in the Bay.

Of course countermeasures are being devised. Monomolecular films spread on the surface of water produce evaporation savings of as much as 65 percent in tests, although wind whipping the water into waves breaks the film and destroys much of its effectiveness. Thin membranes of asphalt set as barriers two feet beneath the surface of loose soil may successfully stop the infiltration of water beyond the root zone. Solar power may be successful in producing electricity. An experimental solar cookstove has been tested by Pima Indian families who report on it favorably, perhaps bemused by it and perhaps impressed with its practicality. Rain runoff can be harvested and used to recharge groundwater supplies, at least partially replacing the fossil resource of water that soaked into the earth for tens of thousands of years. Ocean water can be distilled, perhaps soon on a financially feasible basis. Measures can be taken, and are being taken; but the question nagging the mind is, Will solutions be tempered with wisdom and love, or be merely technologically and economically clever? Does anybody care about the desert as *desert?*

To the arriving Europeans the whole of the North American wilderness was an evil to wrestle against, and even now the desert seems an annoyance that challenges human patience and wit to overcome: a mistake to correct: a land to "reclaim" without regard for its having a valid, distinctive nature of its own. Perhaps Anglo-Americans, and modern Mexicans, have struggled this intently in the desert because its essential leanness brings man squarely against realities he can ignore at least a little longer in gentler, more indulgent lands. Perhaps for this very reason the desert holds special value, and instead of trying to subdue it all and stamp its face with the false green and blue of limitless fields and lakes we should now see the desert for itself. For here is a land where you stand alone between the empty sweep of earth and sky. Your eyes behold bare rock and sand, and the vastness of the night heavens pricked with light; and you puzzle out the relationships between your own frail house of bone and flesh and the awesome, impersonal immensity beyond.

Somehow in regions that are more succoring these questions seem less urgent, even though man now knows that his future on this "spaceship" planet depends on precisely this sort of awareness.

Once, after a long absence from the desert, my husband and I found ourselves again driving the arrow-straight roads that knife for miles across dusty brown flats and climb without a curve up the broad alluvial fans to the passes that notch the mountains. The silence impressed us that trip — silence that was not so much the absence of sound as the positive presence of magnificent hush. Not even wind stirred, although wind can howl against canyon walls and whistle in the thorns of cactus when all other sounds are stilled. Dawn had lit the eastern sky and angular shadows had streaked the land with a strong, masculine sort of beauty. Not the soft, obvious loveliness of an alpine meadow or a quiet woodland, but a more demanding beauty. The desert asks not just your heart but your mind and a bit of your time, since to appreciate the harmonies of so hostile a land you must understand relationships that do not reveal themselves readily. The huge scale of the desert is easily grasped, even by looking only through car windows at seventy miles per hour; but the intricacies and the small miracles withhold themselves — the tiny cascade of sand grains as a lizard bolts for safety, the royal purple spots at the base of each petal of a mallow blossom, the eyes of a kit fox or a kangaroo rat reflecting the glow of your campfire.

True desert is compounded of both the vast and the small. Accept its terms and give yourself to it, and your spirit will find quiet without coddling. No wonder the religions of the desert have been monotheistic: one God with each man standing directly in relation to Him, each charged with effecting his own destiny. In the desert you contemplate earth and time and life. You see the obituary column of the circling vultures, and also the miracle of dawn light catching against thorns and producing halos. You find perspective. And peace.

A Selective List
of Scientific Names

Principal References

Index

A Selective List of Scientific Names

agave, *Agave* sp.

agria, *Machaerocereus gummosus*

antelope brush, *Purshia glandulosa*

arrowweed, *Pluchea sericea*

aspen, *Populus tremuloides*

barrel cactus, *Ferocactus wislizeni*

beavertail cactus, *Opuntia bigelovii*

blackbrush, *Coleogyne ramosissima*

blue palm, *Erythea armata*

boojum tree, *Idria columnaris*

bristlecone pine, *Pinus aristata*

brittlebush, *Encelia farinosa*

buckwheat, *Eriogonum* sp.

bunchgrass, *Hilaria rigida*

burrobush, *Hymenoclea salsola*

bur sage, *Franseria dumosa*

bush lupine, *Lupinus rubens*

California poppy, *Eschscholtzia californica*

caper plant, *Capparis spinosa*

cardon, *Pachycereus pringlei*

carrizo, *Phragmites communis*

catclaw, *Acacia greggii*

"chain cholla," *Opuntia fulgida*

Chihuahua pine, *Pinus leiophylla* var. *chihuahuana*

cholla, *Opuntia* sp.

chuckwalla's delight, *Bebbia juncea*

clubmoss, *Selaginella arizonica*

coldenia, *Coldenia* sp.

condalia, *Condalia* sp.

cottontop cactus, *Echinocactus polycephalus*

cottonwood, *Populus fremontii*

creosote bush, *Larrea tridentata*

datilillo, *Yucca valida*

desert chicory, *Rafinesquia neomexicana*

desert holly, *Atriples hymenelytra*

desert rue, *Thamnosma montana*

devil claw, *Proboscidea parviflora*

dodder, *Cuscuta veatchii*

Douglas-fir, *Pseudotsuga menziesii*

elephant tree, *Bursera microphylla,* *Pachycormus discolor*

Engelmann spruce, *Picea engelmannii*

fan palm, *Washingtonia filifera*

four-wing saltbush, *Atriplex canescens*

gold-poppy, *Eschscholtzia glyptosperma*

greasewood, *Sacobatus vermiculatus*
hackberry, *Celtis* sp.
hairbrush cactus, *Pachycereus pectenaboriginum*
hedgehog cactus, *Echinocereus engelmanni*
iceplant, *Mesembryanthemum crystallinum*
ironwood, *Olneya tesota*
jojoba, *Simmondsia californica*
Joshua tree, *Yucca brevifolia*
juniper, *Juniperus* sp.
lichen, *Usnea* sp.
liverwort, *Riccia* sp.
lupine, *Lupinus* sp.
lycium, *Lycium* sp.
mangrove, *Rhizophora mangle*
manzanita, *Arctostaphylos* sp.
mesquite, *Prosopis juliflora*
Mormon tea, *Ephedra* sp.
morning-glory tree, *Ipomoea arborescens*
night-blooming cereus, *Peniocereus greggii*
oak, *Quercus* sp.
ocotillo, *Fouquieria diguetii*
organpipe, *Lemaireocereus thurberi*
paintbrush, *Castilleja* sp.
palosanto, *Acacia willardiana*
paloverde, *Cercidium* sp.
penstemon, *Penstemon parishii*
pereskia, *Pereskia* sp.
phacelia, *Phacelia crenulata*
phlox, *Phlox* sp.
pickleweed, *Allenrolfea occidentalis*
pincushion, *Chaenactis* sp.
pinyon pine, *Pinus monophylla*

plantain, *Plantago* sp.
ponderosa pine, *Pinus ponderosa*
prickly pear, *Opuntia engelmannii*
primrose, *Oenothera* sp.
puffball, *Podaxon farlowii*
pursley, *Heliotropium* sp.
pygmy cedar, *Peucephyllum schottii*
rabbitbrush, *Chrysothamnus* sp.
sage, *Salvia* sp.
sagebrush, *Artemisia* sp.
saguaro, *Carnegiea gigantea*
salicornia, *Salicornia rubra*
saltbush, *Atriplex* sp.
saltcedar, *Tamarix* sp.
saltgrass, *Distichlis texana*
"sand food," *Ammobromma sonorae*
sand verbena, *Albronia villosa*
sedum, *Sedum* sp.
seepwillow, *Baccharis* sp.
senita, *Lophocereus schottii*
sina, *Rathbunia alamosensis*
smoketree, *Dalea spinosa*
sotol, *Dasylirion wheeleri*
staghorn cholla, *Opuntia veriscolor*
storksbill, *Erodium texanum*
subalpine fir, *Abies lasiocarpa*
sumac, *Rhus* sp.
sycamore, *Platanus racemosa*
teddybear cholla, *Opuntia bigelovii*
thistle, *Cirsium* sp.
tillandsia, *Tillandsia recurvata*
tumbleweed, *Salsola* sp.
watercress, *Nasturtium officinale*
white fir, *Abies concolor*
willow, *Salix* sp.
wire lettuce, *Stephanomeria* sp.
yucca, *Yucca* sp.

MAMMALS

antelope ground squirrel, *Citellus leucurus*

badger, *Taxidea taxus*

bighorn sheep, *Ovis canadensis*

bobcat, *Lynx rufus*

brown bat, *Eptesicus fuscus*

burro, *Equus asinus*

cactus mouse, *Peromyscus eremicus*

coati, *Nasua narica*

coyote, *Canis latrans*

desert cottontail, *Sylvilagus auduboni*

eland, *Taurotragus* sp.

grasshopper mouse, *Onychomys torridus*

gray wolf, *Canis lupus*

hognose bat, *Choeronycteris mexicana*

hognose skunk, *Conepatus leuconotus*

jackrabbit, *Lepus alleni*

kangaroo mouse, *Microdipodops* sp.

kangaroo rat, *Dipodomys* sp.

kit fox, *Vulpes macrotis*

longnose bat, *Leptonycteris nivalis*

Mojave ground squirrel, *Citellus mohavensis*

mountain lion, *Felis concolor*

mule deer, *Odocoileus hemionus*

ocelot, *Felis pardalis*

oryx, *Oryx leucoryx*

packrat, *Neotoma lepida*

peccary, *Pecari angulatus*

pipistrel, *Pipistrellus hesperus*

pocket mouse, *Perognathus* sp.

porcupine, *Erethizon dorsatum*

ringtail cat, *Bassariscus astutus*

roundtail ground squirrel, *Citellus tereticaudus*

AMPHIBIANS

desert slender salamander, *Batrochoseps aridus*

Mexican leaf frog, *Agalychnis dacnicolor*

red-spotted toad, *Bufo punctatus*

spadefoot toad, *Scaphiopus* sp.

REPTILES

Arizona coral snake, *Micruroides euryxanthus*

banded gecko, *Coleonyx variegatus*

brown-shouldered lizard, *Uta stansburiana*

chuckwalla, *Sauromalus obesus*

collared lizard, *Crotaphytus collaris*

desert iguana, *Dipsosaurus dorsalis*

desert tortoise, *Gopherus agassizi*

false coral snake, *Lampropeltis pyromelana*

fringe-toed lizard, *Uma notata*

Gila monster, *Heloderma suspectum*

hognose snake, *Heterodon nasicus*

horned lizard, *Phrynosoma* sp.

kingsnake, *Lampropeltis* sp.

Mexican beaded lizard, *Heloderma horridum*

night lizard, *Xantusia vigiles*
sidewinder, *Crotalus cerastes*
spiny lizard, *Sceloporus magister*
tree lizard, *Urosaurus ornatus*
western diamondback rattlesnake,
 Crotalus atrox

western fence lizard, *Sceloporus occidentalis*
whiptail, *Cnemidiphorus tigris*

FISHES

black bullhead, *Ictalurus melas*
Gila sucker, *Catostomus*
green sunfish, *Lepomis cyanellus*
loach minnow, *Tiaroga cobitis*
longfin dace, *Agosia chrysogaster*
pupfish, *Cyprinodon* sp.

rainbow trout, *Salmo gairdneri*
roundtail chub, *Gila robusta*
Sonora sucker, *Catostomus insignis*
speckled dace, *Rhinichthys osculus*
spikedace, *Meda fulgida*
topminnow, *Peociliopsis occidentalis*

INVERTEBRATES

cactobrosis moth, *Cactobrosis fernaldialis*
centipede, *Scolopendra* sp.
digger wasp, *Bembix* sp.
predaceous diving beetle,
 Cybester explanatus
fairy shrimp, *Eulimnadia* sp.
grasshopper, *Trimerotropis pallidipennis*
harvester ant, *Veromessor* sp.
horsefly, *Tabanus punctifer*
katydid, *Microcentrum* sp.

pinacate beetle, *Eleodes* sp.
pseudoscorpion, *Chelonops* sp.
saguaro mosquito, *Aedes* sp.
scorpion, *Vejovis* sp.; *Centruroides sculpturatus* (deadly); *Centruroides gertschi* (deadly)
solpugid, *Eremobates* sp.
springtail, *Collembola* sp.
tarantula, *Aphonopelma* sp.
yucca borer, *Scyphophorus yuccae*
yucca moth, *Pronuba* sp.

Principal References

Alcorn, Stanley M. "Natural History of the Saguaro," *Arid Lands Colloquia* for 1959–1960, 1960–1961, pp. 23–29. Tucson: University of Arizona.

Alcorn, Stanley M., and Edwin B. Kurtz, Jr. "Some Factors Affecting Germination of Seed in the Saguaro Cactus," *American Journal of Botany,* 46 (1959):526–29.

Alcorn, Stanley M., S. E. McGregor, and George Olin. "Pollination Requirements of the Organpipe Cactus," *The Cactus and Succulent Journal,* 34 (1962):2.

Anderson, Anders H. and Anne. "Life History of the Cactus Wren, Part I:Winter and Pre-nesting Behavior," *The Condor,* 59 (1959):274–96.

———. "Life History of the Cactus Wren, Part II:The Beginning of Nesting," *The Condor,* 61 (1959):186–205.

———. "Life History of the Cactus Wren, Part IV:Development of Nestlings," *The Condor,* 6 (1961):87–97.

Aschmann, Homer. *Central Desert of Baja California:Demography and Ecology.* Berkeley:University of California Press, 1959.

Baegert, Johann Jakob, S.J. *Observations in Lower California.* Berkeley: University of California Press, 1952 (originally published Mannheim, Germany, 1772).

Bancroft, Herbert Eugene. *Spanish Explorations in the Southwest, 1542–1706.* New York: Scribner's, 1916.

Barber, Willard E., and W. L. Minckley. "Fishes of Aravaipa Creek, Graham and Pinal Counties, Arizona," *Southwest Naturalist,* 11 (1966):313–24.

Bartholomew, George A., Jr., and Tom J. Cade. "Temperature Regulation, Hibernation, and Aestivation in the Little Pocket Mouse, *Perognathus longemembris,*" *Journal of Mammalogy,* 38 (1957):60–72.

Bartholomew, George A., Jr., and William R. Dawson. "Body Temperature and Water Requirements in the Mourning Dove," *Ecology,* 35 (1954):181–87.

———. "Body Temperatures in California and Gambel's Quail," *The Auk,* 75 (1958):150–56.

———. "Respiratory Water Loss in Some Birds of the Southwestern United States," *Physiological Zoology,* 26 (1953):162–66.

Bartholomew, George A., Jr., and Jack W. Hudson. "Desert Ground Squirrels," *Scientific American,* May 1961, pp. 107–16.

Bartholomew, George A., Jr., and Richard E. MacMillan. "O$_2$ Consumption, Estivation, and Hibernation in the Kangaroo Mouse, *Microdipodops pallidus,*" *Physiological Zoology,* 34 (1961):177–83.

———. "Water Economy of the California Quail and Its Use of Sea Water," *The Auk,* 78 (1961):505–14.

———. "The Water Requirements of Doves and Their Use of Sea Water and NaCl Solutions," *Physiological Zoology,* 33 (1960):171–78.

Bartholomew, George A., Jr., William R. Dawson, and Edward J. O'Neill. "Field Study of Temperature Regulation in Young White Pelicans, *Pelecanus erythrorhynchos,*" *Ecology,* 34 (1953):554–60.

Bartholomew, George A., Jr., Thomas R. Howell, and Tom J. Cade. "Torpidity in the White-throated Swift, Anna's Hummingbird, and Poor-will," *The Condor,* 59 (1957):145–55.

Beament, J. W. L. "Water Relations of Insect Cuticle," *Biological Reviews,* 36 (1961):281–320.

Beatty, Janice C. "Survival of Winter Annuals in the Northern Mojave Desert," *Ecology,* 48 (1967):745–50.

Belkin, Daniel A. "Anoxia: Tolerance in Reptiles," *Science,* 139 (1963):492–93.

Benson, Seth B. "Three Rodents from the Lava Beds of Southern New Mexico," *Zoology* (University of California), 38 (1932):335–44.

Bentley, P. J. "Adaptations of Amphibia to Arid Environments," *Science,* 152 (1966):619–23.

Blackwelder, Eliot. "Historical Significance of Desert Varnish," Geological Society of America *Bulletin,* 59 (1948):1367.

———. "Mudflow As a Geologic Agent in Semi-Arid Mountains," Geological Society of America *Bulletin,* 39 (1928):465–84.

———. "Origin of the Piedmont Plains of the Great Basin," Geological Society of America *Bulletin,* 40 (1929):168.

Bliss, Wesley L. "In the Wake of the Wheel: Introduction to the Wagon of the Papago Indians of Southern Arizona," in Edward H. Spicer, ed., *Human Problems in Technological Change.* New York: Russell Sage Foundation, 1952.

Bogart, Charles M. "How Reptiles Regulate Their Body Temperature," *Scientific American,* April 1959, pp. 105–20.

Bogart, Charles M., and Rafael Martín del Campo. "The Gila Monster and Its Allies," The American Museum of Natural History *Bulletin,* 109 (1956):5–238.

Bolton, Herbert, *Kino's Historical Memoir: Pimaría Alta.* Berkeley: University of California, 1948.

Bragg, Arthur. "Breeding Habits, Eggs and Tadpoles of *Scaphiopus hurterii,*" *Copeia* (1944), pp. 230–41.

Brattstrom, Bayard H. "Body Temperature of Reptiles," *American Midlands Naturalist,* 73 (1965):376–422.

Brauner, Joseph. "Reactions of Poor-wills to Light and Temperature," *The Condor,* 54 (1952):152–59.

Brown, G. W., ed. *Desert Biology.* New York and London: Academic Press, 1968.

Brown, James H. "The Desert Pupfish," *Scientific American,* May 1971, pp. 104-10.

Buechner, Helmut K. "The Bighorn Sheep in the United States, Its Past, Present, and Future," *Wildlife Monograph,* 4 (1960):1-174.

Bunnell, Sterling. *Pupfish of the Death Valley Region.* San Francisco: California Tomorrow, 1970.

Bustard, H. Robert. "The Eating of Shed Epidermal Material in Squamate Reptiles," *Herpetologica,* 21 (1965):4.

———. "Gecknoid Lizards Adapt Fat Storage to Desert Environments," *Science,* 158 (1967):1197-98.

Buxton, P. A. *Animal Life in the Desert.* London: Arnold, 1923.

Cade, Tom J. "Relations between Raptors and Columbiform Birds at a Desert Water Hole," *The Wilson Bulletin,* 77 (1965):340-45.

Calder, Ritchie. *Man against the Desert.* London: Allen & Unwin, 1951.

Calder, William. "The Diurnal Activity of the Roadrunner," *The Condor,* 70 (1968):84-85.

———. "Nest Sanitation: a Possible Factor in the Water Economy of the Roadrunner," *The Condor,* 70 (1968):279.

———. "There Really Is a Roadrunner," *Natural History,* 77 (1968):50-55.

Cannon, W. A. "Biological Relations of Certain Cacti," *American Naturalist,* 40 (1960):27-46.

Carpenter, Charles C. "Behavior Patterns of Fringe-toed Lizards," *Copeia* (1963) pp. 406-12.

Castetter, Edward R., and Willis H. Bell. "The Aboriginal Utilization of the Tall Cactus in the American Southwest," *Ethnological Studies in the Southwest,* Vol. IV. University of New Mexico *Bulletin.* Albuquerque, 1937.

Chew, Robert M. "Water Metabolism in Desert-Inhabiting Vertebrates," *Biological Reviews,* 36 (1961):1-31.

Chew, Robert M., and Bernard B. Butterworth. "Ecology of Rodents in Indian Cove (Mojave Desert), Joshua Tree National Monument, California," *Journal of Mammalogy,* 45 (1964):203-25.

Chew, Robert M., and Arthur E. Dammann. "Evaporative Water Loss of Small Vertebrates, As Measured with an Infrared Analyzer," *Science,* 133 (1960):384-85.

Childs, Thomas. "Sketch of the 'Sand Indians' As Written by Henry F. Dobyns," *Kiva,* 19, Nos. 2 and 4 (1954):27-29.

Clements, F. E. "The Origin of the Desert Climax and Climate" in T. H. Goodspeed, ed., *Essays in Geobotany.* Berkeley: University of California Press, 1936.

Cloudsey-Thompson, J. L. *Rhythmic Activity in Animal Physiology and Behavior.* New York and London: Academic Press, 1961.

———. *Spiders, Scorpions, Centipedes, and Moths.* New York: Pergamon Press, 1958.

———, ed. *Biology of Deserts.* London: Institute of Biology, Tavistock House, 1954.

Cole, LaMont C. "Experiments of Tolerance of High Temperatures in Lizards with Reference to Adaptive Coloration," *Ecology,* 24 (1943):94–108.

Coolidge, Dane and Mary Roberts. *The Last of the Seris.* New York: Dutton, 1939.

Cott, H. B. *Adaptive Coloration in Animals.* London: Methuen, 1940.

Cottam, Clarence, and James B. Trefethen. *Whitewings.* Princeton: Van Nostrand, 1968.

Cowles, Raymond B. "Note on the Arboreal Feeding of the Desert Iguana," *Copeia* (1946), pp. 172–73.

———. "Observations on the Winter Activities of Desert Reptiles," *Ecology,* 22 (1941):125–40.

———. "Possible Origin of Dermal Temperature Regulation," *Evolution,* 12 (1956):347–57.

———. "The Relation of Birds to Seed Dispersal of the Desert Mistletoe," Madroño, 3 (1936):352–56.

———. "Some Activities of the Sidewinder," *Copeia* (1945), pp. 220–22.

Cowles, Raymond B., and William R. Dawson. "A Cooling Mechanism of the Texas Nighthawk," *The Condor,* 53 (1951):19–22.

Cross, Jack, Elizabeth Shaw, and Kathleen Scheifele. *Arizona, Its People and Resources.* Tucson: University of Arizona Press, 1960.

Cutter, William L. "An Instance of Blood Squirting by *Phrynosoma solare,*" *Copeia* (1959), p. 176.

Davis, William M. "Sheetfloods and Streamfloods," Geological Society of America *Bulletin,* 49 (1938):1337–1416.

Dawson, William R. "The Relation of O_2 Consumption to Temperature in Desert Rodents," *Journal of Mammalogy,* 36 (1955):543–53.

———. "Temperature in the Lizard, *Eumeces obsoletus,*" *Physiological Zoology,* 33 (1960): 87–103.

Deacon, James E. "Studies on the Ecology of Saratoga Springs, Death Valley National Monument." National Park Service Final Report, Research Contract 14–10–0434–0983. Washington, D.C., 1967.

Debenham, Frank. *The Geography of Deserts.* Cambridge, England: Cambridge University Press, 1954.

Deevey, Edward S. "The Human Population," *Scientific American,* September 1960, pp. 195–204.

Dice, Lee R. "Mammal Distribution in the Alamogordo Region, New Mexico," Museum of Zoology *Occasional Papers,* No. 213. Ann Arbor: University of Michigan Press, 1930.

Dice, Lee R., and Philip M. Blossom. "Studies of Mammalian Ecology in Southwestern North America with Special Attention to the Colors of Desert Mammals," Carnegie Institution *Publication 485,* 1937.

Ditmars, Raymond L. *Reptiles of the World,* rev. ed. New York: Macmillan, 1933.

Dobie, J. Frank. "The Roadrunner in Fact and Fiction," *Arizona Highways,* May 1958, pp. 9–15.

Dobyns, Henry F. "Thirsty Indians," *Human Organization,* 11 (1952):33–35.

Druisberg, Peter C. "Creosote Bush," *Plant Physiology,* 270 (1952):769–77.

Dunbier, Roger. *The Sonoran Desert.* Tucson: University of Arizona Press, 1968.

Eaton, W. Clement. "Frontier Life in Southern Arizona, 1858–1861," *The Southwestern Historical Quarterly,* 36 (1933):173–92.

Edgren, Richard A. and Margery K. "Experiences on Bluffing and Death-feigning in the Hognose Snake, *Heterodon platyrhinos,*" *Copeia* (1955), pp. 2–4.

Egoscue, Harold J. "Ecology and Life History of the Kit Fox in Tooele Co., Utah," *Ecology,* 43 (1962):481–97.

Evans, Edna H. "Useful Trees of the Desert," *Pacific Discovery,* March-April 1965, pp. 19–25.

Felger, Richard S., and Charles H. Lowe. "Climal Variation in Surface-Volume Relationships of the Columnar Cactus *Lophocereus schottii* in Northwestern Mexico," *Ecology,* 48 (1967):4.

Fenneman, Nevin M. *Physiography of Western United States.* New York: McGraw-Hill, 1931.

Fletcher, Joel E., and W. P. Martin. "Some Effects of Algae and Mold in the Rain-Crust of Desert Soils," *Ecology,* 29 (1948):95–100.

Frankel, J. "Evaporation Reduction," *Arid Zone.* Paris: UNESCO, 1965.

French, Norman R., Bernardo G. Maza, and Arnold P. Aschwanden. "Life Spans of *Dipodomys* and *Perognathus* in the Mojave Desert," *Journal of Mammalogy,* 48 (1967):537–48.

———. "Periodicity of Desert Rodent Activity," *Science,* 154 (1966):1194–95.

Geiger, Rudolf. *The Climate Near the Ground.* Cambridge: Harvard University Press, 1965.

Getty, Harry T. "Changes in Land Use among the Western Apaches," in Clark Knowlton, ed., *Indian and Spanish American Adjustments to Arid and Semi-arid Environs.* Committee on Desert and Arid Zone Research Contribution No. 7. Lubbock: Texas Technological College, 1964.

Gray, Jane. "Pleistocene Paleoclimate," *Science,* 133 (1961):38–39.

Greene, Robert A., and Charles Raymond. "The Influence of 2 Burrowing Rodents, *Dipodomys spectabilis spectabilis* and *Neotoma albigula albigula,* on Desert Soils in Arizona," Parts 1 and 2, *Ecology,* 13 (1932):73–80, 359–63.

Greenewalt, Crawford H. *Hummingbirds.* New York: Doubleday, 1960.

Gullion, Gordon W. "The Ecology of Gambel's Quail in Nevada and the Arid Southwest," *Ecology,* 41 (1960):518–21.

Hackenberg, Robert A. "Economic Alternatives for Native Peoples in Arid Lands," *Arid Lands Colloquia* for 1959–1960, 1960–1961, pp. 46–57. Tucson: University of Arizona.

Hadley, Neil F., and Stanley Williams. "Surface Activities of Some North American Scorpions in Relation to Feeding," *Ecology,* 49 (1968): 726–47.

Halseth, Odd S. "Prehistoric Irrigation in Central Arizona," *Masterkey,* 5 (1932):165–75.

Harris, David R. "Recent Plant Invasions in the Arid and Semi-Arid Southwest of the United States," *Association of American Geographers Annals,* 56 (1966); 408–22.

Harshbarger, John A. "Geohydrology of Arid Lands: Arizona—a Case Study," *Arid Lands Colloquia* for 1958–1959, pp. 9–18.

Hastings, James Rodney. "Precipitation and Saguaro Growth," *Arid Lands Colloquia* for 1959-1960, 1960-1961, pp. 30-38. Tucson: University of Arizona.

———. "Vegetation Change and Arroyo Cutting in Southeastern Arizona during the Past Century: An Historical Review," *Arid Lands Colloquia* for 1958-1959, pp. 24-39. Tucson: University of Arizona.

Hastings, James Rodney, and Stanley M. Alcorn. "Physical Determinations of Growth and Age in the Giant Cactus," Arizona Academy of Sciences *Journal*, 2 (1961):32-39.

Hastings, James Rodney, and Robert R. Humphrey, eds. *Climatological Data and Statistics for Baja California: Technical Reports on the Meteorology and Climatology of Arid Regions, No. 18.* Tucson: University of Arizona Institute of Atmospheric Physics, 1969.

———. *Climatological Data and Statistics for Sonora and Northern Sinaloa: Technical Reports on the Meteorology and Climatology of Arid Regions, No. 19.* Tucson: University of Arizona Institute of Atmospheric Physics, 1969.

Hastings, James Rodney, and Raymond M. Turner. *The Changing Mile.* Tucson: University of Arizona Press, 1965.

Haury, Emil W. "First Masters of the American Desert: The Hohokam," *National Geographic,* May 1967, pp. 670-95.

———. "Post-Pleistocene Human Occupation of the Southwest," in Terah Smiley, ed., *Climate and Man in the Southwest.* Tucson: University of Arizona Press, 1958.

———. *Stratigraphy and Archaeology of Ventana Cave, Arizona.* Tucson: University of Arizona Press, 1950.

Hawbecker, Albert. "Food and Moisture Requirements of the Nelson Antelope Ground Squirrel," *Journal of Mammalogy,* 28 (1947):115-25.

Hayden, Julian D. "Salt Erosion," *American Antiquity,* 10 (1945):373-78.

———. "A Summary Prehistory and History of the Sierra Pinacate, Sonora," *American Antiquity,* 33 (1967):335-44.

Heald, Weldon F. *Sky Island.* Princeton: Van Nostrand, 1967.

Heath, James Edward. "Head-Body Temperature Differences in Horned Lizards," *Physiological Zoology,* 37 (1964):273-79.

———. "Temperature Fluctuation in the Vulture," *The Condor,* 64 (1962):234-35.

———. "Temperature-Independent Morning Emergence in Lizards of the Genus *Phrynosoma," Science,* 138 (1962):891-92.

———. "Venous Shunts in the Cephalic Sinuses of Horned Lizards," *Physiological Zoology,* 39 (1966):30-35.

Hensley, M. Max. "Ecological Relations of the Breeding Bird Population of the Desert Biome in Arizona," *Ecological Monographs,* 24 (1954):185-207.

Heppner, Frank. "The Metabolic Significance of Differential Absorption of Radiant Energy by Black and White Birds," *The Condor,* 72 (1970):50-59.

Hills, E. S., ed. *Arid Lands: A Geographical Appraisal.* London: Methuen for UNESCO, 1966.

Hodge, Carle, ed. *Aridity and Man.* American Association for the Advancement of Science Publication No. 74. Washington, D.C., 1963.

Holdenried, R. "Natural History of the Bannertailed Kangaroo Rat in New Mexico," *Journal of Mammalogy,* 38 (1957):330-50.

Hollon, W. Eugene. *The Great American Desert, Then and Now.* Oxford: Oxford University Press, 1966.

———. *The Southwest: Old and New.* New York: Knopf, 1961.

Horton, Jerome S. *Notes on the Introduction of Deciduous Tamarisk.* U.S. Forest Service Research Note RM-16. Rocky Mountain Forest and Range Experiment Station, U.S. Department of Agriculture, 1964.

———. *Present Management Problems in the Phreatophyte and Riparian Zones.* Report to the Joint Meeting of the Phreatophyte Subcommittee, Pacific Southwest Interagency Committee. July 22, 1969.

———. "Problems of Land Management in Various Phreatophyte Zones." Phreatophyte Symposium 66-3, August 30, 1966. Albuquerque, New Mexico, 1966.

———. *The Problems of Phreatophytes.* Symposium on woodlands and water-lysimeters held at Hannoversch-Münden, September 8–13, 1959. International Union of Geodesy and Geophysics.

Howell, Thomas R., and George A. Bartholomew. "Further Experiments on Torpidity in the Poor-Will," *The Condor,* 61 (1959):180–85.

Howes, Paul Griswold. *The Giant Cactus Forest and Its World.* Boston: Little, Brown, 1954.

Humphrey, Robert R. "The Cirio: the Tallest Tree in the Sonoran Desert," *Cactus and Succulent Journal,* 42 (1970):99–101.

———. "Comments on an Epiphyte, a Parasite, and Four Independent Spermatophytes of the Central Desert of Baja California," *Cactus and Succulent Journal,* 43 (1971):99–104.

———. "A Detailed Study of Desert Rainfall," *Ecology,* 14 (1933):31–34.

———. "Growth Habits of Barrel Cactus," *Madroño,* 3 (1963):448–52.

———. "Plants of the Vizcaíno Desert of Baja California: Datilillo (*Yucca valida*)," *Capital Cactus Chatter,* 5:1–3. Tucson, 1969.

———. "A Study of *Idria columnaris* and *Fouquieria splendens,*" *American Journal of Botany,* 22 (1935):184–207.

———. "Thorn Formation in *Fouquieria splendens* and *Idria columnaris,*" Torrey Botanical Club *Bulletin,* 58 (1931):263–64.

Humphrey, Robert R. and A. B. "Height and Volume Characteristics of *Idria columnaris* Kellogg," Arizona Academy of Sciences *Journal,* 5 (1969):207–15.

Humphrey, Robert R., and Floyd G. Werner. "Some Records of Bee Visitations to the Flowers of *Idria columnaris,*" Arizona Academy of Sciences *Journal,* 5 (1969):243–44.

Hunt, Charles B. *Physiography of the United States.* New York: W. H. Freeman, 1967.

Hunt, Charles B., T. W. Robinson, Walter A. Bowles, and A. L. Washburn. *Hydrologic Basin, Death Valley, California.* U.S. Geological Survey Professional Paper 494-B. U.S. Department of Interior, Washington, D.C., 1966.

Hutchison, Victor H., and James L. Larimer. "Reflectivity of the Integument of Some Lizards from Different Habitats," *Ecology,* 41 (1960):199–209.

Ives, Ronald L. "Behavior of Dust Devils," American Meteorological Society *Bulletin,* 28 (1947):168–74.

———. "Climate of the Sonoran Desert Region," Association of American Geographers *Annals,* 39 (1949):143–87.

―――. "The Discovery of Pinacate Volcano," *Scientific Monthly*, 54 (1942): 230–37.

―――. "Geologic Verification of a Papago Legend," *Masterkey*, 9 (1935):160–61.

Jackson, Ray D., and C. H. M. van Bavel. "Solar Distillation of Water from Soil and Plant Materials," *Science*, 149 (1965):1377–79.

Jaeger, Edmund C. *Desert Wildlife*. Stanford: Stanford University Press, 1961.

―――. *The North American Desert*. Stanford: Stanford University Press, 1957.

Johns, Richard H. "Collapse Depression of the Pinacate Volcanic Field, Sonora, Mexico," *Southern Arizona Guidebook* Part II, pp. 165–84. Arizona Geologic Society, 1959.

Johnson, Duncan S. "The Influence of Insolation on the Distribution and on the Developmental Sequence of the Flowers of the Giant Cactus of Arizona," *Ecology*, 5 (1924):70–82.

Johnson, Sheldon. "Arroyos," *Scientific American*, June 1952, pp. 71–76.

Johnston, Ivan M. "The Floristic Significance of Shrubs Common to North and South American Deserts," Arnold Arboretum *Journal*, 21 (1940):356–63.

Joseph, Alice, Rosamond Spicer, and Jane Chesky. *Desert People*. Chicago: University of Chicago Press, 1949.

Juhren, Marcella, F. W. Went, and Edwin Phillips. "Ecology of Desert Plants IV: Combined Field and Laboratory Work on the Germination of Annual in the Joshua Tree National Monument, California," *Ecology*, 37 (1956):318–30.

Kalmus, Hans. "More on the Language of the Bees," *Scientific American*, July 1953, p. 60.

Kelly, William H. *The Papago Indians of Arizona: a Population and Economic Study*. Bureau of Ethnic Research, Department of Anthropology, University of Arizona. Tucson, 1963.

Kirmiz, J. P. *Adaptations to Desert Environment: a Study on the Jerboa, Rat, and Man*. London: Butterworth, 1962.

Klauber, Laurence M. "The Geckos of the Genus *Coleonyx* with Descriptions of New Subspecies," San Diego Society of Natural History *Transactions*, 10 (1945):133–216.

―――. *Rattlesnakes, Their Habits, Life Histories, and Influence on Mankind*. 2 vols. Berkeley: University of California Press, 1956.

―――. "The Sidewinder, *Crotalus cerastes*, with Description of a New Subspecies," San Diego Society of Natural History *Transactions*, 10 (1944):91–126.

Krizman, Richard D. "The Saguaro Tree-Hole Microenvironment in Southern Arizona, I: Winter." Master's thesis, University of Arizona, 1964.

Krutch, Joseph Wood. *The Forgotten Peninsula*. New York: Sloane, 1961.

Kurtz, Edwin B. "Chemical Basis for Adaptation in Plants," *Science*, 128 (1958):1115–17.

Lee, Douglas H. K., ed. "Variability in Human Response to Arid Environments," in William G. McGinnies and Bram J. Goldman, eds., *Arid Lands in Perspective*. Tucson: University of Arizona Press, 1969.

Leopold, Starker A. *Wildlife of Mexico*. Berkeley: University of California Press, 1957.

Ligon, J. David, and Russell P. Balda. "Recent Data on Summer Birds of the Chiricahua Mountains Area, Southeastern Arizona," San Diego Society of Natural History *Transactions,* 15 (1969): 41–50.

Lindsay, George E. "The Gulf Island Expedition of 1966," *Pacific Discovery,* May 1966, pp. 2–10.

Logan, Richard F. *The Central Namib Desert of South West Africa.* National Academy of Sciences *Publication* No. 758. Washington, D.C.: National Research Council, 1960.

Lumholtz, Carl. *New Trails in Mexico.* New York: Scribner's, 1913.

Lustick, Sheldon. "Bird Energetics: Effects of Artificial Radiation," *Science,* 163 (1968):387–89.

Lustig, Lawrence K. *Clastic Sedimentation in Deep Springs Valley, California.* U.S. Geological Survey Professional Paper 352-F. U. S. Department of Interior, Washington, D.C., 1966.

———. "Geomorphic and Paleoclimatic Significance of Alluvial Deposits in Southern Arizona," *Journal of Geology,* 74 (1966):95–102.

McClanahan, Lon, Jr. "Adaptations of the Spadefoot Toad, *Scaphiopus couchi,* to Desert Environments," *Comparative Biochemistry and Physiology,* 20 (1967):73–99.

McCoy, Floyd W., Jr., Warren J. Nokleberg, and Robert M. Norris. "Speculations on the Origin of the Algodones Dunes, California," Geological Society of America *Bulletin,* 78 (1967):1039–44.

McDonald, James E. "Climatology of Arid Lands," *Arid Lands Colloquia* for 1958–1959, pp. 3–12. Tucson: University of Arizona.

MacDougal, D. T., and Earl B. Working. "Another High Temperature Record for Growth and Endurance," *Science,* 54 (1921):152–53.

McGee, W. J. "Desert Thirst As a Disease," *Interstate Medical Journal.* St. Louis, 1906.

———. "Sheetflood Erosion," Geological Society of America *Bulletin,* 8 (1897):87–112.

McGinnies, William G. *Deserts of the World.* Office of Arid Land Studies. Tucson: University of Arizona Press, 1969.

McGinnies, William G., and Bram Goldman, eds. *Arid Lands in Perspective.* Tucson: University of Arizona Press, 1969.

McGinnies, William G., Bram Goldman, and Patricia Paylore, eds. *Deserts of the World: An Appraisal into Their Physical and Biological Environments.* Albuquerque: University of New Mexico Press, 1968.

McGinnis, Samuel M., and Larry L. Dickson. "Thermoregulation in the Desert Iguana, *Dipossaurus dorsalis,*" *Science,* 156 (1967):1757–59.

McGregor, S. E., and Stanley M. Alcorn. "Partial Self-Sterility of the Barrel Cactus," *Cactus and Succulent Journal,* 31 (1959):3.

McGregor, S. E., Stanley M. Alcorn, and George Olin. "Pollination and Pollinating Agents of the Saguaro," *Ecology,* 43 (1962):259–67.

McGregor, S. E., Stanley M. Alcorn, Edwin B. Kurtz, Jr., and George D. Butler, Jr. "Bee Visits to Saguaro Flowers," *Journal of Economic Entomology,* 52 (1959):1002–4.

McMillen, Richard E., and Anthony K. Lee. "Australian Desert Mice: Independence of Exogenous Water," *Science,* 158 (1967):383–85.

Mangelsdorf, Paul C. "Ancestor of Corn," *Science,* 128 (1958):1313–19.

Markle, Millard S. "Root Systems of Certain Desert Plants," *Botanical Gazette*, 64 (1917):177–205.

Marshall, Elizabeth Thomas. *The Harmless People*. New York: Knopf, 1959.

Marshall, Joe T., Jr. *Birds of the Pine-Oak Woodland in Southern Arizona and Adjacent Mexico*. Pacific Coast Avifauna, No. 22. Berkeley: Cooper Ornithological Society, 1957.

Martin, Paul S. "Buried Valleys and the Climatic Factor," *Arid Lands Colloquia* for 1958–1959, pp. 40–45. Tucson: University of Arizona.

———. *The Last 10,000 Years*. Tucson: University of Arizona Press, 1963.

Martin, Paul S., and James Schoenwetter. "Arizona's Oldest Cornfield," *Science*, 132 (1960):33–34.

Maximov, N. A. "Symposium on Xeromorphy," *Ecology*, 19 (1931):272–82.

Mayhew, Wilbur W. "Adaptations of the Amphibian *Scaphiopus couchi* to Desert Conditions," *American Midlands Naturalist*, 74 (1965):95–109.

———. "Photoperiodic Response of Female Fringe-toed Lizards," *Science*, 134 (1961):2104–05.

Meigs, Peveril. "Geography of Coastal Deserts," *Arid Zone 28*. Paris: UNESCO, 1966.

Melton, Mark A. "Debris-Covered Hillslopes of the Southern Arizona Desert: Considerations of Their Stability and Sediment Contribution," *Journal of Geology*, 73 (1965):715–29.

Mercer, E.H. "Cocoon-Surrounding Desert-Dwelling Frogs," *Science*, 157 (1967):87–88.

Meyer, Delbert E. "Drinking Habits in the Earless Lizard, *Holbrookia maculata* and in Two Species of Horned Lizard, *Phrynosoma*," *Copeia* (1966), pp. 126–28.

———. "Survival of the Earless Lizard, *Holbrookia maculata*, under Natural and Artificial Anaerobic Conditions," *Copeia* (1967), pp. 163–67.

Migahid, A. M. "The Drought Resistance of Egyptian Desert Plants," *Plant-Water Relationships in Arid and Semi-Arid Conditions*. Madrid Symposium, UNESCO, 1961.

Miller, Alden. "Tribulations of Thorn-Dwellers," *The Condor*, 38 (1936):218–19.

Milne, Lorus J. and Margery. "Notes on the Behavior of Horned Toads," *American Midlands Naturalist*, 443 (1953):720–41.

Moberly, Walter R. "Hibernation in Desert Iguana, *Dipsosaurus dorsalis*," *Physiological Zoology*, 36 (1963):152–60.

Mooney, H. A., and B. R. Strain. "Bark Photosynthesis in Ocotillo," *Madroño*, 17 (1964):230–33.

Mosauer, Walter. "Adaptive Convergence in the Sand Reptiles of the Sahara and of California: A Study in Structure and Behavior," *Copeia* (1932), pp. 72–78.

———. "The Tolerance of Solar Heat in Desert Reptiles," *Ecology*, 17 (1936):56–66.

Mosauer, Walter, and Edgar L. Lazier. "Death from Insolation in Desert Snakes," *Copeia* (1933), p. 149.

Muller, Cornelius H. "The Association of Desert Annuals with Shrubs," *American Journal of Botany*, 40 (1953):53–60.

Muller, Walter H. and Cornelius H. "Association Patterns Involving Desert Plants That Contain Toxic Products," *Journal of Botany,* 43 (1956): 354–61.

Myers, Lloyd E. "Precipitation Runoff Inducement," *Water Supplies for Arid Regions.* Committee on Desert and Arid Zone Research Contribution No. 10. Tucson: University of Arizona Press, 1967.

Nichter, Richard. "The Effect of Variation in Humidity and Water Intake on Activity of *Dipodomys," Journal of Mammalogy,* 38 (1957):502–12.

Norris, Kenneth S. "Ecology of the Desert Iguana, *Dipsosaurus dorsalis," Ecology,* 34 (1953):265–87.

Norris, Kenneth S., and William R. Dawson. "Observations on the Water Economy and Electrolyte Excretion of Chuckwallas," *Copeia* (1964), pp. 638–46.

Norris, Kenneth S., and Charles H. Lowe. "An Analysis of Background Color Matching in Amphibians and Reptiles," *Ecology,* 45 (1964):565–80.

Norris, Robert M. and Kenneth S. "Algodones Dunes of Southeastern California," Geological Society of America *Bulletin,* 72 (1961):605–20.

Ohmart, R. D., and R. C. Lasiewski. "Roadrunners: Energy Conservation by Hypothermia and Absorption of Sunlight," *Science,* 172 (1971):67–69.

Ohmart, R. D., T. E. Chapman, and L. Z. McFarland. "Water Turnover in Roadrunners under Different Environmental Conditions," *The Auk,* 87 (1970):787–93.

Oliver, James A. *The Natural History of North American Amphibians and Reptiles.* Princeton: Van Nostrand, 1955.

Oppenheimer, H. R. "Summer Drought and Water Balance of Plants in the Near East," *Journal of Ecology,* 39 (1951):356–62.

Pearson, Oliver A. "The Daily Energy Requirements of a Wild Anna's Hummingbird," *The Condor,* 56 (1954):1.

Peterson, Roger T. *Birds Over America.* New York: Dodd, Mead, 1948.

Peterson, Willis. "Meet Dipo," *Audubon,* March-April 1968, pp. 28–34.

Petinov, N. S., and U. G. Molotkovsky. "The Protective Processes of Heat-Resistant Plants," Plant-Water Relationships in Arid and Semi-Arid Conditions. Madrid Symposium, UNESCO, 1961.

Pettingill, Olin S. *The Bird Watcher's America.* New York: McGraw-Hill, 1965.

Phillips, Walter S. "Depth of Roots in Soil," *Ecology,* 44 (1963):424.

Porter, Warren P. "Solar Radiation through the Living Body Walls of Vertebrates with Emphasis on Desert Reptiles," *Ecological Monographs,* 37 (1967):273–96.

Porter, Warren P., and Kenneth S. Norris. "Lizard Reflectivity Change and Its Effect on Light Transmission through Body Walls," *Science,* 163 (1969):482–84.

Poulson, T. L., and G. A. Bartholomew. "Salt Balance in the Savannah Sparrow," *Physiological Zoology,* 35 (1962):109–19.

Pumpelly, Raphael. *My Reminiscences,* vol. 2. New York: Holt, 1918.

Quay, W. B. "Integumentary Modification of North American Desert Rodents," in A. G. Lyne and B. F. Short, eds., *Biology of the Skin and Hair Growth.* New York: American Elsevier, 1965.

Rempel, Peter J. "The Crescentic Dunes of the Salton Sea and Their Relation to the Vegetation," *Ecology*, 17 (1936):347–58.

Resnick, Sol. "Economic Evaluation of Water Conservation Practices," *Arid Lands Colloquia* for 1959–1960, 1960–1961, pp. 19–26. Tucson: University of Arizona.

Reynolds, S. E. "Problems of Water Rights As Related to the Water Salvaged by Phreatophyte Control." Phreatophyte Symposium 66-3, August 30, 1966. Albuquerque, New Mexico.

Salt, G. W. "The Lungs and Inflation Mechanism of *Sauromalus obesus*," *Copeia* (1943), p. 193.

Sauer, Carl. "Distribution of Aboriginal Tribes and Languages in Northwest Mexico." *Ibero Americana 5*. Berkeley: University of California Press, 1934.

Schmidt-Nielsen, Knut. *Desert Animals: Physiological Problems of Heat and Water.* London: Oxford University Press, 1964.

Schmidt-Nielsen, Knut and Bodil. "The Desert Rat," *Scientific American*, July 1953, pp. 73–78.

–––. "Water Metabolism of Desert Mammals," *Physiological Review*, 32 (1952):135–36.

Schmidt-Nielsen, Knut, and William A. Calder. "Temperature Regulation and Evaporation in the Pigment of the Roadrunner," *American Journal of Physiology*, 213 (1967):883–88.

Schmidt-Nielsen, Knut, Arieh Borut, Ping Lee, and Eugene Crawford, Jr. "Nasal Salt Excretion and the Possible Function of the Cloaca in Water Conservation," *Science*, 142 (1963):1300–1301.

Sears, Paul. *Deserts on the March.* Norman: University of Oklahoma Press, 1947.

Shantz, H. L. "Drought Resistance and Soil Moisture," *Ecology*, 8 (1927):145–57.

Shields, Lora M. "Leaf Xeromorphy As Related to Physiology and Structural Influence," *Botanical Review*, 16 (1956):399–447.

Shields, Lora M., and Linton J. Gardner, eds. "Bioecology of the Arid and Semi-Arid Land of the Southwest." New Mexico Highlands University *Bulletin*. Las Vegas, New Mexico, 1961.

Shipley, H. *The Long Drink: Water Supplies for Arid Regions.* Tucson: University of Arizona Press, 1967.

Shreve, Edith B. "Seasonal Changes in the Water Relations of Desert Plants," *Ecology*, 4 (1923):266–92.

Shreve, Forrest. "A Comparison of the Vegetational Features of Two Desert Mountain Ranges," *Plant World*, 22 (1919):291–307.

–––. "Conditions Indirectly Affecting Vertical Distribution on Desert Mountains," *Ecology*, 3 (1922):269–74.

–––. "The Desert Vegetation of North America," *Botanical Review*, 8 (1942):195–246.

–––. "Establishment Behavior of the Palo Verde," *Plant World*, 14 (1911):289–96.

–––. "The Influence of Low Temperature on the Distribution of the Giant Cactus," *Plant World*, 14 (1911):136–46.

–––. "Plant Life of the Sonoran Desert," *Scientific Monthly*, 42 (1936):195–213.

———. "Rainfall of Northern Mexico," *Ecology,* 25 (1944):105–11.

———. "Rainfall, Runoff and Soil Moisture under Desert Conditions," Association of American Geographers *Annals,* 24 (1934):131–56.

———. "The Rate of Establishment of the Giant Cactus," *Plant World,* 14 (1911):235–40.

———. "The Transition from Desert to Chaparral in Baja California," *Madroño,* 3 (1936):257–320.

Shreve, Forrest, and Ira L. Wiggins. *Vegetation and Flora of the Sonoran Desert.* 2 vols. Stanford: Stanford University Press, 1964.

Smiley, Terah L. "Status of Cenozoic Geochronology in the Southwest," *Arid Lands Colloquia* for 1959–1960, 1960–1961, pp. 69–73. Tucson: University of Arizona.

Soule, Michael. "Aspects of Thermoregulation in 9 Species of Lizards from Baja California," *Copeia* (1963), pp. 107–15.

Soule, Oscar H. "The Saguaro Tree-Hole Microenvironment in Arizona, II: Summer." Master's thesis, University of Arizona, 1964.

Spalding, Effie Southworth. "Mechanical Adjustment of the Suaharo (*Cereus giganteus*) to Varying Quantities of Stored Water," Torrey Botanical Club *Bulletin,* 32 (1905):57–68.

Spencer, Donald B. "A Small Mammal Community in the Upper Sonoran Desert," *Ecology,* 22 (1941):421–25.

Spicer, Edward H. *Cycles of Conquest.* Tucson: University of Arizona Press, 1962.

———. *Pascua: A Yaqui Village in Arizona.* Chicago: University of Chicago Press, 1940.

Spier, Leslie. *Yuman Tribes of the Gila River.* Chicago: University of Chicago Press, 1933.

Stahnke, Herbert L. "Some Aspects of Scorpion Behavior," Southern California Academy of Sciences *Bulletin,* Vol. 65 (1966), No. 2.

Stebbins, Robert C. "Adaptations in the Nasal Passages for Sand Burrowing in the Saurian Genus *Uma,*" *American Naturalist,* 77 (1943):88–92.

———. "Effects of Pinealectomy in Western Fence Lizards," *Copeia* (1959), pp. 276–83.

———. "Some Aspects of the Ecology of the Iguanid Genus *Uma,*" *Ecological Monographs,* 14 (1944):311–32.

Stewart, Kenneth M. "Mojave Indian Agriculture," *Masterkey,* 40 (1966):5–15.

Stone, Edward C., F. W. Went, and C. L. Young. "Water Absorption from the Atmosphere by Plants Growing in Dry Soil," *Science,* 111 (1950):546–48.

Sumner, F. B. "Desert- and Lava-Dwelling Mice, and the Problem of Protective Coloration in Mammals," *Journal of Mammalogy,* 2 (1921):75–86.

———. "Genetic, Distributional, and Evolutionary Studies of Sub-Species of Deer Mice (*Peromyscus*)," *Bibliographia Genetica,* 9 (1932):1–106.

Sykes, Godfrey. *The Colorado Delta.* New York: Carnegie Institution of Washington and American Geographical Society of New York, 1937.

Taylor, C. R. "The Eland and the Oryx," *Scientific American,* January 1969, pp. 88–95.

Templeton, James R. "Respiration and Water Loss at the Higher Temperatures in the Desert Iguana, *Dipsosaurus dorsalis,*" *Physiological Zoology,* 33 (1960):136–45.

Tevis, Lloyd. "Germination and Growth of Ephemerals Induced by Sprinkling a Sandy Desert," *Ecology,* 39 (1958):681–88.

———. "Herpetological Notes from Lower California," *Copeia* (1944), pp. 6–18.

———. "Interrelations between the Harvester Ant *Veromessor pergandei* (Mayr) and Some Desert Ephemerals," *Ecology,* 39 (1958):695–704.

———. "A Population of Desert Ephemerals Germinated by Less Than One Inch of Rain," *Ecology,* 39 (1958):688–95.

Thorson, Thomas B. "Relation of Water Economy to Terrestrialism in Amphibians," *Ecology,* 36 (1955):100–116.

Thorson, Thomas B., and Arthur Svihla. "Correlation of the Habitats of Amphibians with Their Ability to Survive Loss of Body Water," *Ecology,* 24 (1943):378–81.

Tschirley, Red H., and Wagle, R. F. "Growth Rate and Population Dynamics of Jumping Cholla," Arizona Academy of Sciences *Journal,* 3 (1964):67–71.

Tucker, Vance F. "Diurnal Torpidity in the California Pocket Mouse," *Science,* 136 (1962):380–81.

Turnage, William V. "Desert Soil Temperatures," *Soil Science,* 47 (1939):195–99.

Turnage, William V., and Arthur L. Hinckley. "Freezing Weather in Relation to Plants Distribution in the Sonoran Desert," *Ecological Monograph,* 8 (1938):530–50.

Turner, Frederick B. "Some Features of the Ecology of *Bufo punctatus* in Death Valley, California," *Ecology,* 402 (1959):175–81.

Turner, Raymond M., Stanley M. Alcorn, and George Olin. "Mortality of Transplanted Saguaro Seedlings," *Ecology,* 50 (1969):835–44.

Turner, Raymond M., Stanley M. Alcorn, George Olin, and John A. Booth. "The Influence of Shade, Soil, and Water in Saguaro Seedling Establishment," *Botanical Gazette,* 127 (1966):95–102.

Van der Post, Laurens. *The Lost World of the Kalahari.* New York: Morrow, 1958.

Van Walkenburgh, Sallie. "The Casa Grande of Arizona As a Landmark in the Desert," *Kiva,* 27 (1962):1–31.

Vogl, Richard J., and Lawrence T. McHargue. "Vegetation of California Fan Palm Oasis on the San Andreas Fault," *Ecology,* 47 (1966):533–40.

Von Haartman, Lars. "Adaptation in Hole-Nesting Birds," *Evolution,* 11 (1957):339–47.

Vorhies, Charles T., and Walter P. Taylor. *The Life Histories of Jackrabbits.* Technical Bulletin 49, University of Arizona, College of Agriculture Experiment Station, 1933.

Walker, Lewis W. "Nocturnal Observations of Elf Owls," *The Condor,* 45 (1943):165–67.

Walls, Gordon Lynn. "Ophthalmological Implications for the Early History of the Snake," *Copeia* (1940), pp. 1–8.

———. *The Vertebrate Eye and Its Adaptive Radiation.* Cranbrook Institute of Science Bulletin 19, 1942.

Wauer, Roland H. "A Survey of the Birds in Death Valley," *The Condor,* 64 (1962):220–33.

Weaver, F. G. "*Carpophilus longiventris* in Saguaro Blossoms," *Psyche,* Vol. 66 (1959), No. 3.

Webb, George. *A Pima Remembers.* Tucson: University of Arizona Press, 1959.

Wells, Philip V., and Clive D. Jorgenson. "Pleistocene Woodrat Middens and Climatic Change in the Mohave Desert: A Record of Juniper Woodlands," *Science,* 143 (1964):1171–73.

Went, F. W. "The Dependence of Certain Annual Plants on Shrubs in Southern California Deserts," Torrey Botanical Club *Bulletin,* 69 (1942):100–114.

———. "The Ecology of Desert Plants," *Scientific American,* April 1955, pp. 68–76.

———. "Ecology of Desert Plants, I: Observations on Germination in the Joshua Tree National Monument, California," *Ecology,* 29 (1948):242–53.

———. "The Effect of Rain and Temperature on Germination and Growth," *Ecology,* 30 (1949):1–13.

Winslow, C. E. A., and L. P. Herrington. *Temperature and Human Life.* Princeton: Princeton University, 1949.

Woodbury, Angus M., and Ross Hardy. "Studies of the Desert Tortoise, *Gopherus agassizii,*" *Ecological Monographs,* 18 (1948):145–200.

Woodbury, Richard B. "The Hohokam Canals at Pueblo Grande, Arizona," *American Antiquity,* 26 (1960):267–70.

———. "Prehistoric Agriculture in East-Central Arizona," *Arid Lands Colloquia* for 1959–1960, 1960–1961, pp. 17–22. Tucson: University of Arizona.

———. "Prespanish Human Ecology in the Southwestern Deserts," *Arid Lands Colloquia* for 1958–1959, pp. 82–92. Tucson: University of Arizona.

Woodward, Arthur. *Camels and Surveyors in Death Valley.* Palm Desert: Death Valley '49ers, Inc., 1961.

Zohary, M. "On Hydro-Ecological Relations of the Near East Desert Vegetation," *Plant-Water Relationships in Arid and Semi-Arid Conditions.* Madrid Symposium, UNESCO, 1961.

Index